VOCABULARY, SPELLING and GRAMMAR

CONTENTS

VOCABULARY, SPELLING and GRAMMAR

PART I
INTRODUCTION

WHAT THIS BOOK WILL DO
FOR YOU

There is a definite correlation between language skills and test scores. An extensive vocabulary, a good command of spelling, and knowledge of the rules of grammar and usage are sure to result in higher scores on civil service, military, scholastic and employment tests. This self-teaching text allows you to build and test vocabulary, spelling and grammar skills on your own—in your own home and at your own pace.

The Vocabulary section includes over 2000 words every test-taker should know. The chapter on etymology defines and illustrates 150 prefixes, suffixes and roots to help decipher unfamiliar words that may turn up on tests. Forty practice tests cover synonym, antonym, sentence completion and verbal analogy questions assembled from a variety of previous tests.

The Spelling section offers tips on improving spelling skills, 8 easy rules for spelling any English word, a list of the 400 most commonly misspelled words and practice tests to assess and improve spelling skill.

The Grammar section defines and explains the parts of speech, provides a concise review of the rules of punctuation and capitalization, and tests mastery of the subject with hundreds of previous test questions on correct usage and effective expression.

GETTING STARTED

It is important to determine how much time you have available to prepare for your exam, and then to make up a realistic schedule of how you will spend this study time. Set aside some time every day for your study, and follow your schedule closely.

HOW TO STUDY FOR MAXIMUM
RESULTS

Here are a few suggestions to help you use your study time effectively.

1. **Study alone.** You will concentrate better if you work by yourself. Keep a list of questions you cannot answer and points you are unsure of to talk over with a friend who is preparing for the same exam. Plan to exchange ideas at a joint review session just before the test.

2. **Eliminate distractions.** Disturbances caused by family and neighbor activities (telephone calls, chit-chat, TV programs, etc.) work to your disadvantage. Study in a quiet, private room.

3. **Don't try to learn too much in one study period.** If your mind starts to wander, take a short break and then return to your work.

4. **Review what you have learned.** Once you have studied something thoroughly, be sure to review it the next day so that the information will be firmly fixed in your mind.

5. **Answer all the questions in this book.** Don't be satisfied merely with the correct answer to each question. Do additional research on the other choices that are given. You will broaden your background and be more adequately prepared for the actual exam. It's quite possible that a question on the exam that you are going to take may require you to be familiar with the other choices.

6. **Tailor your study to the subject matter. Skim or scan.** Don't study everything in the same manner. Obviously, certain areas are more important than others.

7. **Organize your material.** Make sure that your notes are in good order. Valuable time is wasted when you can't find quickly what you are looking for.

8. **Keep physically fit.** You cannot retain information well when you are uncomfortable, headachy, or tense. Physical health promotes mental efficiency.

HOW TO TAKE AN EXAM

1. **Get to the examination room about ten minutes ahead of time.** You'll get a better start when you are accustomed to the room. If the room is too cold, or too warm, or not well ventilated, call these conditions to the attention of the person in charge.

2. **Make sure that you read the instructions carefully.** In many cases, test-takers lose credits because they misread some important point in the directions, for example, the *incorrect* choice instead of the *correct* choice.

3. **Skip hard questions and go back later.** It is a good idea to make a mark on the question sheet next to all questions you cannot answer easily, and to go back to those questions later. First answer the questions you are sure about. Do not panic if you cannot answer a question. Go on and answer the questions you know. Usually the easier questions are presented at the beginning of the exam and the questions become gradually more difficult.

If you do skip ahead on the exam, be sure to skip ahead also on your answer sheet. A good technique is periodically to check the number of the question on the answer sheet with the number of the question on the test. You should do this every time you decide to skip a question. If you fail to skip the corresponding answer blank for that question, all of your following answers will be wrong.

Each student is stronger in some areas than in others. No one is expected to know all the answers. Do not waste time agonizing over a difficult question because it may keep you from getting to other questions that you can answer correctly.

4. **Mark the answer sheet clearly.** When you take the examination, you will mark your answers to the multiple-choice questions on a separate answer sheet that will be given to you at the test center. If you have not worked with an answer sheet before, it is in your best interest to become familiar with the procedures involved. Remember, knowing the correct answer is not enough. If you do not mark the sheet correctly, so that it can be machine scored, you will not get credit for your answers.

In addition to marking answers on the separate answer sheet, you will be asked to give your name and other information, including your social security number. As a precaution, bring along your social security number for identification purposes.

Read the directions carefully and follow them exactly. If they ask you to print your name in the boxes provided, write only one letter in each box. If your name is longer than the number of boxes provided, omit the letters that do not fit. Remember, you are writing for a machine; it does not have judgment. It can only record the pencil marks you make on the answer sheet.

Use the answer sheet to record all your answers to questions. Each question, or item, has four or five answer choices labeled (A), (B), (C), (D), (E). You will be asked to choose the letter that stands for the best answer. Then you will be asked to mark your answer by blackening the appropriate space on your answer sheet. Be sure that each space you choose and blacken with your pencil is *completely* blackened. The machine will "read" your answers in terms of spaces blackened. Make sure that only one answer is clearly blackened. If you erase an answer, erase it completely and mark your new answer clearly. The machine will give credit only for clearly marked answers. It does not pause to decide whether you really meant (B) or (C).

5. **Read each question carefully.** The exam questions are not designed to trick you through misleading or ambiguous alternative choices. It's up to you to read each question carefully so you know what is being asked.

6. **Don't answer too fast.** The multiple-choice questions that you will meet are not superficial exercises. They are designed to test not only your memory but also your understanding and insight. Do not place too much emphasis on speed. The time element is a factor, but it is not all-important. Accuracy should not be sacrificed for speed.

7. **Materials and conduct at the test center.** You need to bring with you to the test center your Admission Form, your social security number, and several No. 2 pencils. Arrive on time as you may not be admitted after testing has begun. Instructions for taking the tests will be read to you by the test supervisor and time will be called when the test is over. If you have questions, you may ask them of the supervisor. Do not give or receive assistance while taking the exams. If you do, you will be asked to turn in all test materials and told to leave the room. You will not be permitted to return and your tests will not be scored.

HOW TO MARK ANSWER SHEETS

A typical machine-scored answer sheet is shown below, reduced from the actual size of 8½ × 11 inches. Since it's the only one that reaches the office where papers are scored, it's important that the blanks at the top be filled in completely and correctly.

The chances are very good that you'll have to mark your answers on one of these sheets. Consequently, we've made it possible for you to practice with them throughout this book.

SAMPLE ANSWER SHEET

EXAM TITLE		TODAY'S DATE	
SCHOOL OR BUILDING		ROOM NO.	SEAT NO.

YOUR SOCIAL SECURITY NO.

EXAM NO.

PRINT WITH SOFT PENCIL ONLY. Print, with pencil, your SOCIAL SECURITY NO. and the EXAM. NO. in the boxes at the tops of the columns. ONE NUMBER IN A BOX. In each column, darken (with pencil) the oval containing the number in the box at the top of the column. Only ONE OVAL in a COLUMN should be darkened. Then, using your pencil, print in the: Exam. Title, School or Building, Room No., Seat No., and Today's Date.

Follow the instructions given in the question booklet. Mark nothing ▶ but your answers in the ovals below.

SAMPLE QUESTION: When we add 5 and 3 we get: (A) 11 (B) 9 (C) 8 (D) 2. Since the answer is 8, your answer should be marked like this: Ⓐ Ⓑ ● Ⓓ

WARNING: Be sure that the oval you fill in is in the row numbered the same as the question you are answering. Use a No. 2 pencil (soft pencil).

BE SURE YOUR PENCIL MARKS ARE HEAVY AND BLACK. ERASE COMPLETELY ANY ANSWER YOU WISH TO CHANGE. DO NOT make stray pencil dots, dashes or marks ANYPLACE on this SHEET.

START HERE

1–25, 26–50, 51–75, 76–100, 101–125, 126–150 (answer ovals Ⓐ Ⓑ Ⓒ Ⓓ for each numbered row)

PART II
BUILDING YOUR VOCABULARY SKILLS

INTRODUCTION

This part is designed to help you expand your vocabulary quickly and to give you practice answering vocabulary questions. It is divided into two major sections. The first, Building Your Vocabulary Skills, includes an etymology chart, a word list, and helpful examples of how to answer the different kinds of questions you will encounter on your exam. Read this material through carefully, but don't try to absorb it all at once. Follow the study suggestions. To study effectively, you might divide the word list into sections. Learn each section thoroughly before going on to the next one. For maximum concentration, a half-hour of studying at a time is plenty.

The second section, Testing Your Vocabulary Skills, has a series of eleven practice tests on synonyms, ten practice tests on antonyms, ten practice sentence completion tests, and twelve practice tests on verbal analogies. The second section is followed immediately by answer keys. To get the maximum benefit from the practice tests, space them out. You might take one or two at the beginning to see how well you do. Then spend some time on the vocabulary building section before taking another round of tests. Keep an honest record of your scores so you'll know how much you've improved.

Use the practice tests to help you learn. When you check your answers, make sure you understand why they were wrong, or right. Make a note of any words you're not sure of and look them up in the word list or in a dictionary.

This part is only a starting place. There are many ways you can work to increase your vocabulary. Make it a habit to read as much as you can, and read many different kinds of things. You will not only learn the meanings of new words from their context in actual writing; you will also learn how they are used. If you come across a word that seems mysterious, look it up in a dictionary. Then look again at how it is being used in context. Practice using it yourself so that it becomes a permanent part of your vocabulary. With a little effort you will find your knowledge of words steadily growing.

ETYMOLOGY: THE KEY TO MEANING

Etymology is the study of how words are formed. Many English words, especially the longer and more difficult ones, are built up out of basic parts or roots. One of the most efficient ways of increasing your vocabulary is to learn some of these parts. Once you know some basic building blocks, you will find it easier to remember words you've learned and to puzzle out unfamiliar ones.

Let's look at some examples. The word *biography* is made up of two important parts. *Graphy* comes from a Greek word meaning "writing." Many English words use this root. *Graphology*, for instance, is the study of handwriting. *Graphite* is the carbon material used in "lead" pencils. The *telegraph* is a device for writing at a distance. The *bio* part, also from Greek, means "life." It too is at the root of many English words, such as *biology* (the study of life) and *biochemistry* (the chemistry of life). When we put *bio* and *graphy* together, we get a word meaning "writing about a person's life." We can make another word by adding another part, this time from the Latin word *auto*, meaning "self." An *autobiography* is "a person's written account of his own life."

Looking over the last two paragraphs, can you guess the meaning of the word part *-logy?*

Any good dictionary will give you the etymology of words. When you look up an unfamiliar word, make it a habit to look at how it was formed. Does the word have a root that helps to explain its meaning? Is it related to other words that you already know?

The following chart lists over 150 common word parts. Each part is defined and an example is given of a word in which it appears. Don't try to memorize the whole chart at once. If you study only a small section at a time, you'll get better results. When you've learned one of the building blocks, remember to look for it in your reading. See if you can think of other words in which the word part appears. Use the dictionary to check your guesses. To help you apply what you've learned, there are seven etymology exercises following the chart.

WORD PART	MEANING	EXAMPLE
a, ab, abs	from, away	*abrade*—to wear off
		absent—away, not present
act, ag	do, act, drive	*action*—a doing
		agent—one who acts for another
alter, altr	other, change	*alternate*—to switch back and forth
am, ami	love, friend	*amorous*—loving
anim	mind, life, spirit	*animated*—spirited
annu, enni	year	*annual*—yearly
ante	before	*antediluvian*—before the Flood
anthrop	man	*anthropology*—study of mankind
anti	against	*antiwar*—against war
arbit	judge	*arbiter*—a judge
arch	first, chief	*archetype*—first model

WORD PART	MEANING	EXAMPLE
aud, audit, aur	hear	*auditorium*—place where performances are heard
auto	self	*automobile*—self-moving vehicle
bell	war	*belligerent*—warlike
bene, ben	good, well	*benefactor*—one who does good deeds
bi	two	*bilateral*—two-sided
bibli	book	*bibliophile*—book lover
bio	life	*biology*—study of life
brev	short	*abbreviate*—to shorten
cad, cas, cid	fall	*casualty*—one who has fallen
cede, ceed, cess	go, yield	*exceed*—go beyond *recession*—a going backwards
cent	hundred	*century*—hundred years
chrom	color	*monochrome*—having one color
chron	time	*chronology*—time order
cide, cis	cut, kill	*suicide*—a self-killing *incision*—a cutting into
circum	around	*circumnavigate*—to sail around
clam, claim	shout	*proclaim*—to declare loudly
clin	slope, lean	*decline*—to slope downward
cogn	know	*recognize*—to know
com, co, col, con, cor	with, together	*concentrate*—to bring closer together *cooperate*—to work with *collapse*—to fall together
contra, contro, counter	against	*contradict*—to speak against *counterclockwise*—against the clock's direction
corp	body	*incorporate*—to bring into a body *corpse*—dead body
cosm	order, world	*cosmos*—universe
cre, cresc, cret	grow	*increase*—to grow *accretion*—growth by addition
cred	trust, believe	*incredible*—unbelievable
culp	blame	*culprit*—one who is to blame
cur, curr, curs	run, course	*current*—presently running
de	away from, down, opposite	*detract*—to draw away from
dec	ten	*decade*—ten years
dem	people	*democracy*—rule by the people
dic, dict	say, speak	*dictation*—a speaking *predict*—to say in advance, foretell
dis, di	not, away from	*dislike*—to not like *digress*—to turn away from the subject
doc, doct	teach, prove	*indoctrinate*—to teach
domin	rule	*domineer*—to rule over
du	two	*duo*—a couple
duc, duct	lead	*induct*—to lead in
dur	hard, lasting	*durable*—able to last
equ	equal	*equivalent*—of equal value

WORD PART	MEANING	EXAMPLE
ev	time, age	*longevity*—age, length of life
ex, e, ef	from, out	*expatriate*—one who lives outside his native country
		emit—to send out
extra	outside, beyond	*extraterrestrial*—from beyond the earth
fac, fact, fect, fic	do, make	*factory*—place where things are made
		fictitious—made up or imaginary
fer	bear, carry	*transfer*—to carry across
fid	belief, faith	*fidelity*—faithfulness
fin	end, limit	*finite*—limited
flect, flex	bend	*reflect*—to bend back
flu, fluct, flux	flow	*fluid*—flowing substance
		influx—a flowing in
fore	in front of, previous	*forecast*—to tell ahead of time
		foreleg—front leg
form	shape	*formation*—shaping
fort	strong	*fortify*—to strengthen
frag, fract	break	*fragile*—easily broken
		fracture—a break
fug	flee	*fugitive*—one who flees
gen	birth, kind, race	*engender*—to give birth to
geo	earth	*geology*—study of the earth
grad, gress	step, go	*progress*—to go forward
graph	writing	*autograph*—to write one's own name
her, hes	stick, cling	*adhere*—to cling
		cohesive—sticking together
homo	same, like	*homophonic*—sounding the same
hyper	too much, over	*hyperactive*—overly active
in, il, ig, im, ir	not	*incorrect*—not correct
		ignorant—not knowing
		illogical—not logical
		irresponsible—not responsible
in, il, im, ir	on, into, in	*impose*—to place on
		invade—to go into
inter	between, among	*interplanetary*—between planets
intra, intro	within, inside	*intrastate*—within a state
ject	throw	*reject*—to throw back
junct	join	*juncture*—place where things join
leg	law	*legal*—lawful
leg, lig, lect	choose, gather, read	*legible*—readable
		eligible—able to be chosen
		select—to choose
lev	light, rise	*alleviate*—to make lighter
liber	free	*liberation*—a freeing
loc	place	*location*—place
log	speech, study	*dialogue*—speech for two characters
		psychology—study of the mind

WORD PART	MEANING	EXAMPLE
luc, lum	light	*translucent*—allowing light to pass through *luminous*—shining
magn	large, great	*magnify*—to make larger
mal, male	bad, wrong, poor	*maladjusted*—poorly adjusted *malevolent*—ill-wishing
mar	sea	*marine*—sea-dwelling
ment	mind	*demented*—out of one's mind
meter, metr, mens	measure	*chronometer*—time-measuring device *commensurate*—of equal measure
micr	small	*microwave*—small wave
min	little	*minimum*—least
mis	badly, wrongly	*misunderstand*—to understand wrongly
mit, miss	send	*remit*—to send back *mission*—a sending
mono	single, one	*monorail*—train that runs on a single track
morph	shape	*anthropomorphic*—manshaped
mov, mob, mot	move	*removal*—a moving away *mobile*—able to move
multi	many	*multiply*—to become many
mut	change	*mutation*—change
nasc, nat	born	*innate*—inborn *native*—belonging by or from birth
neg	deny	*negative*—no, not
neo	new	*neologism*—new word
nom	name	*nomenclature*—system of naming *nominate*—to name for office
non	not	*nonentity*—a nobody
nov	new	*novice*—newcomer, beginner *innovation*—something new
omni	all	*omnipresent*—present in all places
oper	work	*operate*—to work *cooperation*—a working together
path, pat, pass	feel, suffer	*patient*—suffering *compassion*—a feeling with
ped, pod	foot	*pedestrian*—one who goes on foot
pel, puls	drive, push	*impel*—to push
phil	love	*philosophy*—love of wisdom
phob	fear	*phobic*—irrationally fearing
phon	sound	*symphony*—a sounding together
phot	light	*photosynthesis*—synthesis of chemical compounds in plants with the aid of light *photon*—light particle
poly	many	*polygon*—many-sided figure
port	carry	*import*—to carry into a country *portable*—able to be carried
post	after	*postmortem*—after death

WORD PART	MEANING	EXAMPLE
pot	power	*potency*—power
pre	before, earlier than	*prejudice*—judgment in advance
press	press	*impression*—a pressing into
prim	first	*primal*—first, original
pro	in favor of, in front of, forward	*proceed*—to go forward *prowar*—in favor of war
psych	mind	*psychiatry*—cure of the mind
quer, quir, quis, ques	ask, seek	*query*—to ask *inquisitive*—asking many questions *quest*—a search
re	back, again	*rethink*—to think again *reimburse*—to pay back
rid, ris	laugh	*deride*—to make fun of *ridiculous*—laughable
rupt	break	*erupt*—to break out *rupture*—a breaking apart
sci, scio	know	*science*—knowledge *conscious*—having knowledge
scrib, script	write	*describe*—to write about *inscription*—a writing on
semi	half	*semiconscious*—half conscious
sent, sens	feel, think	*sensation*—feeling *sentient*—able to feel
sequ, secut	follow	*sequential*—following in order
sol	alone	*desolate*—lonely
solv, solu, solut	loosen	*dissolve*—to loosen the bonds of *solvent*—loosening agent
son	sound	*sonorous*—sounding
spec, spic, spect	look	*inspect*—to look into *spectacle*—something to be looked at
spir	breathe	*respiration*—breathing
stab, stat	stand	*establish*—to make stand, found
string, strict	bind	*restrict*—to bind, limit
stru, struct	build	*construct*—to build
super	over, greater	*superfluous*—overflowing, beyond what is needed
tang, ting, tact, tig	touch	*tactile*—of the sense of touch *contiguous*—touching
tele	far	*television*—machine for seeing far
ten, tain, tent	hold	*tenacity*—holding power *contain*—to hold together
term	end	*terminal*—last, ending
terr	earth	*terrain*—surface of the earth
test	witness	*attest*—to witness
therm	heat	*thermos*—container that retains heat
tort, tors	twist	*contort*—to twist out of shape
tract	pull, draw	*attract*—to pull toward
trans	across	*transport*—to carry across a distance
un	not	*uninformed*—not informed
uni	one	*unify*—to make one

WORD PART	MEANING	EXAMPLE
vac	empty	*evacuate*—to make empty
ven, vent	come	*convene*—to come together
ver	true	*verity*—truth
verb	word	*verbose*—wordy
vid, vis	see	*video*—means of seeing
		vision—sight
viv, vit	life	*vivid*—lively
voc, vok	call	*provocative*—calling for a response
		revoke—to call back
vol	wish, will	*involuntary*—not willed

EXERCISES

In each of the following exercises, the words in the left-hand column are built on roots given in the etymology chart. Match each word with its definition from the right-hand column. Refer to the chart if necessary. Can you identify the roots of each word? If there is any word you can't figure out, look it up in a dictionary.

EXERCISE 1

mutable	able to be touched
culpable	laughable
interminable	empty of meaning or interest
amiable	of the first age
vacuous	holding firmly
vital	necessary to life
primeval	unending
tenacious	stable, not able to be loosened or broken up
tangible	changeable
inoperable	friendly
risible	blameworthy
indissoluble	not working, out of order

EXERCISE 2

infinity	list of things to be done
duplicity	sum paid yearly
levity	a throwing out or from
brevity	shortness
ejection	endlessness
edict	body of teachings
infraction	killing of a race
genocide	lightness of spirit
agenda	a breaking
annuity	doubledealing
microcosm	official decree; literally, a speaking out
doctrine	world in miniature

EXERCISE 3

recede	state as the truth
abdicate	throw light on
homogenize	forswear, give up a power
illuminate	put into words
supervise	make freer
verbalize	go away
liberalize	bury
legislate	oversee
intervene	make laws
inter	draw out
aver	make the same throughout
protract	come between

EXERCISE 4

abduction	arrival, a coming to
fortitude	a pressing together
consequence	a flowing together
confluence	something added to
compression	a coming back to life
locus	place
status	truthfulness
disunity	that which follows as a result
veracity	strength
revival	lack of oneness
advent	a leading away, kidnapping
adjunct	standing, position

EXERCISE 5

nascent	being born
centennial	before the war
prospective	believing easily
circumspect	going against
multinational	in name only
clamorous	hard, unyielding
antebellum	looking forward
contrary	careful, looking in all directions
impassioned	hundred-year anniversary
credulous	having interests in many countries
obdurate	full of strong feeling
nominal	shouting

EXERCISE 6

dislocation	wrong name
misanthropy	withdrawal
misnomer	a knowing in advance
misconception	denial
negation	power of will
propulsion	forerunner
volition	a putting out of place
retraction	wrong idea
arbitration	a judging
inclination	a pushing forward
precognition	hatred of mankind
precursor	a leaning toward

EXERCISE 7

solitary	measuring time
altruistic	all-powerful
beneficial	badly shaped
benevolent	doing good, favorable
malefactor	alone, single
malformed	of the earth
malodorous	serving others
omniscient	bad-smelling
omnipotent	great-spirited, generous
magnanimous	all-knowing
chronometric	evil-doer
terrestrial	well-wishing

WORD LIST FOR VOCABULARY BUILDING

ABACUS—instrument for performing computations by sliding counters along rods or grooves. The *abacus* is still widely used in Japan for computation.

ABASE—to cast down or reduce in estimation, to degrade. The French Revolution *abased* the proud nobility.

ABASH—to discomfit or embarrass. He was *abashed* by the open criticism of his work.

ABATE—to reduce in intensity or number. The tempest *abates* in fury.

ABBREVIATE—to shorten. When he saw that the meeting was running late, he *abbreviated* his comments.

ABDICATE—to give up a power or function. The father *abdicated* his responsibility by not setting a good example for the boy.

ABERRATION—a deviation from the right or normal. Many hospital patients suffer from mental *aberrations*.

ABET—to encourage or countenance the commission of an offense. Aiding and *abetting* an enemy of the country constitutes treason.

ABEYANCE—temporary suspension of action. The strike motion was held in *abeyance* pending contract negotiations.

ABHOR—to regard with horror or loathing. The pacifist *abhors* war.

ABIDE BY—to live up to, submit to. We will *abide by* the decision of the court.

ABILITY—skill or power to do something. Her scores clearly indicated a remarkable *ability* for calculus.

ABJECT—miserable, wretched. Many Asians live in a state of *abject* poverty.

ABJURE—to renounce under oath. A new citizen must *abjure* allegiance to his former country.

ABLUTION—a washing or cleansing. *Ablutions* are a part of many religious rites.

ABNEGATE—to deny or renounce. He must *abnegate* all his former friends.

ABOLISH—to do away with, as an institution. Slavery was *abolished* in Massachusetts shortly after the American Revolution.

ABOMINATE—loathe. I *abominate* all laws that deprive people of their rights.

ABORTIVE—ineffectual. They made an *abortive* attempt to capture the radio station.

ABRADE—rub off, wear away by friction. Sandpaper is used to *abrade* a rough surface.

ABRASIVE—scraping or rubbing, annoyingly harsh or jarring. The high-pitched whine of the machinery was *abrasive* to my nerves.

ABRIDGE—shorten. The pocket book was an *abridged* edition.

ABROGATE—annul or abolish. Congress has the right to *abrogate* laws with the consent of the chief executive.

ABSCOND—to steal off to avoid some penalty. The teller *absconded* with the bank's funds.

ABSENTEEISM—condition of being habitually absent, as from work. *Absenteeism* at the plant becomes more of a problem around holidays.

ABSOLUTION—pardon, forgiveness. The clergy has the right to grant *absolution*.

ABSTAIN—refrain voluntarily from some act. Alcoholics must *abstain* from any indulgence in alcoholic drinks.

ABSTEMIOUS—moderate in eating and drinking. The *abstemious* eater is seldom overweight.

ABSTRUSE—deep, obscure in meaning. The concepts of Albert Einstein were *abstruse* even to physicists.

ABSURD—clearly untrue, nonsensical. The parents dismissed the child's story of meeting men from outer space as *absurd*.

ABUNDANT—plentiful, more than enough. Rich soil and *abundant* rainfall make the region lush and fruitful.

ABUT—to touch, as bordering property. When estates *abut*, borders must be defined properly.

ACCEDE—consent. He *acceded* to their request.

ACCELERATE—to increase in speed. Going downhill, a vehicle will naturally *accelerate*.

ACCEPT—to receive with intent to keep. They *accepted* their responsibility to meet the deadline.

ACCESS—means of approach. Public libraries insure that the people have *access* to vast stores of information.

ACCLAIM—to applaud, approve loudly. The crowd in the square *acclaimed* their hero as the new president.

ACCLIMATE—accustom to a new environment. Visitors to the desert have a hard time *acclimating* themselves to the extreme variations in temperature.

ACCLIVITY—upward slope. He viewed the great *acclivity* with dismay as their car chugged along.

ACCOLADE—an award or praise. He accepted the *accolade* modestly.

ACCOMMODATE—to make room for, adjust. The room can *accommodate* two more desks. We will *accommodate* ourselves to the special needs of those clients.

ACCUMULATE—to gather, pile up. Over the years she has *accumulated* a large collection of antique bric-a-brac.

ACCUSTOM—to get or be used to. The supervisor was not *accustomed* to having her instructions ignored.

ACERBITY—bitterness, sourness. The *acerbity* of her wit won her many enemies.

ACKNOWLEDGE—to admit, recognize as true or legitimate. We do not *acknowledge* the state's authority to legislate people's beliefs.

ACME—the top or high point. Her latest book marked the *acme* of her career.

ACOLYTE—an assistant, especially in a religious rite. The youth was anxious to serve as *acolyte* to a priest.

ACOUSTIC—pertaining to hearing. The *acoustic* qualities of a room may be improved by insulation.

ACQUIESCE—to comply or accept, reluctantly. One must often *acquiesce* to the demands of a superior.

ACQUIT—to set free from an accusation. The jury *acquitted* the defendant.

ACRIMONY—harsh or biting language or temper. His *acrimony* resulted from years of disappointment.

ACRONYM—word formed from initials. Radar is an *acronym* for *ra*dio *d*etecting *a*nd *r*anging.

ACROSTIC—word arrangement in which certain letters read up and down to make another word; e.g. news—
>   North
>   East
>   West
>   South

ACTUARY—an expert who calculates insurance risks. The *actuary* plays an important part in establishing insurance premium rates.

ACTUATE—to put into action, incite. The machine was *actuated* by an electric starter.

ACUMEN—sharpness of mind, keenness in business matters. The *acumen* of many early industrialists accounts for their success.

ADAGE—a proverb, a saying that has been in long use. "A stitch in time saves nine" is an old *adage*.

ADAMANT—inflexible, hard. A man must be *adamant* in his determination to succeed.

ADAPTABLE—able to adjust to new circumstances. Thanks to the intelligence that has made technology possible, humans are more *adaptable* to a variety of climates than any other species.

ADDICTED—to be captive to a habit or substance. Workaholics are *addicted* to their careers.

ADDUCE—bring forward as a reason or example. In their defense they *adduced* several justifications for their actions.

ADEPT—skilled, well-versed. A journalist is *adept* at the use of words.

ADEQUATE—sufficient, enough. Without *adequate* sunlight, many tropical plants will not bloom.

ADHERE—to hold, stick to, cling. Many persons *adhere* to their beliefs despite all arguments.

ADIPOSE—fatty. *Adipose* tissue is often the sign of a glandular defect.

ADJOURN—to suspend proceedings, usually for the day. Since it is now five o'clock, I move that we *adjourn* until tomorrow morning.

ADJUNCT—something joined to a thing but not necessarily a part of it. A rider is an *adjunct* to a legislative bill.

ADJURE—to charge or command solemnly. The witness was *adjured* to weigh his words carefully.

ADMONISH—to warn. The child was *admonished* not to run into the roadway.

ADROIT—skillful in use of the hands or mental faculties. The *adroit* juggler held the attention of the crowd.

ADULATION—praise, flattery, with element of servility. The *adulation* tendered to the wealthy is often aimed at their purses.

ADUMBRATION—a faint outline or foreshadowing. The first atomic bomb was an *adumbration* of a new era of destruction.

ADVANTAGEOUS—useful, favorable. Our opponent's blunders have been *advantageous* to our campaign.

ADVENT—coming, arrival. The *advent* of spring is always a gay time.

ADVENTITIOUS—coming from outside. The *adventitious* economic aid given by the United States was instrumental in saving many nations from Communism.

ADVERSE—opposing, contrary. *Adverse* winds are a hazard to sailing craft.

ADVERSITY—misfortune, poverty. Shakespeare praised the "sweet uses" of *adversity*.

ADVOCATE—plead for or urge. Socialists *advocate* public ownership of utilities.

AESTHETIC—pertaining to the beautiful as distinguished from the practical. Modern design seeks to produce machines which have *aesthetic* as well as functional appeal. Also: esthetic.

AFFABLE—amiable, pleasant, easy to talk to. The smiling face and *affable* manner of the agent put the child at ease.

AFFECT—to influence. The judge did not allow his personal feelings to *affect* his judgment of the case's legal merits.

AFFIDAVIT—a sworn statement in writing. An *affidavit* may serve in place of a personal appearance.

AFFILIATION—connection, as with an organization. His *affiliation* with the club has been of long standing; he has been a member for over ten years.

AFFINITY—relationship, kinship. There is a close *affinity* among many European languages.

AFFIRMATION—solemn avowal, especially by one who will not take an oath. Quakers and others may testify in court on *affirmation*.

AFFIX—to attach, fasten. A price tag was *affixed* to each item.

AFFLUENT—abundant, wealthy. The United States is an *affluent* nation.

AGENDA—list of things to be done. The *agenda* of the conference included the problem of tariffs.

AGGLOMERATE—gather into one mass. It was necessary to *agglomerate* all the minerals into one product to produce the necessary weight.

AGGRAVATE—to annoy or make worse. His sarcasm only *aggravated* an already touchy situation.

AGGREGATE—mass or sum. The *aggregate* of uranium ores in the Colorado plateau amazed prospectors.

AGGRESSION—unprovoked attack. The invasion of Afghanistan was denounced in the Western press as *aggression*.

AGITATE—to stir up or disturb. Rumors of change in the government *agitated* the population.

AGNOSTIC—one who does not think it possible to know whether or not God exists. Many *agnostics* are converted to religion in their later years.

AGORAPHOBIA—unreasonable fear of open places. A person suffering from *agoraphobia* may be unable to go outdoors without experiencing panic.

AGRARIAN—having to do with land. *Agrarian* reforms were one of the first measures proposed in the economic rehabilitation of the country.

AGRONOMY—the science and practice of field crop production and soil management. Many positions in *agronomy* are offered by the Federal government.

AKIMBO—position with hand on hip. He stood with arms *akimbo*, his elbows touching the sides of the hallway.

ALACRITY—cheerful briskness. The *alacrity* shown by the new employee gratified the manager.

ALBINO—white, without pigment. *Albino* deer are extremely rare.

ALCHEMY—medieval chemistry. A goal of *alchemy* was the transmutation of base metals into gold.

ALIBI—a defensive excuse. His *alibi* was iron-clad; he was in the hospital at the time of the murder.

ALIENATE—to estrange, make inimical or indifferent. One purpose of the offer to the East was to *alienate* the Western nations.

ALLAY—pacify, calm. Therapy will often *allay* the fears of the neurotic.

ALLEGATION—assertion without proof. He was unable to prove his wild *allegations*.

ALLEGORY—a story that teaches through symbols. Animal fables are usually *allegories* of human behavior.

ALLEVIATE—lessen, make easier. The morphine helped to *alleviate* the pain.

ALLOCATE—to distribute or assign. The new serum was *allocated* among the states by population.

ALLUDE—to refer indirectly or by suggestion. The report *alludes* to a later document.

ALLUVIAL—left by departing water. *Alluvial* deposits are marked by stratified rock.

ALOOF—distant, reserved, or cold in manner. Her elegant appearance and formal politeness made her seem *aloof*, though in reality she was only shy.

ALTERCATION—angry dispute. The *altercation* stopped just short of physical violence.

ALTITUDE—height, especially above sea level or the earth's surface. The plane had reached an *altitude* of four miles.

ALTRUISM—regard for the interest of others. The *altruism* of the nursing profession is taken for granted.

AMALGAMATE—make into a single unit. We will have to *amalgamate* all our groups in order to be strong.

AMASS—to collect, pile up. Through careful investment he had *amassed* a sizable fortune.

AMATORY—pertaining to sexual love. The *amatory* emphasis in films disturbed some groups.

AMBIDEXTROUS—able to use both hands equally well. *Ambidextrous* tennis players have a great advantage.

AMBIGUOUS—having more than one meaning. The *ambiguous* nature of many legislative acts requires clarification by the courts.

AMBIVALENT—having conflicting feelings. I am *ambivalent* about the job; although the atmosphere is pleasant, the work itself is boring.

AMBULATORY—moving about, able to walk. *Ambulatory* patients require organized activities to speed their recovery.

AMELIORATE—make better, improve. It will take more than a few new textbooks to *ameliorate* the crisis in the schools.

AMENABLE—open to suggestion. He was *amenable* to any proposition.

AMEND—to correct or improve. She *amended* the situation by paying for the lamp she had broken.

AMENITY—pleasantness, courteous act. One must observe the *amenities* in dealing with strangers.

AMENTIA—mental deficiency. *Amentia* should not be confused with neurotic disorders.

AMICABLE—friendly. Courts often seek to settle civil suits in an *amicable* manner.

AMNESTY—pardon for a large group. The president granted *amnesty* to the rebels.

AMORAL—nonmoral, with no sense of sin. To the new settlers, the islanders seemed to lead a carefree, *amoral* existence, doing whatever they pleased.

AMPERSAND—the symbol for *and*, &. Many firms use an *ampersand* instead of *and* on their letterheads.

AMPLIFY—to enlarge, expand. Congressmen may *amplify* their remarks for appearance in the Record.

AMULET—a charm worn to protect against evil. The tooth of an animal was a popular *amulet* among primitive tribes.

ANACHRONISM—something out of its proper time. An abstract picture in an early American home is an *anachronism*.

ANALECTS—fragments forming a literary collection. The Dickens *analects* from the estate brought high prices at the auction.

ANALGESIA—insensibility to pain while retaining consciousness. Drugs to induce *analgesia* are widely used in dentistry.

ANALOGY—a similarity, partial likeness. Countless poets have pointed out the *analogy* between youth and springtime.

ANARCHY—absence of government and law. When the police union strikes, *anarchy* may soon follow.

ANATHEMA—a solemn curse, or the thing or person cursed. Even the mildest socialist program is *anathema* to his way of thinking.

ANEMIA—deficiency of red blood corpuscles or hemoglobin in the blood. Before it was treated, her *anemia* caused her to tire easily.

ANEROID—using no fluid. The *aneroid* barometer is suitable for cold weather areas because there is nothing to freeze.

ANEURISM—permanent swelling of artery. An *aneurism* may be caused when part of the wall of the blood vessel is destroyed. Also: aneurysm.

ANIMADVERSION—adverse criticism, blame. Although it had its flaws, the film did not deserve such *animadversion* from the critics.

ANIMOSITY—ill will, resentment. The *animosity* of the population of the occupied territories made the value of its labor doubtful to the conqueror.

ANNALS—chronological records. The *annals* of the scientific societies reflect the advance of our era.

ANNIHILATE—to destroy completely. If the government does not act to preserve the few remaining herds, the whole species will have been *annihilated* by the end of the century.

ANNOTATE—provide explanatory notes. *Annotations* are sometimes the most interesting part of a text, but they are often overlooked.

ANNUAL—yearly, once a year. The company holds an *annual* picnic on the Fourth of July.

ANNUITY—an amount of money payable yearly. Investment in an *annuity* provides an income for one's old age.

ANNUL—to wipe out, make void. The Supreme Court can *annul* a law which is unconstitutional.

ANODYNE—pain reliever. Morphine, ether, and bullets are famous *anodynes*.

ANOMALOUS—out of place, inappropriate to the surroundings. An *anomalous* jukebox stood rusting in the square of the primitive village.

ANONYMOUS—bearing no name, unsigned. Little credence should be given to an *anonymous* accusation.

ANTECEDENT—something preceding. All history is a repetition of *antecedents*.

ANTEDILUVIAN—very old (lit. before the Flood). The *antediluvian* man attracted attention with his long beard and flowing robe.

ANTEPENULTIMATE—third from the end. In a series of six words, the fourth is *antepenultimate*.

ANTERIOR—before in time, prior, toward the front. The *anterior* section of the boy's brain was damaged in the accident.

ANTHOLOGY—a collection of literary selections. The publisher of an *anthology* must use judgment in his selections.

ANTHROPOLOGY—the science of man. *Anthropologists* study the development and cultures of the human race.

ANTICIPATE—to foresee, give thought to in advance, expect. We *anticipate* that this movie will be a box office hit.

ANTIPATHETIC—opposite in disposition. Siblings are often *antipathetic*.

ANTIPATHY—dislike. She had an *antipathy* toward men.

ANTITHESIS—direct opposite. Black is the *antithesis* of white.

APARTHEID—South African policy of racial segregation. The oppression of blacks is enforced by law under *apartheid*.

APATHETIC—without feeling, indifferent. The *apathetic* attitude of voters enables a minority to control the election.

APERTURE—opening. The woman walked through an *aperture* between two rocks and found herself in a cave.

APEX—summit, peak. Some men reach the *apex* of their careers before forty.

APHORISM—a witty maxim. An *aphorism* is often remembered when its context is forgotten.

APIARY—place where bees are kept. An *apiary* provides an interesting and sometimes profitable hobby.

APLOMB—self-assurance, poise. His *aplomb* is characteristic of the successful urbanite.

APOCALYPSE—revelation. *Apocalypse* gets its meaning from the last book of the New Testament.

APOCRYPHAL—of doubtful authority. This is the second *apocryphal* Van Dyck presented for sale at the gallery.

APOGEE—highest point in an orbit. The moon is at its *apogee* when it is at the point in its orbit farthest from earth.

APOSTASY—a forsaking of beliefs. After her *apostasy* she never again set foot in a church.

APOTHEGM—a practical maxim. "Early to bed" is an *apothegm*.

APOTHEOSIS—the making of a human being into a god. After the Senate declared his *apotheosis*, the late Emperor Augustus was worshipped at temples in Rome.

APPARITION—phantom, anything that appears suddenly or unexpectedly. Dressed in the antique gown, the woman looked like an *apparition* from her grand-mother's era.

APPEASE—to give in to satisfy or make peace, to pacify. Only a heartfelt apology will *appease* his rage at having been slighted.

APPELLANT—one who appeals from a judicial decision. The *appellant* is responsible for costs of the action if his appeal fails.

APPELLATION—name, designation. Use of a nickname deprives a person of his true *appellation*.

APPEND—attach, affix. Exhibits should be *appended* to the report.

APPENDIX—extra material added at the end of a book. A chronology of the events described may be found in the *appendix*.

APPOSITE—fitting, relevant. Since he hadn't followed the discussion, his comments were not *apposite*.

APPRAISE—set a value on. The price at which authorities *appraise* a building determines its taxes.

APPREHEND—to arrest, also to understand. To *apprehend* a culprit is the first step toward his trial.

APPREHENSIVE—fearing some coming event. She was *apprehensive* about the examination.

APPRISE—give notice. He was captured because none could *apprise* him of the enemy advance.

APPROBATION—approval. The act was performed with the *approbation* of his superiors.

APROPOS—pertinent, to the point. His remarks were *apropos* and logical.

AQUILINE—hooked, like an eagle's beak. His *aquiline* features gave him a piratical appearance.

ARBITER—a person having power to determine a dispute. The *arbiter* ruled in favor of neither contestant.

ARBITRARY—despotic, arrived at through will or caprice. An *arbitrary* ruling of a civil commission may be reviewed by the courts.

ARBITRATION—referring disagreement to an outsider for decision. Under their agreement, disputes were to be settled by *arbitration*.

ARBOREAL—living in trees, pertaining to trees. The South American sloth is an *arboreal* mammal.

ARCHAIC—out of use. Some words like "thou" are *archaic*.

ARCHETYPE—prime example, original model. Solomon is the *archetype* of the wise man.

ARCHIVES—historic records. A separate building houses the United States *archives* in Washington.

ARDENT—passionately enthusiastic. His *ardent* patriotism led him to risk his life in the underground resistance movement.

ARGOT—specialized language of a particular line of work or way of life. New members of the police force quickly learn the *argot* of the criminal.

ARMADA—a fleet of armed ships. The Spanish *Armada* sailed against England in 1588.

AROMA—fragrance. The *aroma* of good coffee stimulates the salivary glands.

ARRAIGN—bring before a court. A person arrested must be *arraigned* within 24 hours.

ARROGATE—claim without right. He *arrogates* to himself the judicial power.

ARROYO—dry river bed. The horse followed the *arroyo* as the most convenient path.

ARTIFACT—man-made object. *Artifacts* found by archaeologists enable them to learn much about the daily lives of primitive peoples.

ARTIFICE—trickery, clever device. He used every *artifice* to win the contract.

ASCERTAIN—to find out with certainty. Because the woman's story was so confused, we have been unable to *ascertain* whether a crime was committed or not.

ASCETIC—person who practices self-denial. As an *ascetic*, he ate only the simplest foods and never touched alcohol.

ASCRIBE—to attribute, or assign as a cause. His death was *ascribed* to poison.

ASEPTIC—free from bacteria. The doctor ordered an *aseptic* preparation.

ASININE—stupid, silly. The argument was too *asinine* to deserve a serious answer.

ASPERITY—harshness. The *asperity* of his decisions made the judge no friends.

ASPERSION—a disparaging remark. Every pioneer in science has had *aspersions* cast on his work.

ASPHYXIATION—death or loss of consciousness caused by lack of oxygen. The flames never reached that part of the building, but several residents suffered *asphyxiation* from the smoke.

ASSAILANT—attacker. Faced with a line-up, the victim picked out his alleged *assailant*.

ASSAY—determination of weight, quality, etc. An *assay* precedes any attempt to extract ores from the ground.

ASSEMBLAGE—a group or collection of things or persons. Out of the *assemblage* of spare parts in the garage, we found the pieces to repair the bicycle.

ASSENT—concur, comply, consent. All parties involved *assented* to the statement.

ASSERT—claim or state positively. He *asserted* his title to the property.

ASSESS—to set a value on. The house has been *assessed* for taxes at far below its market value.

ASSIDUOUS—performed with constant diligence. *Assiduous* attention to his assignment won him a promotion.

ASSIGN—to appoint, prescribe. The new reporters were *assigned* to cover local sports events.

ASSIMILATE—absorb and convert into the parent body. In time, each generation of immigrants becomes *assimilated* into the American population.

ASSUAGE—ease or mitigate. The medicine should *assuage* his pains.

ASSUMPTION—something taken for granted or supposed to be fact. I prepared dinner on the *assumption* that they would be home by seven.

ASSURE—to make something certain, guarantee; to promise with confidence. The fact that they left their tickets *assures* that they will return. I *assured* her that someone would be there to meet her.

ASTRAL—relating to the stars. The number of *astral* bodies is beyond computation.

ASTUTE—difficult to deceive. It takes an *astute* man to succeed in poker.

ATAXIA—inability to coordinate movements. Victims of *ataxia* find it difficult to drive a car and sometimes even to walk.

ATONE—make amends for an offense. He *atoned* for his crime by serving his sentence.

ATROPHY—a wasting away. The untreated snake bite resulted in the *atrophy* of his arm.

ATTAIN—to get through effort, to achieve or reach. Thanks to their generous contribution, the campaign has *attained* its goal.

ATTENUATE—make thin, dilute, weaken. His mumbling delivery and hesitant manner *attenuated* the force of his remarks.

ATTEST—bear witness to by oath or signature. Disinterested witnesses must *attest* to the signing of a will.

ATTRITION—a gradual wearing down. With the armies dug into the trenches, World War I became a war of *attrition*.

ATYPICAL—not normal or usual. The usually calm man's burst of temper was *atypical*.

AUCTION—to sell to the highest bidder. Bidding started at five dollars, but the chair eventually was *auctioned* for thirty.

AUGMENT—increase. He *augments* his wealth with every deal.

AUGUR—portend, prophecy. His excellent education *augured* well for his success in law.

AURAL—of the ear or hearing. Since the sound system was not working properly, the *aural* aspect of the performance was a disappointment.

AUREATE—gilded. The *aureate* ceiling glowed in the light.

AUSPICIOUS—indicating success. The first week's business was an *auspicious* start for the whole enterprise.

AUSTERITY—quality of being strict, rigorous, very simple, or unadorned. To save money they went on an *austerity* program, cutting down on driving and nonessential purchases.

AUSTRAL—southern. Some *austral* stars are never seen by Canadians.

AUTHORIZE—to give official permission. The guard is *authorized* to demand identification from anyone entering the building.

AUTOCRAT—a despot, a domineering person. The *auto-cratic* attitude of the Russian ruling class elicited resentment from the people.

AUTOPSY—examination and partial dissection of a body to determine the cause of death. The *autopsy* revealed a brain tumor.

AUXILIARY—an appendage to another organization. The woman's *auxiliary* of the church maintained the school.

AVARICE—greed for wealth. In many novels, *avarice* leads to destruction.

AVERSE—having a dislike or reluctance. The perennial bachelor is *averse* to matrimony.

AVERT—to turn aside or ward off. By acting quickly we *averted* disaster.

AVOCATION—hobby. The person who can earn a living from his *avocation* is indeed fortunate.

AVOW—declare openly. He *avowed* his belief in the political party.

AVUNCULAR—like an uncle. He displayed an *avuncular* interest in the children of the neighborhood.

BACKGAMMON—a game played with pieces on a board. Dice are used in the game of *backgammon*.

BADGER—to tease or annoy. The students *badgered* the teacher.

BADINAGE—banter. The *badinage* which accompanied the tennis match left no scars.

BAFFLE—to perplex, frustrate. The intricacies of the game *baffle* description.

BALEFUL—destructive, deadly. The *baleful* glance of a witch was feared.

BANAL—commonplace, trite. The use of *banal* remarks will dull any conversation.

BANEFUL—actively evil. The ex-convict exerted a *baneful* influence on the other members of the group.

BANTER—tease in a light, good-natured way. *Bantering* comments are popular among juveniles.

BAROQUE—highly ornate. *Baroque* decorations are characteristic of the last century.

BARREN—unfruitful, unproductive. Only a few scrubby trees clung to the rocky soil of that *barren* landscape.

BARRISTER—British term for a lawyer. In England, a *barrister* is superior to a solicitor or attorney.

BARTER—to trade by direct exchange of one commodity for another. In a *barter* transaction, no money is involved.

BASTION—type of fortification. The *bastion* projects outward from the main enclosure.

BAUBLE—trifle, piece of finery or jewelry. He gave up his self-respect for a *bauble*.

BAZAAR—an exchange market place in the East. The *bazaar* is the center of political and social as well as business life in many countries.

BEDIZEN—deck with vulgar finery. The gypsies were *bedizened* in costumes of many colors.

BEDLAM—scene of wild confusion and uproar. The students' riot created a *bedlam* on the campus.

BEGUILE—mislead, deceive. Where he found himself weak, he would *beguile* the opposition into applauding his propositions.

BELABOR—to beat soundly. In the book, the poor servant was constantly *belabored* without cause.

BELIE—to lie about, to show to be false. Her laughing face *belied* her pretense of annoyance.

BELITTLE—to make smaller or less important. He *belittled* the actress's talent by suggesting that her beauty, rather than her acting ability, was responsible for her success.

BELLICOSE—warlike. The *bellicose* attitude of the man involved him in many fights.

BENEDICTION—blessing. Many sought the *benediction* of their pastor during troubled times.

BENEFICIARY—one who benefits, especially one who receives a payment or inheritance. The man named his wife as the *beneficiary* of the insurance policy.

BENIGN—kindly. His *benign* influence helped to alleviate the suffering of the poor.

BERATE—scold vehemently. The teacher who *berates* his class is rationalizing his own faults.

BESTOW—to grant or confer. The republic *bestowed* great honors upon its heroes.

BIBLIOGRAPHY—list of sources of information on a particular subject. She assembled a *bibliography* of major works on American history published since 1960.

BICAMERAL—consisting of two bodies. The United States legislature is a *bicameral* body.

BIENNIAL—happening every two years. Many state legislatures convene on a *biennial* basis.

BIGOT—narrow-minded, intolerant person. A *bigot* is not swayed from his beliefs by rational argument.

BIPED—a two-footed animal. Man and birds are listed among the *bipeds*.

BLANCH—to bleach, make white. You can *blanch* plants by excluding light.

BLASPHEMY—irreverence, sacrilege. *Blasphemy* is the strongest term for intentional indignity offered toward God or a sacred object.

BLATANT—too noisy, obtrusive. The herds of cattle filled the air with their *blatant* bellowing.

BLITHE—joyous, glad, cheerful. Her *blithe* spirit provided an air of gaiety to the whole event.

BOGUS—false, counterfeit. Using a *bogus* driver's license, she had opened an account under an assumed name.

BOLSTER—to prop up, support. The announcement that refreshments were being served *bolstered* the flagging spirits of the company.

BOMBASTIC—pompous, high-sounding, using inflated language. The *bombastic* politician sounds like a fool on television.

BOURGEOIS—middle-class. Thriftiness, respectability, and hard work are often thought of as *bourgeois* traits.

BOVINE—cowlike. Persons with a sluggish disposition are called *bovine*.

BOYCOTT—to refuse to do business with or use. Consumers *boycotted* the company's products to show support for the striking workers.

BRACE—a couple or pair. *Brace* is applied to ducks, dogs, pistols.

BRAZEN—brassy, shameless. A *brazen* contempt for law is found among teen-age delinquents.

BREACH—opening or gap; failure to keep the terms, as of a promise or law. When they failed to deliver the goods, they were guilty of a *breach* of contract.

BREVITY—conciseness, terseness. *Brevity* is the essence of journalistic writing.

BROACH—to tap or pierce a cask to let out the liquor; to open up for the first time, as in conversation. He did not *broach* the subject.

BROCHURE—a pamphlet. *Brochures* on many topics are available free of charge.

BROMIDE—a type of sedative; a trite statement. His conversation was full of *bromides*.

BRUIT—to rumor. The story of his failure was *bruited* around town.

BRUNT—force or shock. The *brunt* of the attack was borne by the infantry.

BRUSQUE—blunt, curt in manner. A *brusque* manner displeases many persons.

BUCOLIC—pertaining to a farm, rural. The *bucolic* personality is usually thought of as hearty, simple, and lusty.

BUDGET—plan for the spending of income during a certain period. The present *budget* allocates one-fourth of our joint income for rent and utilities.

BUFFOON—a clown. The *buffoon* provides comic relief in many tragedies.

BULLION—gold or silver in the form of bars. Nations exchange *bullion* to pay their trade balances.

BUOYANT—rising or floating; cheerful. His *buoyant* nature would not allow him to remain glum for long.

BURGEON—to sprout. Plants *burgeon* with the coming of spring.

BURNISH—polish by rubbing. *Burnished* metal will gleam in the light.

BUTT—the object of a jest. The dullard is the *butt* of his classmates' tricks.

CABAL—secret association. The ministry of Charles II was made up of five unpopular ministers, whose names began with the letters *C, A, B, A, L,* and who were thus given a sinister mien by the acronym *cabal*.

CABALA—a Jewish occult philosophy; any occult science. A Hebrew *cabala* that grew up in medieval times found mysterious significances in the arrangements of certain Biblical phrases.

CACHE—a hiding place for loot or supplies. The *cache* left by the expedition was found many years later.

CADAVER—a dead body. The *cadaver* was dissected by the medical students.

CADENCE—rhythmic flow, modulation of speech, measured movement. The low and musical *cadence* of her voice was a delight to hear.

CADRE—a framework, a skeleton organization. A *cadre* of commissioned and non-commissioned officers was maintained.

CADUCEUS—a staff, symbol of the medical profession. Members of the Army medical corps wear the *caduceus* as part of their insignia.

CAIRN—heap of stones used as landmark or tombstone. The *cairns* of England are a tourist attraction.

CAJOLE—coax, persuade by artful flattery. He was *cajoled* into betting on the game.

CALIBER—capacity of mind, quality. Men of the highest *caliber* are wanted for these positions. Also: calibre.

CALK—fill a seam with paste. He *calked* the windows to keep the waters from seeping through. Also: caulk.

CALLIGRAPHY—penmanship. The *calligraphy* of the monks is the basis of many printing typefaces today.

CALLOW—immature, inexperienced. A *callow* youth often grows into a sophisticated man.

CALUMNIATE—to slander. He was known to *calumniate* anyone who disagreed with him.

CALUMNY—slander, false, accusation. Many honest persons are the victims of *calumny*.

CAMISOLE—ornamental woman's underbodice. *Camisoles* return to style periodically when open blouses are in fashion.

CANDID—true to the real facts. He spoke *candidly* of his financial difficulties.

CANDOR—frankness, impartiality. *Candor* and innocence often go hand-in-hand.

CANT—jargon, secret slang, empty talk. The conversational *cant* of the two social scientists was unintelligible to everyone else at the party.

CANTILEVER—a horizontal projection extending beyond the support. His sun deck was built on a *cantilever* over the stream.

CAPACIOUS—spacious. The *capacious* railroad terminals offer a bright welcome to tourists.

CAPACITY—ability or aptitude. His prudent decisions proved his *capacity* for the top job.

CAPITAL—most significant; wealth. That was a *capital* idea! An outlay of *capital* is necessary when starting a business.

CAPITOL—a legislative building. The state Senate convened in the *capitol* today.

CAPITULATE—surrender. The city *capitulated* to the victors.

CAPRICIOUS—changing suddenly, willfully erratic. The lady is *capricious;* today she likes me, tomorrow she likes someone else.

CAPTIOUS—fault-finding. His *captious* criticisms were motivated by an unreasoning jealousy.

CARAFE—bottle. The *carafe* is now popular for an individual service of coffee.

CARCINOGENIC—producing cancer. In tests on laboratory animals, the drug was shown to be *carcinogenic*.

CARCINOMA—a malignant tumor. *Carcinoma* has become synonymous with cancer.

CAREEN—tip to one side. The ship *careened* with each new wave.

CARICATURE—a distorted sketch. *Caricature* is the weapon of the political cartoonist.

CARNAGE—destruction of life. The *carnage* of modern warfare is frightful to consider.

CARNAL—of the body or flesh. The *carnal* pleasures of Babylon were deplored by the ancients.

CARNIVOROUS—flesh-eating. Tigers are among the *carnivorous* animals.

CARRION—decaying flesh of a dead body. Vultures feed on *carrion*.

CARTE BLANCHE—unrestricted authority. French aristocrats had *carte blanche*.

CARTILAGE—firm elastic tissue. The *cartilage* in the nose may become as hard as bone.

CASEOUS—pertaining to cheese. Welsh rarebit is a *caseous* recipe.

CASSOCK—long, close-fitting church garment. The monk wore a black *cassock*.

CASTIGATE—to criticize severely. The judge *castigated* the plaintiff before he fined him for contempt of court.

CASUISTRY—application or misapplication of general ethical principles to specific cases; e.g., If a man and wife are legally one, why must we buy two tickets?

CATACLYSM—a sudden, violent change in the earth. Pompeii was visited by a *cataclysm* that destroyed the entire city.

CATALYST—substance that causes change in other substances without itself being affected. Platinum is a *catalyst* in many processes; it speeds chemical changes without being affected itself.

CATECHISM—elementary book of religious principles. Most parochial school students must learn their *catechism* early.

CATEGORICAL—not conditional. He made these statements *categorically:* that he was at home all night and that he had made no phone calls.

CATEGORY—class or division in a system of classification. Patients are listed according to *categories* which designate the seriousness of their condition.

CATHOLIC—universal, widespread. His taste in literature was *catholic*, encompassing all fields.

CAUDAL—near the tail. He was kicked soundly in the *caudal* region.

CAUSTIC—biting, burning, stinging. The surface of the wood had been marred by some *caustic* substance.

CAUTERIZE—to burn to prevent infection. The surgeon *cauterized* the wound, removing dead tissue.

CAVEAT—a legal notice preventing some action, a warning. A *caveat* may be entered to stop the reading of a will.

CAVIL—to find fault with unnecessarily, quibble. He obstructs the meeting by his *caviling* comments.

CEDE—yield, assign, transfer. A bill of sale will *cede* title of the property.

CELERITY—swiftness. Act with all *celerity* to take advantage of the opportunity.

CELESTIAL—heavenly. Planets are *celestial* bodies.

CELIBATE—unmarried, refraining from sexual activity. The Roman Catholic Church requires that its priests be *celibate*.

CENOTAPH—monument for the dead. They built a *cenotaph* for the heroes lost at sea.

CENSURE—blame, condemnation. An act of *censure* may be enacted by the Senate.

CEPHALIC—pertaining to the head. Among his other *cephalic* injuries, he suffered a mild concussion.

CERAMIC—pertaining to clay. The *ceramic* industry produces dishes, figures, vases, and other forms of pottery.

CEREBRAL—pertaining to the brain. The stroke was the result of a *cerebral* hemorrhage.

CEREBRATION—process of thought. The higher sciences require concentrated *cerebration*.

CHAGRIN—disappointment, vexation. The failure of the play filled the backers with *chagrin*.

CHALLIS—a lightweight fabric, usually printed, of wool, rayon, or cotton. She bought three yards of *challis* to make a dress.

CHAMBRAY—a fine gingham fabric. *Chambray* weaves are commonly used in dresses.

CHAMELEON—a lizard able to change its coloring; a changeable person. The detective was so famous for his disguises that they called him Dr. *Chameleon*.

CHAMP—to bite and chew with force and noise. Many horses *champ* at the bit.

CHANDLER—a candle-seller, a retailer of groceries and other supplies. The ship *chandler* delivered the goods to the pier the day before the ship was to sail.

CHAOTIC—completely confused. Lack of management will result in a *chaotic* state of affairs.

CHARACTERISTIC—typical trait, identifying feature. The curved yellow bill is a *characteristic* of this species.

CHARLATAN—one who pretends to know more than he does. *Charlatans* who pretend they can cure cancer have been responsible for many deaths.

CHARNEL—a burial place. A *charnel* house is a place for bodies or bones of the dead.

CHARY—careful. He is always *chary* with a new acquaintance.

CHASSIS—frame, wheels, and machinery of an automobile. The appearance of the *chassis* may belie the riding qualities of a car.

CHASTE—sexually virtuous, simple in style. A *chaste* design is one that is restrained and unadorned.

CHASTISEMENT—physical punishment. *Chastisement* of delinquent children is considered necessary by some teachers.

CHATTEL—an item of property, not real estate. A *chattel* mortgage would protect a loan made on such property.

CHAUVINISM—zealous unreasoning patriotism. *Chauvinism* is the cause of many unnecessary wars.

CHICANERY—unethical methods, legal trickery. He accused the winning candidate of *chicanery* in the election.

CHIDE—rebuke, scold. Parents should *chide* a disobedient child.

CHIMERICAL—imaginary. The pessimists labeled his reports of prosperity *chimerical*.

CHIROPODY—treatment of foot ailments. He visited a *chiropodist* to have his corns removed.

CHIROPRACTIC—system of healing by manipulating body structures, particularly the spine. The *chiropractic* profession is licensed in some states but not in others.

CHIVALRY—medieval system of knighthood; virtues of knighthood such as courage, courtesy, respect for women. His *chivalry* would not let him take unfair advantage of his opponent's weakness.

CHOLERIC—angry. His *choleric* features augured an eventual heart attack.

CHRONIC—long-lasting, recurring. His *chronic* asthma flares up at certain times of the year.

CHRONOLOGY—arrangement by time, list of events by date. The book included a *chronology* of the poet's life against the background of the major political events of his age.

CHUTNEY—East Indian relish, seasoning. He ordered Bombay duck with *chutney*.

CICADA—a family of insects including crickets. You could hear the chirping of the *cicada* all through the night.

CIRCUITOUS—roundabout. Sometimes a *circuitous* route is the fastest way to reach your destination.

CIRCUMLOCUTION—talking around a subject. The audience was restive as the speaker's *circumlocution* went on and on without making a point.

CIRCUMSPECT—watchful in all directions, wary. A public official must be *circumspect* in all his actions.

CIRCUMVENT—go around, frustrate. By devious dealings, they were able to *circumvent* the regulations.

CIRRUS—a thin, fleecy cloud consisting of ice crystals. *Cirrus* clouds foretell cold weather.

CITADEL—fortress. In the Middle Ages, every town had its *citadel*.

CITATION—summons to appear in court; an official

praise, as for bravery; reference to legal precedent or authority. Caught for speeding, I received a *citation*. Three firefighters received *citations* for the heroic rescue effort. The attorney asked the clerk to check the *citations* to cases in the Supreme Court.

CITE—quote, for support or authority. The lawyer *cited* a previous decision to support his point.

CLAIRVOYANCE—ability to foretell the future. It was believed that the oracles had the power of *clairvoyance*.

CLANDESTINE—secret. The conspirators held a *clandestine* meeting.

CLAQUE—hired applauders. The *claque* applauded at each appearance of the new star.

CLAUSTROPHOBIA—fear of enclosed places. He could not enter an elevator because he suffered from chronic *claustrophobia*.

CLAVICLE—collarbone. Football players sometimes suffer a broken *clavicle*.

CLAVIER—musical keyboard. He selected the notes on the *clavier*.

CLEAVE—this word has two opposite meanings: (1) to adhere. Let us *cleave* together. (2) to split asunder. The blow *cleaved* the limb in two.

CLEMENCY—leniency. The governor granted *clemency* to the prisoners.

CLICHÉ—a trite, overworked expression. "White as snow" is a *cliché*.

CLIMACTIC—of a climax. At the *climactic* moment of the film, the heroine walks out and slams the door.

CLIMATIC—of a climate. Over eons, *climatic* changes turned the swamp into a desert.

COADJUTOR—helper. The cardinal appointed a *coadjutor* to assist the bishop.

COALESCE—grow together. The *coalescence* of the American states is one of the secrets of our nation's progress.

COALITION—temporary union of groups for a specific purpose. Various environmentalist groups formed a *coalition* to work for the candidate most sympathetic to their cause.

CODICIL—an amendment to a will. A *codicil* must be witnessed in the same manner as the original will.

COERCE—compel. The confession was obtained under *coercion*.

COGENT—conclusive, convincing. A debater must present *cogent* arguments to win his point.

COGITATE—think. Take time to *cogitate* before you answer.

COGNATE—having the same ancestor or origin. English and German are *cognate* languages; both are derived from an earlier language known as Germanic.

COGNITION—perception, process of knowing. The mere *cognition* of a problem is only the first step toward a solution.

COGNIZANT—having knowledge. He was *cognizant* of all the facts before he made a decision.

COHERENT—logically connected. They were too distraught to give a *coherent* account of the crash.

COHESION—sticking together. The *cohesion* of molecules creates surface tension.

COHORT—a company or band, a single associate or colleague. The leader arrived with one of his *cohorts*.

COINCIDE—to be alike, to occur at the same time. This year Thanksgiving *coincides* with her birthday.

COLANDER—container with holes for allowing liquids to drain off. She drained the spaghetti in a *colander* over the sink.

COLLABORATE—to work together on a project. The friends decided to *collaborate* on a novel.

COLLATE—collect in order, check that pages of a text are in order. The photocopies have been *collated* and are ready to be stapled.

COLLATERAL—side by side; securities for a debt. He cited *collateral* court decisions. He offered bonds as *collateral* for his loan.

COLLEAGUE—fellow worker in a profession. The biologist enjoyed shoptalk with her *colleagues* at the conference.

COLLOQUIAL—of speech and informal writing, conversational. Having only studied formal French, she was unable to understand many of her host's *colloquial* expressions.

COLLOQUY—conversation, conference. The faculty held a *colloquy* on grading methods.

COLLUSION—secret agreement, conspiracy. Higher prices were set by *collusion* among all the manufacturers.

COLOPHON—inscription in a book giving information on its production. The publisher's *colophon* identified the kind of type used in printing the volume.

COMATOSE—lethargic, of or like a coma. The drug left him in a *comatose* state.

COMITY—friendly feeling as between neighbors. He described the *comity* among Latin American countries as largely illusory.

COMMEND—to praise. The supervisor *commended* them for their excellent work.

COMMENSURATE—equal. He asked for compensation *commensurate* with his work.

COMMINUTE—reduce to fine particles. The talc was *comminuted* before it could be used cosmetically.

COMMISERATION—sympathy for suffering. One can *commiserate* with the victim of an accident.

COMMISSION—to authorize, especially to have someone perform a task or to act in one's place. I have *commissioned* a neighbor to collect the mail while I'm away.

COMMODIOUS—roomy. The *commodious* closets impressed the prospective tenants.

COMMUTATION—substitution of one thing for another; regular travel between home and work. His prison sentence was *commuted* to hard labor. *Commutation* is a daily routine for most working people.

COMPACT—agreement. The *compact* included a three-year no-strike clause.

COMPARABLE—equivalent, able or worthy to be compared. His degree from a foreign university is *comparable* to our master's degree.

COMPATIBLE—harmonious. *Incompatibility* is sometimes grounds for divorce.

COMPEL—to force. He was *compelled* by law to make restitution.

COMPENSATE—be equal to, make up for. Money could not *compensate* for his sufferings.

COMPETENT—fit, capable, qualified. I am not *competent* to judge the authenticity of this document; you should take it to an expert.

COMPETITION—rivalry for the same object. The theory of free enterprise assumes an unrestricted *competition* for customers among rival businesses.

COMPLACENT—self-satisfied. A *complacent* student seldom attains the heights of success in his scholastic efforts.

COMPLEMENT—that which completes, a full set or quantity. An expensive wardrobe is the *complement* to his impeccable grooming. A *complement* of twelve citizens made up the jury.

COMPLEX—a whole made up of interconnected or related parts. The school grew from a few classrooms to a whole *complex* of buildings organized around the computer center.

COMPLIANT—yielding to others. A *compliant* person may gain popularity at the cost of character.

COMPLICITY—partnership in wrongdoing. By withholding evidence she became guilty of *complicity* in the crime.

COMPONENT—a part, constituent. The *components* of the machine were tooled to perfection.

COMPOSE—to put together, create. I spent an hour *composing* a formal letter of protest.

COMPREHENSIBLE—able to be understood. The episode was only *comprehensible* to those who knew the story thus far.

COMPRISE—include, be made up of, consist of. The test will be *comprised* of the subject matter of the previous lessons.

COMPROMISE—a settlement of a difference in which both sides give up something. We are willing to make some concessions in order to reach a *compromise*.

COMPULSORY—required, forced. Attendance is *compulsory* unless one has a medical excuse.

COMPUNCTION—remorse, uneasiness. He showed no *compunction* over his carelessness.

CONCATENATE—join in a chain. They created a *concatenation* of flowers for the festival.

CONCEDE—to yield, as to what is just or true. When the candidate realized she could not win, she *conceded* gracefully.

CONCENTRIC—with the same center. The orbits of the planets are *concentric*.

CONCEPT—idea, general notion. The *concept* that all individuals have inherent and inalienable rights is basic to our political philosophy.

CONCEPTION—beginning, original idea, mental image. The *conception* of the plan was originally his.

CONCERTED—mutually agreed upon. The *concerted* plan of action was carried out by all the parties involved.

CONCILIATE—gain good will, pacify. The adjustor's task is to *conciliate* the client with a legitimate complaint.

CONCISE—brief, expressing much in a few words. A précis must be *concise* yet cover the topic.

CONCLAVE—a private meeting. International diplomacy is still conducted at *conclaves*.

CONCOCTION—combination of various ingredients. The drink was a *concoction* of syrup, soda, and three flavors of ice cream.

CONCOMITANT—something that accompanies. Due consideration must be given to *concomitant* conditions.

CONCORDAT—a compact, formal agreement. Italy signed a famous *concordat* with the Pope.

CONCURRENT—running together, happening at the same time. *Concurrent* action by the police and welfare authorities reduced juvenile crime.

CONDIGN—well-deserved. The *condign* penalty was applauded by the courtroom audience.

CONDIMENT—spice, seasoning. The *condiment* shelf is part of every well-equipped kitchen.

CONDOLE—express sympathy. His friends gathered to *condole* his loss.

CONDONE—pardon, overlook an offense. The law will not *condone* an act on the plea that the culprit was intoxicated.

CONDUCIVE—leading to, helping. The waterbed was *conducive* to a restful sleep.

CONDUCT—behavior. Her cool *conduct* in the emergency inspired confidence in those around her.

CONDUIT—pipe. The cables were inserted into a *conduit*.

CONFESS—to admit. She *confessed* to having a weakness for junk food.

CONFIDANT—one to whom secrets are confided. One should use care in selecting a *confidant*.

CONFIDENTIAL—private, secret. Respondents were assured that the census was *confidential* and would be used for statistical purposes only.

CONFISCATE—to seize, appropriate. The government has no right to *confiscate* private property without just compensation.

CONFLAGRATION—large fire. New York City was almost destroyed in the 1835 *conflagration*.

CONFORMITY—harmony, agreement. In *conformity* with the rule, the meeting was adjourned.

CONFUTE—to overwhelm by argument. His logical rebuttal *confuted* the reasoning of the opposition.

CONGEAL—to change from a fluid to a solid, to curdle. The horrible scene *congealed* his blood.

CONGENITAL—inherent, dating from birth. The patient's tendency to schizophrenia is *congenital*.

CONGLOMERATE—mixture of many things. The rock sample was a *conglomerate* of quartz pebbles.

CONGRUENT—in agreement, in harmony. *Congruent* figures coincide entirely throughout.

CONIC—in the form of a cone. The *conic* shape of the object reminded him of a pyramid.

CONJECTURE—make a guess based on information at hand. He *conjectured* that vocabulary questions would appear on the test.

CONJOIN—unite. The leader asked that all tribes *conjoin* to meet the enemy.

CONJUGAL—of marriage. The *conjugal* state is often thought preferable to bachelorhood.

CONJURE—to practice magic. He waved his wand and *conjured* up the image of a man.

CONNIVE—pretend ignorance of or assist in wrongdoing. The builder and the agent *connived* in selling the overpriced homes.

CONNUBIAL—of marriage, conjugal. After the honeymoon they moved into a cottage and settled down to *connubial* bliss.

CONSANGUINEOUS—having a blood relationship. The conglomerate of *consanguineous* females was called a cousin's club.

CONSCIENTIOUS—honest, faithful to duty or to what is right. He is *conscientious* in his work and so has won the trust of his employers.

CONSECRATE—render sacred, dedicate. We *consecrate* our lives and fortunes to this endeavor.

CONSERVATIVE—tending to preserve what is, cautious. At the annual conference, they presented their *conservative* views on the future of education.

CONSIDERABLE—important, large, much. The director has *considerable* clout among the members of the board; they value her recommendations highly.

CONSIGN—entrust, hand over. The child was *consigned* to the care of her elder sister until the court could appoint a guardian.

CONSONANCE—harmony, pleasant sounds together. Their *consonance* of opinion in all matters made for a peaceful household.

CONSORT—a wife or husband. The *consort* shares the honors of the monarch.

CONSTANT—unchanging, fixed, continual. It is difficult to listen to his *constant* complaining.

CONSTITUENCY—body of voters. The congressman went home to discuss the issue with his *constituency*.

CONSTITUTE—to set up, make up, compose. In industrialized countries, farmers *constitute* only a small percentage of the population.

CONSTRAIN—restrain, compel. He felt *constrained* to make a full confession.

CONSTRUE—interpret, analyze. His attitude was *construed* as one of opposition to the proposal.

CONSUL—an official representative of a foreign government. The Swedish *consul* attended the opening of the museum's Scandinavian exhibit.

CONSUMMATE—bring to completion, make actual. The agreement was *consummated* when all the parties involved had signed.

CONTAGIOUS—transmittable by direct or indirect contact. Leprosy was long considered a very *contagious* disease.

CONTAMINATE—to pollute, make unclean, or unfit. The pesticide seeped into the water table, *contaminating* the wells.

CONTEMN—view with contempt. Those who *contemn* the purposes of a group should not share in its benefits.

CONTENTIOUS—quarrelsome. One *contentious* student can ruin a debate.

CONTIGUOUS—next to, adjoining. Alaska is not *contiguous* to other states of the United States.

CONTINGENT—depending upon something's happening. His plans were *contingent* upon the check's arriving on time.

CONTORT—to twist out of shape. Rage *contorted* her features into a frightening mask.

CONTRACT—a formal agreement, usually written. The company signed a *contract* to operate a bookstore on campus.

CONTRAVENE—oppose by direct opposition. His actions *contravene* the policy set by the Board.

CONTRITE—sincerely remorseful. An upset stomach helped to make him *contrite* about the disappearing cookies.

CONTRIVE—devise, plan. They *contrived* a way to fix the unit using old parts.

CONTROVERSY—highly charged debate, conflict of opinion. A *controversy* arose over whether to use the funds for highway improvement or for mass transit.

CONTROVERT—to dispute. He can *controvert* that argument with a hundred others.

CONTUMACIOUS—stubbornly disobedient. *Contumacious* children often disrupt their classes.

CONTUMELY—humiliating treatment or language. He heaped *contumely* on the captured king.

CONTUSION—bruise. He suffered from severe *contusions* as a result of the accident.

CONVENE—gather together, assemble. The graduates will *convene* on the campus.

CONVERGE—move nearer together, head for one point. The flock *converged* on the seeded field.

CONVERSANT—familiar, having knowledge of. The accountant is *conversant* with the tax laws.

CONVEYANCE—a deed transferring title to property, a

vehicle. A real property *conveyance* must bear a tax stamp.

CONVIVIAL—gay, festive. Class reunions are *convivial* affairs.

CONVOKE—summon, call together. The conference was *convoked* to consider amending the constitution of the organization.

CONVULSION—violent, involuntary contracting and relaxing of the muscles. Epilepsy is accompanied by *convulsions*.

COOPERATE—to work together for a common goal. If everyone *cooperates* on decorations, entertainment, and refreshments, the party is sure to be a success.

COORDINATE—to bring different elements into order or harmony. In a well-run office, schedules are *coordinated* so that business is uninterrupted.

COPIOUS—plentiful. The table was *copiously* set.

CORDILLERA—chain of mountains. The *cordillera* known as the Andes is the principal range on the South American continent.

CORDOVAN—a type of soft leather. She wore expensive boots of Spanish *cordovan*.

CORNUCOPIA—great horn symbolic of plenty. The *cornucopia* has become a harvest symbol.

CORONARY—pertaining to the arteries. He suffered from a *coronary* thrombosis, a blood clot.

CORPORAL—of the body. *Corporal* punishment of children in public schools is bitterly resented by many parents.

CORPS—an officially associated group of people. Members of the diplomatic *corps* represent the United States wherever they are.

CORPULENT—very fat. The *corpulent* individual must choose his clothes with great care.

CORRELATION—mutual relation, connectedness. The doctor explained the *correlation* between smoking and lung disease.

CORRIGIBLE—capable of being reformed. *Corrigible* offenders should be separated from hardened criminals.

CORROBORATE—provide added proof. Laws of evidence require that evidence of a crime must be *corroborated* by other circumstances.

CORRUGATE—to bend into folds. *Corrugated* paper boxes are widely used for packaging.

CORTEGE—procession. The funeral *cortege* was headed by a band of musicians.

COSMOPOLITAN—belonging to all portions of the world. New York is a *cosmopolitan* city, but many midwest cities are not.

COTERIE—a small, informal social group. The *coteries* of college boys organized themselves into a fraternity.

COTILLION—social dance. The debutantes were introduced annually at a formal *cotillion*.

COTTER—pin which fits into a hole to hold two parts together. The *cotter* pin on the axle kept the wheel from falling off.

COUCHANT—lying down. The Romans received visitors *couchant*, but modern practice requires the host to greet his guests standing.

COULEE—gulch. The deep, cliff-flanked *coulee* was a constant tourist attraction.

COUNCIL—a group assembled for discussion. The church *council* voted to raise funds for a new altar.

COUNSEL—(v.) to give advice to; (n.) a legal advisor. To *counsel* a stubborn child is often exasperating. Mr. Ramirez will act as my *counsel* during the trial.

COUNTERMAND—revoke an order or command. The wise executive will not hesitate to *countermand* an unwise order.

COUP D' ÉTAT—sudden change of government by force. The *coup d'état* was the usual method of governmental change in South America only a few generations ago.

COUTURIER—dressmaker. Paris is famous for its *couturiers*.

COVENANT—a solemn agreement between parties. Where a *covenant* calls for an illegal act, it may not be enforced.

COVERT—hidden, secret. To avoid a public outcry, the president ordered a *covert* military action and publicly denied that he was sending combat troops.

COVETOUS—desiring greedily what belongs to another. He was so *covetous* of attention that he would interrupt anyone else who tried to speak.

COWER—shrink from fear. At the sound of thunder, the dog would *cower* in a corner.

CRANIUM—the skull of a vertebrate. The *cranium* is designed by nature to afford great protection to the brain.

CRASS—stupid, unrefined. The *crass* behavior of some tourists casts discredit on their nation.

CRAVEN—cowardly. His *craven* conduct under stress made him the butt of many jests.

CREDENCE—faith, belief. One could have little *credence* in the word of a known swindler.

CREDIBLE—worthy or able to be believed. The tale, though unusual, was entirely *credible,* considering the physical evidence.

CREDULOUS—inclined to believe on slight evidence. The *credulous* woman followed every instruction of the fortuneteller.

CREED—statement of faith. The Apostles' *creed* is the basis of their belief.

CREMATE—burn a dead body. He left instructions that he was to be *cremated* upon his death.

CRITERION—standard of judging. His answer was used as a *criterion* for grading the test papers.

CROUTON—small piece of toasted bread. Onion soup is invariably served with *croutons*.

CRUCIAL—of utmost importance. The discovery of the letter was *crucial* to the unraveling of the whole mystery.

CRUCIATE—cross-shaped. Many plants have *cruciate* leaves and petals.

CRYPTIC—having a hidden meaning, mysterious. The *cryptic* message was deciphered by the code expert.

CULINARY—relating to the kitchen or to cooking. The proper use of condiments is an important aspect of *culinary* skill.

CULL—to select, pick out from a group. From the pile we *culled* all the mail for local delivery.

CULMINATION—acme, highest attainment. Graduation with highest honors was the *culmination* of his academic efforts.

CULPABLE—faulty, deserving of blame. The *culpable* parties should not escape punishment.

CULT—group with a similar belief, especially an outlandish or faddish one. Nudists are a *cult*.

CUPIDITY—greed for wealth, avarice. The *cupidity* of the miser cannot be satisfied.

CURATIVE—concerning or causing the cure of disease. The grandmother had faith in the *curative* powers of certain herbs.

CURMUDGEON—churlish person. The old *curmudgeon* had no friends.

CURSORY—superficial, hurried. *Cursory* examination of the scene revealed little information.

CURTAIL—reduce, shorten. Classes were reduced to *curtail* teaching costs.

CYGNET—young swan. The grace of the *cygnet* makes it a favorite for decorative lakes.

DACTYL—a metrical foot of one stressed and two unstressed syllables. The word "harmony" is a *dactyl*.

DAGUERREOTYPE—type of early photograph. Many famous mid-19th century personalities posed for *daguerreotypes*.

DALE—a small valley. He trudged over hill and *dale*.

DAMASK—a fine fabric with a figured weave. The crystal bowls were displayed on a fine *damask* tablecloth.

DANK—unpleasantly damp. Dungeon walls are often described as *dank*.

DAPPLED—marked with small spots. The *dappled* horse won the race.

DASTARD—coward. Some *dastard* stabbed him in the back.

DAWDLE—waste time, trifle. Do not *dawdle* at your tasks.

DEARTH—scarcity. A *dearth* of water can create a desert in a few years.

DEBASE—reduce in dignity. Do not *debase* yourself by answering him.

DEBATE—to argue formally for and against. The candidate challenged the incumbent to *debate* the issues on television.

DEBAUCH—corrupt. The temptations they offered could not *debauch* her.

DEBILITATE—enfeeble, weaken. Constant excesses will *debilitate* even the strongest constitution.

DEBONAIR—courteous. Suave and *debonair,* the gentleman impressed the ladies with his city manners.

DECAMP—depart suddenly. The patrol prepared to *decamp* before daylight.

DECANT—pour off gently. *Decant* the wine just before serving it.

DECANTER—ornamental wine bottle. They poured port from the *decanter*.

DECEIVE—to trick, be false to. They *deceived* us by telling us that our donations would be used to provide food to the needy; in reality, the money was used to supply guns to the rebels.

DECIDUOUS—leaf-shedding. Most trees are *deciduous,* but evergreens retain their foliage throughout the winter.

DECIMATE—to destroy a large part (literally, one-tenth) of a population. The Black Death had *decimated* the town.

DECLIVITY—downward slope. The *declivity* offered fine skiing.

DECOLLETÉ—low-necked. The *decolleté* dress attracted much attention from the men.

DECOROUS—proper. *Decorous* conduct is the mark of a gentleman.

DECREPIT—broken down by old age. His *decrepit* appearance branded him as unimportant.

DECRY—clamor against. Critics *decry* the lack of emotion on the stage.

DEDUCE—derive by reasoning. From the facts presented, we *deduce* this conclusion.

DEDUCT—to subtract, take away. Because the package was damaged, the seller *deducted* two dollars from the price.

DEEM—have an opinion, think. They did not *deem* him worthy of the honors he received.

DE FACTO—actual as opposed to legal. Although the *de facto* government was not duly elected, it was in power.

DEFALCATION—embezzlement. The *defalcation* of the cashier ruined the bank.

DEFAMATION—act of ruining another's reputation. Law suits may be brought to collect damages for *defamation* of character.

DEFAULT—failure to do what is required. In *default* of the payment, the property was seized by the creditor.

DEFERENCE—act of respect, respect for another's wishes. Out of *deference* to her age, we rose when she entered.

DEFICIENT—not up to standard, inadequate. The child is *deficient* in reading but excels in arithmetic.

DEFILE—befoul, make profane. A man is not allowed to wear shoes in a mosque, lest he *defile* it.

DEFINITIVE—decisive, conclusive. After exhausting all possible leads, the reporter wrote a *definitive* exposé.

DEFOLIATE—to strip of leaves. All the trees in the yard had been *defoliated* by an infestation of moths.

DEFRAY—to pay (costs). The company *defrayed* the costs of a vacation trip for the winner of the essay contest.

DEFUNCT—dead, no longer functioning. The business has been *defunct* since the big fire.

DEGENERATE—to decline from a higher or normal form. The discussion eventually *degenerated* into a shouting match.

DEGRADE—to lower in status, value, or esteem. The celebrity refused interviews, feeling that it was *degrading* to have her personal life publicly discussed.

DEIFY—to make as a god. They would *deify* Caesar.

DEIGN—condescend. He *deigned* to reply to their criticism.

DE JURE—according to law. Although the government was in power, it was not considered a government *de jure* by the neighboring countries.

DELECTABLE—delightful. The food is delicious, the girls *delectable,* and the music delirious.

DELEGATE—to authorize or assign to act in one's place. Since I will be unable to attend the conference, I have *delegated* my assistant to represent me.

DELEGATION—a group of persons officially authorized to act for others. Our *delegation* to the United Nations is headed by the ambassador.

DELETE—strike out, erase. The proofreader *deleted* the superfluous word.

DELETERIOUS—injurious, harmful. DDT, when taken internally, has a *deleterious* effect on the body.

DELIBERATE—intended, meant. It was no accident, but a *deliberate* act.

DELINEATE—mark off the boundary of. They asked him to *delineate* the areas where play was permitted.

DELINQUENT—delaying or failing to do what rules or law require. Since she was *delinquent* in paying her taxes, she had to pay a fine.

DEMAGOGUE—leader who uses mob passions. Hitler was a *demagogue.*

DEMEAN—degrade, debase. Could you *demean* yourself by joining in their crude pastimes?

DEMONSTRABLE—able to be shown. The tests showed that the consumers' preference was justified by that brand's *demonstrable* superiority.

DEMOTE—to lower in rank. He was stripped of his rank and *demoted* to private.

DEMUR—hesitate, object. Once he *demurred,* we knew we had the advantage of additional time to prepare.

DEMURE—serious, sober. The *demure* maiden was an object of their admiration, but not their affection.

DENIGRATE—to blacken, defame. The lawyer tried to *denigrate* the character of the witness by implying that he was a liar.

DENIZEN—inhabitant, dweller. The *denizens* of the forest fashioned their shelter from the available resources.

DEPLETE—to empty, use up. At the present rates of consumption, the known reserves will be *depleted* before the end of the century.

DEPLORE—to lament, disapprove strongly. Pacifists *deplore* violence even on behalf of a just cause.

DEPOSITION—written testimony taken outside court. A *deposition* had to be taken from the hospitalized witness.

DEPRAVED—sordid, corrupt. Only a *depraved* mind would think of committing a heinous crime.

DEPRECATE—detract from. Do not *deprecate* what you cannot understand.

DEPRECIATE—lessen in value. Property will *depreciate* rapidly unless kept in good repair.

DEPREDATION—ravaging, plundering. The *depredations* of the Huns left a bloody path across the continent.

DERANGED—insane, disordered. The working of the *deranged* mind baffles even those trained in mental care.

DERELICT—a wreck, a thing or person abandoned as worthless. In winter the city's *derelicts* frequent the bus station to stay warm.

DERIDE—mock, laugh at. Many would *deride* the street-corner preacher.

DEROGATORY—disparaging, disdainful. His *derogatory* remarks hid feelings of envy.

DESCRY—spy out, discover by eye. In the distance we could *descry* a small cabin.

DESECRATE—violate, profane. Hoodlums attempted to *desecrate* the cemetery.

DESIGNATE—to name, appoint. We will rendezvous at the time and place *designated* on the sheet.

DESPICABLE—contemptible. The villain in melodramas is always a *despicable* character.

DESPOIL—plunder. The army threatened to *despoil* the city unless it surrendered.

DESPOT—an absolute ruler. The *despot* is out of place in modern monarchy.

DESTITUTE—in extreme want. Even the most *destitute* person has hope for the future.

DESUETUDE—lack of use. The law, which had never been repealed, had fallen into *desuetude* and was never enforced.

DESULTORY—jumping around, aimless. *Desultory* reading will seldom create a well-read individual; reading must be planned.

DETERRENT—a thing that discourages. The absolute certainty of apprehension is a powerful *deterrent* to crime.

DETONATE—to explode. An electrical charge may be used to *detonate* certain explosives.

DETRACT—take away a part, lessen. The old-fashioned engraving *detracted* from the value of the piece of jewelry.

DETRIMENT—a thing which damages or harms. The support of some groups can be a *detriment* to the campaign of an office-seeker.

DEVIATE—stray, turn aside from. The honest man will never *deviate* from the path of rectitude.

DEVIOUS—roundabout, indirect, underhanded. When no one would tell her anything, she resorted to *devious* means to uncover the truth.

DEVISE—contrive, invent. I will *devise* a plan of escape.

DEVOID OF—completely without. The landscape was flat and barren, *devoid of* interest or beauty.

DEVOLVE—be transferred, be handed down. The duties of the position *devolved* upon the new sales manager.

DEXTERITY—quickness, skill and ease in some act. The art of juggling is one that calls for the highest degree of *dexterity*.

DIABOLIC—devilish, fiendish. The ancients used charms to ward off the influence of *diabolic* creatures.

DIADEM—a crown, regal power. The emperor's *diadem* was richly encrusted with gems.

DIAPHANOUS—almost transparent, sheer. Her *diaphanous* negligee revealed the outlines of a beautiful figure.

DICHOTOMY—division into two parts, often opposed. The *dichotomy* of his position, half instructor, half administrator, made efficient work in either field impossible.

DICTUM—an authoritative statement. The professor's *dictum* ended the debate.

DIDACTIC—instructive, intended to teach. The *didactic* approach may be well suited for a text book but should be avoided in books aimed at the general public.

DIFFIDENCE—timidity, humility. His *diffidence* caused him to miss many opportunities.

DIFFUSE—to spread out, scatter widely. When the bottle broke, the fragrance *diffused* throughout the room.

DIGRESS—wander from the subject. To *digress* from the main topic may lend interest to a theme, but at the cost of its unity.

DILAPIDATED—in disrepair, partial ruin. A *dilapidated* building will bring down the value of neighboring property.

DILATE—expand. Some drugs will cause the pupil of the eye to *dilate*.

DILATORY—delaying action. The filibuster is an effective legislative tool in *dilatory* campaigns.

DILEMMA—choice of two unpleasant alternatives, a problem. Even a wrong decision may be preferable to remaining in a *dilemma*.

DILETTANTE—a dabbler, or aimless follower of the fine arts. A *dilettante* may be more interested in talking of his artistic pursuits than following them.

DILUVIAL—pertaining to a flood. The histories of many ancient races speak of a *diluvial* period during which only a few chosen persons survived.

DIMINUTION—reduction in size, lessening. The *diminution* of international armies is a long-sought goal of statesmen.

DIPSOMANIAC—one with an uncontrollable desire for alcohol. The *dipsomaniac* is said to drown his sorrows in liquor.

DISABILITY—loss of ability. The accident resulted in a temporary *disability;* the employee was out for two weeks.

DISCERNIBLE—perceivable, identifiable. The other cars were barely *discernible* in the fog.

DISCIPLE—follower of a teacher. The renowned economist won over many *disciples* with his startling theories.

DISCLAIM—renounce, give up claim to. In order to obtain United States citizenship, one must *disclaim* any title or rank of nobility from another nation.

DISCLOSE—to reveal. The caller did not *disclose* the source of her information.

DISCOMFIT—defeat, frustrate, confuse. Truth may *discomfit* a political opponent more than bombast.

DISCONCERT—throw into confusion. An apathetic audience may *disconcert* even the most experienced performer.

DISCORDANT—harsh, not harmonious. The *discordant* cries of wild birds may make summer vacationers long for the familiar sounds of the city.

DISCREET—prudent, diplomatic. She countered the rude question with a soft-spoken and *discreet* denial.

DISCRETE—separate, unrelated. The process is divided into six *discrete* steps.

DISCRETION—power of decision, individual judgment. The penalty to be imposed in many cases is left to the *discretion* of the judge.

DISCURSIVE—rambling, passing from one subject to another. A debater must check the tendency to *discursive* remarks.

DISDAIN—to reject as unworthy. Many beginners *disdain* a lowly job that might in time lead to the position they desire.

DISINGENUOUS—sophisticated, not innocent. The slip of the tongue indicated that he was not as *disingenuous* as he wished to appear.

DISINTERESTED—not involved in, unprejudiced. A *disinterested* witness is one who has no personal involvement in the outcome of the matter under dispute.

DISJOIN—to separate. The links of the chain were *disjoined.*

DISMANTLE—to take apart. The machine must be *dismantled,* cleaned, repaired, and reassembled.

DISPARAGE—speak slightingly of, belittle. A teacher who *disparages* the efforts of beginners in her subject is not helping them.

DISPARITY—inequality, difference in degree. A *disparity* in age need not mean an incompatible marriage.

DISPATCH—to send on an errand. The bank *dispatched* a courier to deliver the documents by hand.

DISPEL—to drive away, make disappear. The good-humored joke *dispelled* the tension in the room.

DISPENSE WITH—to get rid of, do without. Let's *dispense* with the formalities and get right down to business.

DISPUTATION—a controversy, debate. In his *disputation*, he defended the theories expressed in his paper.

DISQUIETING—disturbing, tending to make uneasy. There have been *disquieting* reports of a buildup of forces along the border.

DISSEMBLE—disguise, make pretence of, simulate. A skillful publicity man will *dissemble* his propaganda to appear as impartial information.

DISSEMINATE—spread, broadcast. With missionary zeal, they *disseminated* the literature about the new religion.

DISSENSION—lack of harmony or agreement. There was *dissension* among the delegates about which candidate to support.

DISSERTATION—an extended treatment of a subject, a formal essay. The *dissertation* is an important requirement for an advanced degree.

DISSIMULATE—disguise. He tried to *dissimulate* his intentions in order to gain his ends.

DISSIPATE—scatter aimlessly, spend foolishly. He soon *dissipated* his inheritance.

DISSOLUTE—immoral. The *dissolute* young man was soon without friends or reputation.

DISSONANT—inharmonious, discordant. Much contemporary music seems *dissonant* to unaccustomed ears.

DISSUADE—advise against, divert by persuasion. His friends *dissuaded* him from that unwise plan of action.

DISTEND—stretch. If you *distend* a balloon beyond a certain point, it will break.

DISTINCT—clear, notable. There is a *distinct* difference between these two musical compositions.

DISTORTION—a twisting out of shape, misstatement of facts. The *distortions* of the historians left little of the man's true character for posterity.

DISTRACT—to divert, turn aside. The loud crash *distracted* the attention of the students.

DISTRAUGHT—crazed, distracted. The young woman, *distraught* at the tragedy of her husband's death, threatened suicide.

DIURNAL—daily, recurring every day. The movement of the sun in the sky is a *diurnal* phenomenon.

DIVA—prima donna, a leading woman singer in opera. The *diva* took another bow.

DIVERGE—extend in different directions from a common point. The map showed a main lode with thin veins *diverging* in all directions.

DIVERSITY—variety, unlikeness. A university should encourage a *diversity* of opinion among the faculty.

DIVEST—deprive, strip. After the court martial, he was *divested* of his rank and decorations.

DIVINATION—a foretelling of the future by occult means. The ancients believed that certain oracles had the power of *divination*.

DIVISIVE—tending to divide, causing disagreement. The issue of abortion, on which people hold deep and morally-based convictions, was *divisive* to the movement.

DIVOT—turf cut out by a stroke. He tore a big *divot* when he tried to hit the golf ball.

DIVULGE—reveal, make public. Newspapermen have long fought the courts for the right not to *divulge* their sources of information.

DOCILE—easily led. The child was *docile* until he discovered his mother was gone.

DOCTRINAIRE—an impractical theorist. He was considered a *doctrinaire* since none of his ideas could be easily implemented.

DOGMA—system of beliefs. Church *dogma* is usually accepted by members of the congregation.

DOGMATIC—arbitrary. His *dogmatic* statements were not supported by evidence.

DOLDRUMS—dullness, gloomy listlessness. The *doldrums* of life at the office drove him to distraction.

DOLE—a free distribution of food or money. Some people live on the *dole*.

DOLEFUL—sorrowful. Her *doleful* eyes brought tears to mine.

DOLOROUS—grievous. Her *dolorous* experiences excited sympathy.

DOMICILE—residence. Some people have one *domicile* in the winter, another in the summer.

DOOMSDAY—day of judgment. You'll wait until *doomsday* before I admit you're right.

DORMANT—sleeping, inactive. Perennial flowers such as irises remain *dormant* every winter and burgeon in the spring.

DORSAL—referring to the back. The *dorsal* fin serves some fish as a rudder.

DOSSIER—file on a subject or person. The French police kept a *dossier* on every person with a criminal record.

DOTAGE—senility. The grandfather is in his *dotage*.

DOTARD—senile person. The old man is a *dotard*.

DOUBLET—a type of fitted man's coat. The *doublet* was an important part of a gentleman's wardrobe.

DOUGHTY—valiant. My *doughty* men fought through the night.

DOUR—sullen. His *dour* features marked him as a man who had failed in life.

DOWRY—money, goods, or estate that a woman brings to her husband in marriage. During the 19th century, the *dowry* was usually contracted for before an engagement to marry was announced.

DRAPER—dealer in dry goods. The *draper* has become almost an anachronism in America, where most people buy their dresses and drapes already made.

DRAY—open cart without sides. They carried the wood in a huge *dray*.

DRIBLET—small amount. He handed out the nuts in *driblets*.

DRIVEL—flowing saliva or foolish talk. Whenever he opened his mouth, you could hear the *drivel* flow.

DROLL—quietly amusing. The British are noted for their *droll* sense of humor.

DROSS—waste matter, scum. The process of separating the valuable metal from the *dross* may be so expensive that a claim is worthless.

DRYAD—wood nymph. *Dryads* and leprechauns are more likely to be found in books than in the forest.

DUBIOUS—in doubt, doubtful. He had the *dubious* distinction of being the best liar at the school.

DUCTILE—capable of being drawn out or hammered. The *ductile* quality of gold makes it possible to manufacture fine gold leaf for artists' frames.

DUDGEON—resentment. Since everything went wrong at work, he left the office feeling high *dudgeon*.

DUENNA—Spanish female chaperone. She was allowed to go nowhere without her *duenna*.

DUPLICITY—hypocrisy, double-dealing. The *duplicity* of the marketplace may shock the naive.

DURANCE—imprisonment. His *durance* left him pale and resentful.

DYNAMIC—in motion, forceful, energetic. A *dynamic* leader can inspire followers with enthusiasm and confidence.

EASEMENT—right to use land owned by another; an easing. His *easement* allowed him to cross his neighbor's property to get to his own.

EBULLIENCE—a boiling up, overflow. The *ebullience* of youth can be wearying to older persons.

ÉCLAT—brilliancy of achievement. She handled the difficult role with *éclat*.

ECLECTIC—drawing from diverse sources or systems. His *eclectic* record collection included everything from Bach cantatas to punk rock.

ECOLOGY—science of the relation of life to its environment. Persons concerned about *ecology* are worried about the pollution of the earth's environment and the effect this will have on life.

ECSTASY—extreme happiness. The lovers were in *ecstasy* just in touching each other's hands.

EDICT—a public notice issued by authority. The *edict* issued by the junta dissolved the government.

EDIFY—instruct. Some teachers *edify;* others merely try.

EDUCE—elicit, draw out. Can you *educe* any information from her notes?

EFFACE—obliterate, wipe out. The tablets honoring Perón were *effaced* after his fall from power.

EFFECT—(v.) to bring about. New regulations have *effected* a shift in policy on applications. (n.) a result. The headache was an *effect* of sinus congestion.

EFFICACIOUS—able to produce a desired effect. The drug is *efficacious* in the treatment of malaria.

EFFIGY—image of a person, especially of one who is hated. They burned his *effigy* in the public square.

EFFRONTERY—audacity, rude boldness. He had the *effrontery* to go up to the distinguished guest and call him by his first name.

EFFULGENT—radiant, intensely bright. The lamp bathed the room in an *effulgent* brightness.

EFFUSIVE—gushing, demonstrative. Her *effusive* greeting seemed overdone.

EGOCENTRIC—self-centered. The *egocentric* individual has little regard for the feelings of others.

EGOTISM—tendency to attract attention to oneself. His *egotism* demanded that he always be the center of attention.

EGRESS—exit. Barnum put the sign "*egress*" on the door so that the crowd would move on, expecting to see another exhibit.

ELATE—make joyful, elevate in spirit. A grade of 100% will *elate* any student.

ELECTIVE—filled or chosen by election. Although she had served on several commissions by appointment, she had never held *elective* office.

ELECTORATE—the body of persons entitled to vote in an election. His strong appeal to the *electorate* assured his party of victory.

ELEGY—a poem of praise for the dead, a mournful poem. The poet composed the moving *elegy* after his young bride's death.

ELICIT—draw out, evoke. Her direct question only *elicited* further evasions.

ELIGIBLE—fit to be chosen, qualified. Veterans are *eligible* for many government benefits, including low-cost loans.

ELOCUTION—style of speaking, especially in public. His *elocution* was so clear that everyone in the assembly could hear every word.

ELUCIDATE—make clear, explain. The explanation served to confuse rather than to *elucidate*.

ELUDE—to avoid or escape notice. The thief *eluded* the police by darting into a crowded theater.

ELUSIVE—hard to find or grasp. Because the problem is so complex, a definitive solution seems *elusive*.

EMACIATED—very thin, wasted away. He had a tall, bony figure, as *emaciated* as a skeleton.

EMANATE—derive from, issue forth. American law *emanates* largely from English common law.

EMBARGO—governmental restriction or prohibition of trade. In retaliation for the invasion, the government imposed an *embargo* on grain shipments to the Soviet Union.

EMBELLISH—decorate, adorn. He would *embellish* his narratives with fanciful events.

EMBODY—render concrete, incorporate. He tried to *embody* his ideas in the theme.

EMBOLISM—blood clot. *Embolisms,* now known to be responsible for many heart attacks, are preventable in some cases by blood-thinning drugs.

EMENDATION—change or correction in a text. The author corrected typographical errors and made a few other *emendations* in his manuscript.

EMETIC—inducing vomiting. An *emetic* is prescribed for most poisons taken by mouth.

EMIGRATE—to leave a country permanently to settle in another. Many people applied for visas, wishing to *emigrate* and escape persecution at home.

EMISSARY—one sent to influence opponents politically. The rebels sent an *emissary* to negotiate a truce.

EMOLLIENT—soothing. An *emollient* lotion is good for sunburn.

EMOLUMENT—reward for work. Teachers receive comparatively greater *emoluments* in the Soviet Union than in the United States.

EMPATHY—sense of identification with another person. Her *empathy* with her brother was very strong; she generally knew what her sibling was feeling without his having to explain.

EMPIRICISM—the gaining of knowledge through experiment and observation; the doctrine that all knowledge comes through experience. *Empiricism,* requiring that theories about the nature of the universe be tested against experience, was the basis of the modern scientific revolution.

EMPLOY—to use. The artist *employed* charcoal in many of her sketches.

EMPORIUM—principal trade center. In many small towns, one general store will serve as the *emporium* of the community.

EMPYREAL—celestial. In mythology, *empyreal* forces often play a part in human destiny.

EMULATE—vie with, try to equal. He tried to *emulate* the feats of the older boys.

ENACT—to put into law, do, or act out. A bill was *enacted* lowering the voting age to eighteen.

ENCLAVE—an independent area within foreign territory. The Vatican is an *enclave* within Italy.

ENCOMIUM—formal praise. He heaped *encomiums* on the returning hero but refused to find a job for him.

ENCROACH—infringe or invade. Property values fall when industries *encroach* upon residential areas.

ENCYCLOPEDIC—covering a wide range of subjects. The knowledge of a good instructor must be *encyclopedic,* ranging beyond his own specialized field.

ENDEAVOR—to attempt by effort, try hard. I *endeavored*

to contact them several times but they never returned my calls.

ENDEMIC—peculiar to or prevalent in an area or group. Malaria is *endemic* in many southern countries.

ENDIVE—a lettuce-like plant. An *endive* salad is a gourmet's delight.

ENDOGENOUS—originating from within. An ulcer is usually *endogenous.*

ENDORSE—to declare support or approval for. Community leaders were quick to *endorse* a project that would bring new jobs to the neighborhood.

ENERVATE—weaken, enfeeble. A poor diet will *enervate* a person.

ENFORCE—to make forceful, to impose by force. Because of the holiday, parking restrictions are not being *enforced* today.

ENGENDER—produce, cause, beget. Angry words may *engender* strife.

ENGROSS—fully absorb, monopolize. He was so *engrossed* in his hobbies that he neglected his studies.

ENGULF—swallow up. The rising waters *engulfed* the village.

ENHANCE—improve, augment, add to. The neat cover *enhanced* the report.

ENIGMA—a riddle, anything inexplicable. The origin of the statues on Easter Island is an *enigma.*

ENLIGHTENED—free from prejudice or ignorance, socially or intellectually advanced. No *enlightened* society could condone the exploitation of children as it was once practiced in American industry.

ENMITY—state of being an enemy, hostility. The *enmity* between China and Vietnam is traditional and unabated.

ENNUI—weariness, tedium, boredom. Imagination and curiosity are the antidotes for *ennui.*

ENORMITY—state of being enormous; outrageous. The age of the victim added to the *enormity* of the crime.

ENSNARE—catch, trap. He was *ensnared* in the fabric of his lies.

ENSUE—to follow immediately or as a result. One person raised an objection and a long argument *ensued.*

ENTAIL—to involve or make necessary. Getting the report out on time will *entail* working all weekend.

ENTHRALL—enslave, captivate, hold fast. He was *enthralled* by the exciting plot of the book.

ENTITLE—to give a right or claim to. This pass *entitles* the bearer to two free admissions.

ENTRENCHED—firmly established. Protestant fundamentalism is deeply *entrenched* in the lives of those people.

ENTREPRENEUR—employer, one who assumes the risk of a business. The strike by his employees forced the *entrepreneur* to upgrade the benefits.

ENUMERATE—to count, specify in a list. In her essay she

enumerated her reasons for wanting to attend the school.

ENUNCIATE—to pronounce clearly. He could not *enunciate* certain sounds.

ENVENOM—make poisonous, embitter. Out of jealousy he tried to *envenom* the relationship between his friend and his rival.

ENVIRONS—surroundings, suburbs. The *environs* of the city added to its charms as a place to live.

EPHEMERAL—short-lived, temporary. *Ephemeral* pleasures may leave lasting memories.

EPICURE—one with fastidious tastes in food or drink. The life of the *epicure* is centered around his table.

EPIGRAM—a bright or witty thought, tersely expressed. Oscar Wilde is noted for his *epigrams*.

EPILOGUE—the concluding portion of a novel or play. The *epilogue* is delivered at the conclusion of the drama.

EPISTLE—a formal and instructive letter. She wrote a lengthy *epistle* to her newly married daughter, advising her on how best to keep within her household budget.

EPITHET—a descriptive adjective or a significant name, e.g., Richard the Lionhearted.

EPITOME—an abstract; a part that typically represents the whole. He prepared an *epitome* of his work to show to the editor.

EPOCH—a distinctive period of time. Hemingway's writings marked an *epoch* in American literature.

EQUANIMITY—calm temper, evenness of mind. Adversity could not disturb his *equanimity*.

EQUESTRIAN—of horses or riding; on horseback. Polo and fox hunting are both *equestrian* sports.

EQUIPOISE—equilibrium, balance. The tightrope artist's *equipoise* was so assured that he decided not to use a net.

EQUIVOCAL—having more than one possible meaning, deliberately misleading while not literally untrue. His *equivocal* statements left us in doubt as to his real intentions.

ERADICATE—pluck up by roots, wipe out. They tried to *eradicate* the hordes of wild rabbits by introducing a deadly epidemic.

ERODE—eat into, wear away. The glaciers *eroded* the land, leaving deep valleys.

EROTIC—concerning sexual love, amatory. *Erotic* literature is often censored.

ERSATZ—substitute, imitation. The burger consisted of *ersatz* beef made from soybeans.

ERUCT—to belch. It is not considered polite to *eruct* audibly.

ERUDITE—scholarly, with bookish knowledge. The *erudite* person may find it difficult to communicate his thoughts to those less educated.

ERUPT—break out. The volcano *erupted* streams of lava.

ESCADRILLE—airplane squadron. The Lafayette *Escadrille* won fame in World War I.

ESCAPADE—an adventurous prank, reckless adventure for amusement. Relieved from duty at last, the soldiers went on a three-day *escapade*.

ESCHEW—avoid, shun. She *eschewed* any social activities and lived in total seclusion.

ESCULENT—edible. Since many of the wild fruits were *esculent*, they were able to sustain themselves in the wilderness.

ESCUTCHEON—a shield with a coat of arms. The *escutcheon* of old families is the symbol of honor.

ESOTERIC—limited to a few, secret. The *esoteric* rites of the fraternity were held sacred by the members.

ESPALIER—a fruit tree trained to grow flat in a design. *Espalier* pear trees are the pride of European gardens.

ESSENTIAL—necessary, basic. A person must eat a variety of foods to obtain all the *essential* vitamins and minerals.

ESTIMATE—rough calculation. The contractor submitted a written *estimate* of the cost of a new roof.

ESTRANGED—alienated, separated. Her *estranged* husband had been gone for two years.

ESTUARY—part of a river that meets the sea. The ship was caught in the currents of the *estuary* when the tides were going in.

ETHEREAL—spirit-like, celestial. The heroine of his book was endowed with *ethereal* beauty.

ETHICAL—conforming to high moral standards. Although many members of his administration were corrupt, he adhered to strong *ethical* principles.

ETHNIC—belonging to the customs and way of life of a distinct national or social group. Of all the *ethnic* foods available in this city, Italian pizza and Middle Eastern falafel are the most important.

ETIOLOGY—study of causes or origins. The *etiology* of the common cold, man's biggest nuisance, has not been a heavily endowed endeavor.

ETYMOLOGY—the origin and history of a word; the study of the changes in words. The *etymology* of "bedlam" has been traced back to "Bethlehem," the name of a London hospital for the mentally ill.

EUGENIC—producing improvement in offspring. *Eugenics* has provided us with improved animals in every class except the human race.

EULOGY—high praise, laudation. He asked that no *eulogy* be delivered at his funeral.

EUPHEMISM—substitution of an inoffensive or mild expression for a more straightforward one. Like many other people, he used "gone" and "passed away" as *euphemisms* for "dead."

EUPHONIC—pleasant-sounding. Her *euphonic* singing had a soothing effect on the guests.

EUPHORIA—sense of well-being. Their *euphoria* at being

the first to ever climb the mountain was heightened by their narrow escape from death.

EUTHANASIA—painless death administered to one suffering from a painful disease. *Euthanasia* is not legal.

EVACUATE—to empty, clear out. The authorities ordered the town *evacuated* when the waters rose.

EVALUATE—to determine the value of. The purpose of the survey is to *evaluate* the effect of the new teaching methods on the students' progress.

EVANESCENT—transitory. His success was *evanescent*—here today, gone tomorrow.

EVASION—a subterfuge or equivocal statement, an avoiding. His indirect answers were an attempt at *evasion*.

EVINCE—make evident, display. His curt reply *evinced* his short temper.

EVISCERATE—disembowel. Animals must be *eviscerated* before they can be cooked or smoked.

EVOLUTION—gradual change. Through the discovery of ancient bones and artifacts, anthropologists hope to chart the *evolution* of the human species.

EXACERBATE—to make worse, aggravate. A generous portion of french fries is sure to *exacerbate* an upset stomach.

EXACTING—severe in making demands. The *exacting* schoolmaster was the cause of their discontent.

EXCEED—to go beyond, surpass. The business's profits for this year *exceeded* last year's profits by $16,000.

EXCEPT—to exclude. He *excepted* the damaging remarks from his speech.

EXCESS—amount beyond what is necessary or desired. When the prices are in place, wipe away the *excess* glue.

EXCHEQUER—funds, treasury. The reforms were approved but the state of the *exchequer* made it impossible to carry them out.

EXCLUDE—to shut out, not permit to enter or participate. The children made a pact that all adults were to be *excluded* from the clubhouse.

EXCORIATE—remove the skin from; denounce harshly. The principal *excoriated* the student as a juvenile delinquent.

EXECRABLE—extremely bad. Although her acting was *execrable*, she looked so good on stage that the audience applauded.

EXECRATE—curse, abhor. The captors who had lost all sense of humanity deserved to be *execrated*.

EXECUTE—to put into effect, perform. He *executed* the duties of his office conscientiously.

EXEMPLARY—serving as a pattern, deserving imitation. The leader's *exemplary* behavior in both his private and public life made him a model for all to follow.

EXEMPT—excused. Having broken his leg, the child was *exempt* from gym for the rest of the term.

EXHIBIT—to show, display. The paintings were *exhibited* in the municipal museum.

EXHORT—to incite by words or advice. He *exhorted* the mob to attack the station.

EXHUME—dig out, disinter. He obtained a court order to *exhume* the body.

EXIGENCY—necessity, urgent requirement. The *exigencies* presented by four growing children forced him to take another job.

EXISTENTIALISM—a philosophy that urges personal decisions in a purposeless world. *Existentialism* was a popular philosophy of post-war France.

EXOGENOUS—derived externally. His delusions seemed to have no internal cause and were thus termed *exogenous*.

EXONERATE—to free from blame. The confession of one prisoner *exonerated* the other suspects.

EXORBITANT—excessive, going beyond the scope of the law. The *exorbitant* rates of the moneylenders kept the peasants in a state of poverty.

EXORCISE—expel evil spirits. The priest was called upon to *exorcise* the demon from the child.

EXPANSIBLE—capable of being extended, dilated, or diffused. Bodies are not *expansible* in proportion to their weight.

EXPEDIENT—advantageous, appropriate to the circumstances, immediately useful though not necessarily right or just. Under pressure to reduce the deficit, the mayor found it *expedient* to cut funds for social services.

EXPEDITE—to speed, facilitate. In order to *expedite* delivery of the letter, he sent it special delivery.

EXPEL—to push or force out. When a ballon bursts, the air is *expelled* in a rush.

EXPENDITURE—a spending. The finished mural more than justified the *expenditure* of time and money necessary for its completion.

EXPERTISE—skill or technical knowledge of an expert. The *expertise* with which he handled the animal delighted the spectators.

EXPIATE—endure a penalty to pay for a crime. He chose to *expiate* his crime by wearing a hair shirt for ten years.

EXPLICATE—explain, develop a principle. He could not *explicate* a philosophy that depended on doing evil.

EXPLICITLY—openly, without disguise. When the annoying visitor refused to take a hint, the host told him *explicitly* that it was time he left.

EXPLOIT—to use, especially unfairly or selfishly. Some employers *exploit* the labor of illegal immigrants, who are afraid to complain about long hours and substandard wages.

EXPOSTULATE—remonstrate, argue strongly to a person against his actions, etc. He *expostulated* loudly and clearly with his students about their poor working habits.

EXPRESSLY—specifically. I wrote it *expressly* for you.

EXPULSION—the act of driving out. The *expulsion* of the students from the university was unfair.

EXPURGATE—remove objectionable matter. The censors *expurgated* the portions of the book they considered obscene.

EXQUISITE—perfect, especially in a lovely, finely tuned, or delicate way; very intense. The handmade lace was *exquisite* in every detail.

EXTEMPORANEOUS—made with little or no preparation. The speaker who was expected to make the presentation didn't show up, so he gave an *extemporaneous* speech.

EXTENSIVE—broad, of wide scope, thorough. Several hundred persons were interviewed as part of an *extensive* survey.

EXTENUATE—to partially excuse, seem to lessen. His abrupt rudeness was *extenuated* by his distraught state of mind; no one could blame him for it.

EXTIRPATE—destroy entirely. The soldier threatened to *extirpate* the entire village if they refused to surrender.

EXTRICATE—to free from an entanglement. Carefully removing each prickly branch, she *extricated* herself from the briars.

EXTRINSIC—external, coming from the outside and therefore not of prime importance. Her complaints about one particular teacher are *extrinsic* to an evaluation of the program as a whole.

EXTRUDE—expel, push out, protrude. The volcanic upheaval *extruded* molten lava over a vast area.

FACADE—the front of a building. People come from miles around to admire the *facade* of St. Mark's church.

FACETIOUS—amusing, joking at an inappropriate time. His *facetious* remarks failed to impress the company.

FACILE—expert, able to work quickly and easily. He never turned down an opportunity to make a speech because he was such a *facile* orator.

FACILITATE—make easy or less difficult, free from impediment, lessen the labor of. This piece of machinery will *facilitate* production.

FACILITY—ease. Her *facility* in reading several languages made her ideal for the cataloguing job.

FACSIMILE—exact copy. A *facsimile* edition of a book is a photographic reproduction of an original manuscript or printed version.

FACTIOUS—inclined to act for one group or party, producing dissension. His *factious* attitude made him unsuitable for a judicial position.

FACTOTUM—employee with miscellaneous duties. He was the chief *factotum* of the plant.

FAINT—feeble, languid, exhausted. The children were *faint* with fatigue and hunger.

FALLACIOUS—untrue, misleading. His arguments were transparently *fallacious*.

FALLIBLE—capable of erring or being deceived in judgment. All men are *fallible*.

FALTER—to hesitate, stammer, flinch. He speaks with a *faltering* tongue.

FANATIC—person with an unreasoning enthusiasm. Some credos seem to create *fanatic* followers among the discontent.

FANTASTIC—fanciful, produced or existing only in the imagination. His story was absolutely and completely *fantastic*.

FARRIER—blacksmith. He took his horse to a *farrier*.

FASTIDIOUS—disdainful, squeamish, delicate to a fault. He considered her *fastidious* because her feelings were offended by such trifling defects and errors.

FATHOM—a measure of length used chiefly at sea, about six feet. The water was twenty *fathoms* deep.

FATIGUE—weariness from bodily labor or mental exertion. After a full day's work, their *fatigue* was understandable.

FATUOUS—conceitedly foolish, silly in an obnoxious way. Insisting on a Cadillac you can't afford is *fatuous*.

FAVORITISM—unfair favoring of one person over others. In the office, *favoritism* based on personal friendship is resented.

FEASIBLE—able to be performed or executed by human means or agency, practicable. It is *feasible* to complete the project by July.

FECKLESS—weak, spiritless, irresponsible. A *feckless* soldier is a liability to his outfit.

FECULENT—abounding in dregs, foul with impure substances, muddy. The water was *feculent* with raw sewage.

FELICITATIONS—congratulations on a happy occasion. They extended their *felicitations* to the bride.

FERRET—a type of weasel used in hunting rabbits; also, to search. They tried to *ferret* out the truth.

FERROUS—containing iron. The non*ferrous* metals include gold, silver, copper, lead, and zinc.

FETISH—an object or ceremony of blind reverence. He asked the group to forget their *fetishes* and apply modern methods.

FETUS—unborn animal in the womb. Damage to the *fetus* may be caused by any shock to a pregnant female. Also: foetus.

FIASCO—ridiculous failure. The rain turned the picnic into a *fiasco*.

FICKLE—likely to change. None is so *fickle* as a neglected lover.

FINESSE—artifice, subtlety of contrivance to gain a point. She attained her high position through the use of great *finesse*.

FINITE—having a limit, bounded. There were only a *finite* number of men to be considered.

FISCAL—financial, having to do with public funds. The

administration's *fiscal* policy entailed tighter controls on credit.

FISSURE—a crack. The earthquake created a two-foot *fissure* down the center of the street.

FLAGITIOUS—causing public odium, vile, scandalous. His defamation of the president was considered *flagitious*.

FLAMMABLE—capable of being kindled into flame. They were careful to keep the material away from the sparks because it was *flammable*.

FLATULENT—causing gas in the alimentary canal; also, pretentious in speech. Cauliflower, cabbage, and tomatoes are *flatulent* foods.

FLAUNT—to display freely, defiantly, or ostentatiously. *Flaunting* expensive jewelry in public may be an invitation to robbery.

FLORESCENCE—flowering. The *florescence* of the roses is a signal for much sneezing among those suffering from allergies.

FLOTSAM—floating ship wreckage. He met the *flotsam* and jetsam of humanity on skid row.

FLOUT—to mock, show contempt for. He *flouted* public opinion by appearing with his lover in public.

FLUCTUATE—change continually from one direction to another. *Fluctuations* in stock market prices create many paper losses and profits.

FLUORESCENCE—property of giving off light after bombardment by certain rays. *Fluorescent* signs are used in some areas, particularly when they must be invisible to air observation.

FORAY—plundering raid. The bandits made a *foray* into town.

FORECLOSE—to rescind a mortgage for failure to keep up payments. The bank *foreclosed* the mortgage and repossessed the house, putting it up for sale.

FORESIGHT—a looking ahead. She had the *foresight* to realize that the restaurant would be busy, so she called ahead for reservations.

FORFEIT—to lose because of a fault. The team made a couple of decisive errors and so *forfeited* their lead.

FORMALITY—fixed or conventional procedure, act, or custom; quality of being formal. Skipping the *formality* of a greeting, she got straight to the point. The *formality* of his attire was entirely appropriate to the ceremonious occasion.

FRAUD—intentional deceit for the purpose of cheating. The land development scheme was a *fraud* in which gullible investors lost thousands of dollars.

FRENETIC—frenzied. *Frenetic* activity is evident in the dormitory just before exam time.

FRIVOLOUS—not serious. The atmosphere of the gathering was entirely *frivolous* and gay.

FROND—a fern leaf, any finely divided leaf. The fern's spores are visible on the underside of its *fronds*.

FUGUE—contrapuntal musical composition. They listened while voices joined in Bach's *fugue* in B minor.

FURIOUS—full of madness, raging, transported with passion. The animal was *furious* when confined.

FUTILE—trifling, useless, pointless. The entire matter was dropped because the arguments were *futile*.

GABBLE—to prate, talk fast or without meaning. The young children *gabbled* happily whether anyone was listening or not.

GAINSAY—deny. It was impossible to *gainsay* the truth of the statement the man made.

GALL—chafe, rub sore; annoy, vex. That saddle will *gall* the back of your horse.

GAMUT—the complete range. The singer was able to demonstrate the entire *gamut* of her vocal ability in her performance of the operetta.

GARISH—flashy. Everyone noticed her *garish* clothes.

GARRULOUS—talkative, loquacious. She was so *garrulous* that she said everything at least three times.

GAUCHE—without social grace, tactless. It is considered *gauche* to ask acquaintances how much they earn or how much they paid for something.

GENEALOGY—history of family descent, a family tree. They were able to trace their *genealogy* back four generations to a small village in Sicily.

GENERALIZATION—induction, a general conclusion drawn from specific cases. *Generalizations* are apt to be as dangerous as they are tempting.

GENERATE—beget, procreate, propagate, produce. Every animal *generates* its own species.

GENERIC—pertaining to a race or kind. The *generic* characteristics of each animal enables us to distinguish them.

GENIAL—pleasant, friendly. The president's rotund and *genial* face made him the perfect Santa Claus.

GENUS—a kind or class. There are many species in each *genus*.

GERIATRICS—science of care for the aged. Our longer life span in modern times makes the study of *geriatrics* a necessity.

GERMANE—pertinent. The facts were not *germane* to the argument.

GERUND—a verbal noun. A *gerund*, a verb used as a noun, is formed with *ing;* e.g., *Swimming* is hard work.

GIBBER—to chatter incoherently. The idiot *gibbered* incessantly.

GIST—essential part. That all men are not equal was the *gist* of his speech.

GLAUCOUS—gleaming sea-green. The color of the cabbage leaf had a *glaucous* tone.

GLUCOSE—sugar occurring in fruit, less sweet than cane sugar. The doctor ordered intravenous injections of *glucose* to sustain the patient who could not eat.

GLUTTONOUS—greedy for food and drink. The man was much too *gluttonous* to stick to any kind of diet.

GOAD—drive with a stick, urge on. Although the man

was naturally lax, he was *goaded* on to success by the nagging of his wife.

GONAD—sex gland. The *gonads* secrete hormones that affect our attitude and actions.

GOSSAMER—sheer. The cobwebs were *gossamer* threads strung from the ceiling.

GOURMET—a judge of food. The *gourmet* is to food what a hot rod enthusiast is to engines.

GRACIOUS—socially graceful, courteous, kind. A *gracious* host puts his guests at ease and is concerned only that they enjoy themselves.

GRAFT—illegal use of position of power for gain. He was charged with *graft* in selling contracts for public works projects.

GRANDEUR—splendor, magnificence, stateliness. The *grandeur* of the lofty mountains was admired by all.

GRANULAR—having a crystalline or grain-like texture. The *granular* texture of the limestone made the statue a thing of beauty.

GRAPHOLOGY—study of handwriting. Some *graphologists* claim to read character in handwriting.

GRAPPLE—seize, lay fast hold on, either with the hands or with mechanical devices. He *grappled* with the man who had attacked him.

GRATUITOUS—free, voluntary; granted without compensation, claim or merit. His *gratuitous* insults were resented very highly.

GRATUITY—tip. He left a *gratuity* for the chambermaid.

GREGARIOUS—fond of company. They are a *gregarious* couple who cultivate many friendships among diverse people.

GRIMACE—distort the features. She *grimaced* until her face assumed a crabbed look.

GRIMLY—fiercely, ferociously. The work was tackled *grimly*.

GROMMET—a metal ring. The duffle bag had a *grommet*, through which a cord could be pulled to close it.

GROUSE—complain. There is no use *grousing* over your own mistakes.

GRUELING—exhausting. The labor was so *grueling* that two workers fainted.

GRUFF—rough. His manner was so *gruff* that most of the children feared him.

GUDGEON—one easily duped or ensnared. He was no *gudgeon* but the victim of a carefully planned confidence game.

GUIDON—small signal flag. His golf ball hit the *guidon* on the ninth hole.

GUILE—deceit, cunning. His brief success was due to flattery and *guile* rather than to genuine talent.

GULLIBLE—easily deceived. Naive people are often *gullible*.

GUSTY—windy, blustery. March is usually a very *gusty* month.

GUZZLE—to drink much, to drink frequently, to swallow immoderately. He *guzzled* his liquor like a man dying of thirst.

GYNECOLOGY—science of women's diseases. As a result of complications resulting from the birth of a child, she went to a doctor specializing in *gynecology*.

GYRATE—revolve about a point, whirl. The tornado *gyrates* about a central point.

GYROSCOPE—rotating wheel apparatus that maintains direction regardless of position of surrounding parts. The automatic *gyroscope* holds an airplane on its course even when the machine is upside down.

HABITABLE—capable of being inhabited or dwelt in, capable of sustaining human beings. The climate of the North Pole makes it scarcely *habitable*.

HAFT—handle. He took the knife by the *haft*.

HAGGARD—gaunt, careworn; wasted by hunger, pain, or terror. After three days of being lost on the mountain, the *haggard* campers staggered into the village.

HALBERD—long, axlike, 15th-century weapon. The firemen of today use a *halberd* similar to that used by knights.

HALCYON—calm, quiet, peaceful, undisturbed, happy. The *halcyon* days of that summer will always be remembered.

HALLUCINATION—apparent perceiving of things not present. In his *hallucinations* he heard voices calling to him that no one else could hear.

HAPHAZARD—random. He studied in such a *haphazard* manner that he learned nothing.

HARASS—annoy with repeated attacks. The students perpetually *harassed* the teacher with unnecessary questions.

HARBINGER—something that precedes and forecasts. The dark sky proved to be the *harbinger* of this rainy day.

HARP—perpetually dwell on a particular subject. The employee *harped* so continually on the difficulty of his job that he was eventually fired.

HARRIDAN—shrewish old woman. The word *harridan* always brings to mind an old witch.

HARROWING—severely hurtful or trying, emotionally or physically. The survivors of the crash went through a *harrowing* ordeal before their rescue.

HASSOCK—cushion used as stool. A *hassock* is used in modern living rooms as a pull-up chair.

HAUTEUR—haughty manner. The *hauteur* of her demeanor frightened the servants.

HAWSER—a large rope used for towing light objects. The boy in the rowboat asked his friend to pull him to shore with the *hawser*.

HAYCOCK—small conical pile of hay. They sat on the *haycock* in the field.

HECTIC—fevered, hurried, and confused. The tour turned out to be somewhat *hectic*, covering three cities in as many days.

HEGEMONY—predominance. Hitler's aim was German *hegemony* over the world.

HEINOUS—hateful, atrocious. The deed was so *heinous* that everyone despised him for it.

HELIX—spiral line, coil of wire. The wire was wound into a *helix*.

HENEQUEN—fiber used in making rope. The Indians harvested *henequen* in the Yucatan.

HEPTAGON—seven-sided polygon. The fortress was built in the shape of a *heptagon* with seven bastions.

HERALD—to announce the arrival of, usher in. Crocuses *herald* the advent of spring.

HERBIVOROUS—feeding on plants. A vegetarian is *herbivorous*.

HERETIC—one who believes contrary to his church. A man who is a *heretic* displeases his minister.

HERMAPHRODITE—having both male and female organs. A *hermaphrodite* has the physical characteristics of both sexes.

HERMITAGE—place where a hermit lives. The monk retired to the *hermitage*.

HETERODOX—not orthodox; not conforming, especially in religious belief. Her *heterodox* opinions and outlandish behavior earned her a reputation as an eccentric.

HETEROGENEOUS—composed of unlike elements. The school favored *heterogeneous* groupings, so there was a very wide range of ability and achievement in every class.

HEXAPOD—having six feet. All the true insects are *hexapods*.

HIDALGO—Spanish nobleman. In Spain, a man is either born a *hidalgo* or he never gets the title.

HIERATIC—priestly. Anything pertaining to priests is *hieratic*.

HINDER—retard, slow down, prevent from moving forward by any means. Cold weather *hinders* the growth of plants.

HINDSIGHT—a looking backward. With *hindsight* I realize that everything she said to me was true, though I could not accept it at the time.

HIRSUTE—hairy. His *hirsute* chest made him look like a beast.

HISTOLOGY—science of organic tissue. The microscope is necessary for studying *histology*.

HISTRIONIC—pertaining to acting, overly theatrical, affectedly melodramatic. She indulged in a *histrionic* display of temper in order to make her point.

HOARY—white with great age. The two little old ladies were wrinkled and *hoary*.

HOLOCAUST—a great destruction of living beings by fire. As the fire raged out of control, thousands of lives were lost in the *holocaust*.

HOLOGRAPH—personally handwritten document. A *holograph* attached to a will needs no witnesses.

HOMAGE—respect, a feudal acknowledgment of underl-ing to lord. The entire population paid *homage* to the kind king.

HOMBURG—man's felt hat with curled brim. The *homburg* the man wore made him look very dignified.

HOMEOPATHY—method of treating disease with small quantities of drugs. A vaccination uses the principle of *homeopathy*.

HOMICIDE—killing of one person by another. Killing in self-defense is considered justifiable *homicide*.

HOMILETICS—art of preaching. A religious leader must be well versed in *homiletics*.

HOMILY—discourse on a moral problem, sermon. The judge read the boy a *homily* on his behavior before sentencing him.

HOMOGENEOUS—same, uniform throughout. The entering class was fairly *homogeneous;* nearly all the students were the same age and from similar middle-class homes.

HOMOGRAPH—word written the same but of different origin and meaning. The English language has many homographs, such as *bill* (list of charges) and *bill* (bird's beak).

HOMOLOGOUS—similar in position, origin, structure, etc. The limbs of humans and animals, although they look different, are said to be *homologous*.

HOMOPHONE—word pronounced the same as another. English *homophones* include to/too/two and bare/bear.

HONE—stone for sharpening. A *hone* is necessary to keep the razor sharp.

HORIZONTAL—flat, parallel to the horizon. *Horizontal* stripes are frequently unflattering because they make the figure appear wider.

HORMONE—chemical substance formed in some organ and having a specific effect in regulating the body. Birth control pills act in the body as *hormones*.

HORTATORY—giving advice, encouraging, inciting. With his *hortatory* speech, the orator incited his listeners to riot.

HOSPICE—shelter for pilgrims. The Swiss Alps have many *hospices* in which one can find shelter and entertainment.

HOSPITABLE—welcoming, generous to guests. It was a *hospitable* room, with a soothing color scheme and deep, comfortable chairs.

HOSTILE—conflicting, antagonistic, expressing enmity. Most North American Indians were *hostile* to the white settlers.

HOYDEN—tomboy. The awkward, rough ways of the girl made her seem like a *hoyden*.

HUDDLE—crowd together, press together without order or regularity. The mob *huddled* to get out of the rain.

HUMANITIES—the branch of learning concerned with philosophy, literature, the arts, etc., as distinguished from the sciences and sometimes the social sciences.

The essence of the *humanities* is a concern with human nature, experience, and relationships.

HUMERUS—bone from shoulder to elbow. The *humerus* of the arm is often covered with excess flesh as we get older.

HUMILITY—humbleness of spirit. The minister spoke to the members of his congregation with such sincere *humility* that he impressed them greatly.

HUMMOCK—small hill. The storm blew the sand into many *hummocks*.

HUMUS—decomposed organic material in the soil. *Humus* applied to a lawn makes the grass greener.

HYDROUS—containing water. Watermelon is a *hydrous* gourd.

HYGROSCOPE—instrument indicating changes in humidity. A *hygroscope* can tell us that humidity is present but cannot measure the amount.

HYPERBOLE—obvious exaggeration as a figure of speech. "He was as big as a house" is an example of *hyperbole*.

HYPERTENSION—high blood pressure. *Hypertension* is often a cause of serious diseases.

HYPOCHONDRIA—abnormal anxiety about health. Since no doctor could find anything organically wrong with him, he was labeled a *hypochondriac*.

HYPOTHESIS—an unproved explanation. She started with the *hypothesis* that the earth was spheroid and concluded it would be possible to go east by sailing west.

IAMB—metrical foot of one short and one long syllable. Most English poetry is *iambic* like Keats' line, "The poetry of earth is never dead."

IBIDEM—Latin word meaning in the same place, used in footnotes and abbreviated *ibid*.

ICHTHYOLOGY—science of fish. In water miles deep, the *ichthyologists* found species thought to be extinct.

ICONOCLAST—one who attacks old beliefs as superstition. Abraham was considered an *iconoclast* in his day.

IDEOLOGUE—one who believes in and propagates a social doctrine. The communist *ideologue* argued that the state was more important than any individual.

IDEOLOGY—the body of a social doctrine. The Communist *ideology* holds the State important and the individual inconsequential.

IDIOSYNCRASY—peculiar tendency of an individual. His *idiosyncrasies* were sufficient to label him eccentric but not sufficient to classify him as insane.

IDOLATRY—worship of idols or false gods. His awestruck respect for the older boy amounted to *idolatry*.

IDYLLIC—pleasantly simple or rustic, charmingly picturesque. The *idyllic* landscape of fields and woods seemed to promise a life of simple enjoyment.

IGNEOUS—formed by great heat. The Palisades of the Hudson Valley are of *igneous* origin.

IGNOBLE—without honor. The *ignoble* purpose of his slander multiplied the crime.

IGNOMINIOUS—discrediting, disgraceful. His *ignominious* activities could lead only to his removal from office.

ILLEGIBLE—impossible to read. The letter was so water stained that the handwriting was *illegible*.

ILLICIT—not licensed. *Illicit* love is the root of many divorce actions.

ILLUMINATE—to throw light on, explain. The editor's notes *illuminated* the more obscure passages in the text.

ILLUSION—a vision that is misleading. It isn't difficult to create an optical *illusion* in which lines of equal length seem to be unequal.

ILLUSORY—unreal. The dollar we hope to make is *illusory* until we earn it and have it.

IMBECILITY—weakness of mind. The *imbecility* of the travelers was quickly revealed when they began to express their opinion on the matter.

IMMOLATE—to kill as a sacrifice. The Buddhist monk *immolated* himself in a public square as a gesture of protest against the war.

IMMUNE—not susceptible, protected, as from disease. An inoculation for smallpox makes one *immune* to the disease.

IMPALE—fix on a pointed instrument. Pieces of pickled lamb *impaled* on a skewer make a dramatic serving of shish kebab.

IMPALPABLE—not able to be felt. The seismograph can measure tremors in the earth's crust *impalpable* to humans.

IMPARTIAL—not favoring one side or another. The squabbling children appealed to the babysitter for an *impartial* judgment.

IMPASSIONED—animated, excited, expressive of passion or ardor. The *impassioned* performance of the actor was thoroughly enjoyable.

IMPEACH—to challenge one's honesty or reputation, to call before a tribunal on a charge of wrongdoing. President Nixon resigned before he could be *impeached* by the Senate for high crimes and misdemeanors.

IMPECCABLE—faultless. Successful comedy depends on *impeccable* timing.

IMPECUNIOUS—penniless. His *impecunious* aunt was a drain on his purse.

IMPEDE—hinder, obstruct. The flying shrapnel *impeded* the progress of the troops.

IMPEDIMENT—something that slows progress, an obstacle. The loss of two front teeth caused a speech *impediment*.

IMPEL—to drive forward, push, incite. Although she was not personally involved, her sense of justice *impelled* her to speak out.

IMPERATIVE—of greatest necessity or importance. This

is an emergency; it is *imperative* that I reach them at once.

IMPERIL—to put in danger. The incompetence of the pilot *imperiled* the safety of all on board.

IMPERISHABLE—not subject to decay, indestructible. His fame is *imperishable* because his deeds are so mighty.

IMPERTURBABLE—not easily excited. His poker face was aided by an *imperturbable nature*.

IMPERVIOUS—not to be penetrated or passed through. Heavy cardboard is *impervious* to light.

IMPETUOUS—impulsive. The *impetuous* action often leads to trouble.

IMPLEMENT—to put into effect, to realize in practice. When they *implemented* the program, they realized that some of the planned procedures were not practicable and would have to be modified.

IMPLY—to suggest, say without stating directly. Although they said nothing about it, their cool manner *implied* strong disapproval of the scheme.

IMPONDERABLE—not capable of being weighed or measured. Some skills, for instance typing speed, are easy to measure, but others, such as the talent for getting along with fellow workers, are *imponderable*.

IMPORTUNE—beg. Do not *importune* me for what you can earn so easily.

IMPOTENT—lacking power. The disease left him *impotent* even to walk across the room.

IMPOVERISH—to make poor. She was an exceptionally effective administrator; the company has been *impoverished* by her loss.

IMPRECATION—a curse. He uttered an *imprecation* that sent shudders through the superstitious mob.

IMPRECISE—not precise, vague, inaccurate. The description was *imprecise* because the witness had had only a fleeting glimpse of the man.

IMPRESARIO—manager of a muscial company. The *impresario* brought the ballet company to America.

IMPRESSIVE—having the power of affecting, or of exciting attention and feeling. The view was so *impressive* that he never forgot it.

IMPRIMATUR—license to publish. He was given an *imprimatur* for all the works of Benjamin Franklin.

IMPROMPTU—spontaneous, not planned or prepared in advance. *Impromptu* remarks, spoken on the spur of the moment, often tell voters more about a candidate's real opinions than his carefully edited speeches do.

IMPUDENCE—shamelessness, want of modesty, assurance accompanied with a disregard for the opinions of others. His *impudence* made them all uncomfortable.

IMPUGN—cast doubt on someone's motives or veracity. Do not *impugn* his testimony unless you have substantiation for your charges.

IMPUNITY—exemption from punishment, penalty, injury, or loss. No person should be permitted to violate the laws with *impunity*.

IMPUTE—attribute, ascribe. The difficulties were *imputed* to his negligence.

INADEQUATE—not equal to the purpose, insufficient to effect the object. He could not maintain his car because of his *inadequate* resources.

INADVERTENCE—oversight due to negligence. The bookkeeper's *inadvertence* caused several checks to be returned unpaid.

INALIENABLE—not transferable. We are endowed with certain *inalienable* rights.

INARTICULATE—not uttered with coordination of the organs of speech, not distinct. The sounds uttered by birds and beasts are, for the most part, *inarticulate*.

INCARCERATE—imprison. The sheriff ordered the prisoner *incarcerated*.

INCEPTION—beginning. The scheme was harebrained from its *inception;* it was no surprise when it was abandoned.

INCESSANT—unceasing, uninterrupted, continual. The *incessant* rain kept the children indoors all day.

INCIDENCE—range of an occurrence or effect. The *incidence* of reported alcoholism in teenagers is increasing.

INCISION—cut. The surgeon made an *incision* above the navel.

INCOGNITO—with identity concealed. The prince traveled *incognito*.

INCOMMENSURABLE—not able to be compared, having no common divisor. The number 27 is *incommensurable* with 4.

INCOMMENSURATE—not of equal measure, not adequate. Our means are *incommensurate* to our wants.

INCOMPATIBILITY—inconsistency. There is a permanent *incompatibility* between truth and falsehood.

INCONSIDERABLE—not worthy of consideration or notice, unimportant, small, trivial. There was an *inconsiderable* distance between the cities of Minneapolis and St. Paul.

INCONTESTABLE—not able to be disputed or denied. With the development of the atomic bomb, U.S. military superiority became *incontestable*.

INCORRIGIBLE—beyond reform. Some delinquents are *incorrigible*.

INCRIMINATE—to accuse or implicate in a crime or fault. Picked up by the police, the boy *incriminated* his companions by naming them as accomplices in the theft.

INCUBUS—a demonic weight, a nightmare. He carried the *incubus* of a mortal sin.

INCULCATE—to instill, to impress on the mind by repetition. From earliest childhood they had been *inculcated* with the tenets of the community's belief.

INCULPATE—blame, incriminate. To *inculpate* others in your troubles may bring some ego satisfaction, but it never brings a solution.

INCUR—to acquire through one's own actions. The debts *incurred* in the legal proceedings were to be paid off in monthly installments.

INDENTURE—contract binding an apprentice to service. The *indentured* servant was virtually a slave.

INDICT—accuse formally. The Grand Jury issues an *indictment.*

INDIGENOUS—native to a country. The *indigenous* trees of the Rockies are largely evergreens.

INDIGENT—poor. The home is for the *indigent* aged.

INDISCRIMINATE—not selective. He is *indiscriminate* in the choice of his friends.

INDOCTRINATE—to instruct in a set of principles or beliefs. Children are sent to Sunday school to be *indoctrinated* in the basic tenets of a particular religion.

INDOLENT—lazy. An *indolent* lad never learns much.

INDUBITABLE—undeniably true. That $2 \times 2 = 4$ is *indubitable.*

INDUCT—bring in, initiate a person. The Army *inducts* 100 men a week in New York.

INDUCTION—initiation; logical reasoning from individual facts to a general conclusion. The annual *induction* of new members is always a festive event. Through *induction,* a judge arrives at his decision after examining all of the evidence and testimony.

INDURATE—hardened. He was an *indurate* criminal.

INEBRIATE—make drunk. The accident was caused by an *inebriated* driver.

INEPT—incompetent, clumsy, inefficient. The basketball team's center is tall and powerful but so physically *inept* that he frequently loses the ball.

INEXHAUSTIBLE—unfailing. The city has an *inexhaustible* supply of water.

INEXORABLE—relentless. The *inexorable* logic of history points to a period of decadence for every satisfied nation.

INFERENCE—conclusion drawn from reasoning; also, implication. The *inference* to be drawn from his statement was that I was wrong.

INFILTRATE—to pass through or into, especially secretly or as an enemy. The radical organization had been *infiltrated* by federal agents who monitored its membership and activities.

INFLAMMATORY—tending to arouse to anger or violence. An *inflammatory* speech incited the crowd to riot.

INFLATE—to blow up or swell, to increase beyond what is right or reasonable. The store is able to get away with charging *inflated* prices because of its convenient location and long hours.

INFRACTION—violation, breaking of a law or regulation. The building inspector noted several *infractions* of the health and safety codes.

INGENUOUS—free from dissimulation or trickery. An *ingenuous* approach is often better than guile.

INGRATIATE—establish in favor. He tried to *ingratiate* himself with his teacher by bringing her apples.

INHERENT—inborn, existing as a basic or natural characteristic. A love of hunting is *inherent* in cats.

INHIBITION—restraint. *Inhibition* is particularly important for emotional people.

INIQUITOUS—not right, vicious. His *iniquitous* activities were legal but wicked.

INITIATION—beginning, introduction. The *initiation* of new members into the fraternity will be held soon and the old members can hardly wait.

INNOCUOUS—harmless. His words were *innocuous*, but his temper vile.

INNOVATION—something new, a change, as in custom or method. The celebration of the Mass in languages other than Latin is a major 20th-century *innovation* in the Roman Catholic Church.

INNUENDO—indirect intimation, hint. There was an *innuendo* in his speech that might be construed as a threat.

INQUEST—judicial investigation. The state held an *inquest* to examine the cause of the disaster and determine whether charges should be brought against any parties.

INQUISITIVE—curious, asking questions. Private eyes in detective fiction often get into trouble by being too *inquisitive.*

INSATIABLE—never satisfied, always greedy. His appetite for wealth was *insatiable;* no matter how rich he became, he always craved more.

INSCRUTABLE—unfathomable. His face was *inscrutable* when he doubled his bet.

INSENSATE—without sensation, without ability to reason or feel. In his *insensate* rage he did not yet feel the pain of his injury.

INSIDIOUS—secretly dangerous, tending to entrap. The casino games were *insidious;* before he had realized it, he had gambled away all of his savings.

INSINUATE—suggest subtly. When you say I remind you of Lincoln, are you *insinuating* that I'm dead?

INSOLVENT—unable to meet debts. The corporation was *insolvent* after the loss of the ship.

INSOUCIANT—carefree. Paris is called the *insouciant* city.

INSTIGATE—urge a bad action. The propaganda was designed to *instigate* a riot.

INSUBORDINATE—failing to obey. Ignoring a direct order is an *insubordinate* act with grave consequences.

INSUFFICIENT—inadequate to any need, use, or purpose. The provisions are *insufficient* in quantity.

INSULAR—pertaining to an island. Puerto Rico is an *insular* commonwealth.

INSURE—to make certain, guarantee. Bail is set to *insure* the defendant's appearance in court. *Also:* ensure.

INTANGIBLE—not able to be touched or easily defined. The company's goodwill among its customers is a genuine but *intangible* asset.

INTEGRAL—necessary to the whole. Alaska is an *integral* part of the United States.

INTEGRATE—absorb into the organization. Vertical *integration* results from the merger of companies that perform different operations in the manufacture of a product.

INTEND—to mean, signify, plan. They *intend* to make repairs on their old car.

INTENSIVE—concentrated, intense. *Intensive* private tutoring is needed to take care of this student's reading problem.

INTERCEDE—interpose in behalf of. He asked his preacher to *intercede* with the judge.

INTERCEPT—to cut off, meet something before it reaches its destination. The missile was *intercepted* and destroyed before it reached its target.

INTERDICT—official order prohibiting. He issued an *interdict* on carrying arms.

INTERPOLATE—change a text by inserting new material. The editor *interpolated* the latest news into the proofs.

INTERREGNUM—interval between reigns of succeeding sovereigns. He asked for a regency in the *interregnum*.

INTRACTABLE—stubborn. An *intractable* person is slow to learn a new way of life.

INTRANSIGENT—uncompromising. The *intransigent* attitude of the abolitionists did much to antagonize the South.

INTRAVENOUS—through a vein. The patient was given an *intravenous* feeding of glucose because he could not swallow.

INTREPID—brave, fearless. The *intrepid* explorers stepped out onto the lunar surface.

INTRINSIC—belonging naturally. The *intrinsic* value of diamonds lies in their hardness.

INTROVERT—a person whose thoughts are directed inward. The *introvert* makes friends with difficulty; the extrovert makes friends with ease.

INUNDATE—to flood. When the craze was at its height, the police were *inundated* daily with reports of UFO sightings.

INVEIGH—attack vehemently with words. He *inveighed* against the bias expressed by the group.

INVENTORY—the stock or goods of a business, list of stock or property. The annual *inventory* check showed that several cartons of paper had been damaged by water.

INVERSE—in reversed position. Work gets done in direct ratio with the number working, in *inverse* ratio with the amount of chatter involved.

INVESTIGATION—close examination and observation, inquiry. The *investigation* showed that arson was the cause of the blaze.

INVIDIOUS—likely to arouse resentment. His tactlessness was *invidious*.

INVOCATION—calling on a deity for aid. The minister delivered the *invocation* at the beginning of the ceremony.

INVOICE—a bill, itemized list of goods sent to a buyer. The book was packed with the *invoice* charging $24.00, including shipping.

IRONY—figure of speech saying the opposite of what is meant; e.g., He said he didn't like vacations because he liked school so much.

IRRADIATE—to spread out, expose to radiant energy, heat by radiant energy. The heat from the fireplace *irradiated* the room, warming us all.

IRRECONCILABLE—unable to be harmonized. His statements about liking school were *irreconcilable* with the distaste he expressed for books in general.

IRRITATE—to annoy, inflame. The harsh cleansers used in the job can *irritate* the skin.

ISTHMUS—narrow land strip bordered by water. The *isthmus* of Panama is pierced by a canal.

ITERATE—repeat. Let me *iterate*: this road is dangerous.

ITINERANT—traveling on a circuit. The *itinerant* judge heard cases in Somerville on the first Tuesday of the month.

ITINERARY—plan or schedule of travel. Our *itinerary* includes three days in Florence and a week in Rome.

JADED—wearied, sated with overuse. *Jaded* with the pleasures of the idle rich, he decided to find a worthwhile occupation.

JARGON—confusing, unintelligible talk, usually a specialized language used by experts. The computer programmers spoke what they called computerese, a *jargon* rife with undecipherable acronyms.

JAUNDICE—marked by a sour mental state in which judgment is distorted. His *jaundiced* outlook resulted from an undisciplined childhood.

JEOPARDY—risk, danger, especially the legal situation of a person on trial. Do not put your health in *jeopardy* by exposing yourself to infection needlessly. A person shall not be put in *jeopardy* twice for the same offense.

JEREMIAD—a long and angry complaint. Stop the *jeremiad* and do something to overcome your troubles.

JETTISON—cast overboard. They had to *jettison* the cargo to lighten the plane.

JINGO—advocate of warlike foreign policy. Teddy Roosevelt's "carry a big stick" policy was said to be *jingoism*.

JOCOSE—humorous, joking. She had the sense not to take his *jocose* teasing seriously.

JOLLITY—noisy mirth, gaiety, merriment. The *jollity* of the occasion will always be remembered.

JUDICIAL—having to do with courts or judges. Chief

Justice of the Supreme Court is the highest *judicial* position in the United States.

JUDICIOUS—prudent. His policy was *judicious* and the results effective.

JURISPRUDENCE—philosophy or theory of law. The courses for the most part emphasize the practical application of the law rather than *jurisprudence* or legal history.

JUSTIFY—prove by evidence, verify, absolve. The defendant was able to *justify* the truth of his statement.

JUXTAPOSITION—a placing close together. The *juxtaposition* of the Capitol and White House was avoided in planning the city of Washington to emphasize the separation of the legislature from the executive branch.

KALEIDOSCOPE—toy or optical instrument containing bits of colored glass that form patterns through the use of mirrors. He could see colored patterns in his *kaleidoscope*.

KINDRED—alike, related. Though from diverse backgrounds, they were *kindred* spirits, alike in intellect and ambition.

KINETIC—of or caused by motion. *Kinetic* energy is produced by a stream turning a water wheel.

KIOSK—a small structure open on one side. A newsstand is usually a *kiosk*.

KNEAD—mix, squeeze, and press with the hands. She *kneaded* the dough before shaping it into four loaves for baking.

KRAAL—South African native village, usually surrounded by a stockade. Apartheid policy is said to be driving natives back to the *kraal*.

LABYRINTH—maze, complex and confusing arrangement. The ancient town within the city walls was a *labyrinth* of narrow, winding streets.

LACERATE—tear tissue roughly. The baby swallowed the safety pin, which caused an intestinal *laceration*.

LACONIC—terse, pithy. His *laconic* replies conveyed much in few words.

LAMENT—bewail, mourn for. The boy *lamented* the death of his father.

LANDED—having an estate in land. He was a *landed* gentleman

LANGUID—listless. His *languid* walk irritated his companions, who were in a hurry.

LANGUISH—become weak, suffer with longing and melancholy. He *languished* for weeks in miserable disappointment, refusing to leave the house or to see anybody.

LAPSE—slip, minor or temporary fault or error. I was embarrassed by a momentary *lapse* of memory when I could not recall her name.

LARCENY—legal term for theft. The shoplifter was apprehended and charged with petty *larceny*.

LASCIVIOUS—wanton, lewd, lustful. The woman was followed with *lascivious* eyes.

LASSITUDE—feeling of weariness, languor. The heat created a *lassitude* among the tourists that caused them to postpone their sightseeing.

LATENT—hidden from ordinary observation. He could see the *latent* possibilities of the situation.

LATEX—the milky fluid secreted by some plants when leaves or stems are broken. Opium is the dried *latex* of the poppy. Rubber is a processed *latex*.

LAUDABLE—praiseworthy. The girl listened to the old man's endless and repetitive stories with *laudable* patience.

LAXITY—looseness, lack of strictness. In summer, when business was slow, the manager allowed the employees some *laxity* in their hours.

LEGACY—something inherited. He acquired the house as a *legacy* from his grandmother.

LEGERDEMAIN—a deceptive performance that depends on dexterity of hand. His feats of *legerdemain* required considerable adroitness.

LEGIBLE—written clearly, able to be read. Please print or type if your handwriting is not easily *legible*.

LEGISLATURE—lawmaking body. The federal *legislature* of the United States, the Congress, has two houses.

LEGITIMATE—lawful, genuine. The government of the country is *legitimate*.

LENIENCY—mercy, gentleness, lack of strictness. The *leniency* of the court in suspending the sentence was well repaid by the convicted man's later contribution to the community.

LETHARGIC—drowsy, slothful. The convalescent moved in a *lethargic* manner.

LEVITY—lightness of spirit, frivolity, playfulness. The party toys and silly costumes epitomized the *levity* of the occasion.

LEVY—to impose by force of law. In spite of his constituents' protests, the congressman voted to *levy* the new tax.

LIABLE—exposed to. A physician is *liable* to contagion.

LIABILITY—debt, something disadvantageous. An older person returning to the job market may find his or her age a *liability*.

LIAISON—connection, linking. He had served as a *liaison* between the Allied command and the local government.

LIBEL—defamation, anything having a tendency to lower reputation or lead to disrepute. The report seemed a *libel* on the man's professional standing.

LIMITATION—restriction, finitude. There is a *limitation* to the strength of human beings.

LITHE—gracefully flexible. His *lithe* figure covered the distance in half the time it takes to tell about it.

LITIGATION—lawsuit, process of carrying on a lawsuit. As long as the estate is tied up in *litigation* by the would-be heirs, no one has use of the property.

LIVID—black and blue, discolored, lead-colored. His face was *livid*.

LONGEVITY—life span, long life. The Bible credits the first generations of men with a *longevity* unheard of today.

LONGITUDINAL—pertaining to length. They measured the *longitudinal* distance carefully.

LOQUACIOUS—talkative. A *loquacious* employee is a double time-waster; he invariably engages others as listeners.

LUCID—clear, transparent. The directions were written in a style so *lucid* that a child could follow them.

LUCRATIVE—profitable. A *lucrative* enterprise is attractive to investors.

LUDICROUS—apt to raise laughter, ridiculous. The play was intended to be *ludicrous*.

LUGUBRIOUS—excessively mournful. The bloodhound had an endearingly *lugubrious* look.

LURID—shocking, sensational, tastelessly violent or passionate. The cheap novel told a *lurid* tale of murder and lust.

MACABRE—gruesome, ghastly. The cannibals joined in a *macabre* dance around the boiling pot.

MACADAMIZE—to cover with small broken stones so as to form a smooth, hard surface. The road was *macadamized*.

MACERATE—soften by dipping in liquid; e.g., dipping doughnuts in coffee. Papier-mâché is merely *macerated* newsprint.

MACHINATION—scheme or secret plot, especially an evil one. The *machinations* of his influential uncle landed him a well-paid sinecure in a prestigious company.

MAELSTROM—whirlpool. The ship was twisted in the *maelstrom*.

MAGISTERIAL—authoritative, arrogant, dogmatical. One who is *magisterial* assumes the air of a master toward his pupils.

MAGMA—molten rock within the earth. Far beneath the earth's surface, the *magma* flows.

MAGNANIMOUS—noble-minded, extremely generous, especially in overlooking injury. The painter was *magnanimous* enough to praise the work of a man he detested.

MAGNATE—important business person. The steel *magnate* refused to approve the consolidation.

MAGNITUDE—size. The apparent *magnitude* of the moon is greater near the horizon than at the zenith.

MALADROIT—tactless in personal relations. His *maladroit* remarks embarrassed the hostess.

MALAISE—general bodily weakness. She complained of a *malaise* that was attributed to the hot weather.

MALAPROPISM—word misused ridiculously. This word is derived from the character Mrs. *Malaprop*, who continually used long words incorrectly in Richard Sheridan's play, *The Rivals*.

MALFEASANCE—wrongdoing, especially in public office. The governor was accused of acts of *malfeasance*, including taking graft.

MALIGN—(adj.) evil, malicious, very harmful. *Malign* comments are often motivated by jealousy. (v.) to speak ill of. The students often *maligned* the strict professor.

MALIGNANT—very malicious. A *malignant* person is dangerous, even as a friend.

MALLEABLE—able to be shaped, adaptable. Children are more *malleable* than adults and adapt to new environments more readily.

MALPRACTICE—improper professional conduct. The surgeon was sued for *malpractice* after a sponge was found in his patient's abdomen.

MANDATE—a specific order. Some islands are still ruled by League of Nations or U.N. *mandate*.

MANGE—a parasitic skin disease. The dog has the *mange*.

MANIFEST—to appear, make clear, show. He claims a greater devotion to that cause than his actions *manifest*.

MANTILLA—silk or lace head scarf. Spanish ladies wear *mantillas*.

MAR—to damage. The floor had been *marred* by scratches and scuff marks.

MARQUEE—roof projecting from building over sidewalk. The *marquee* protects guests from the rain.

MARSUPIAL—type of mammal having an abdominal pouch for its young. The kangaroo is the best-known *marsupial*.

MARTINET—rigid, petty disciplinarian. The captain was a *martinet* who considered an unpolished button criminal negligence.

MASOCHISM—sexual satisfaction derived from suffering pain. *Masochism* has been associated with cases of extreme penitence.

MASTICATE—chew. *Mastication* is the first step in preparing food for the body's use.

MATERIEL—tools and equipment needed for work. Combat forces need a steady supply of *materiel* such as ammunition and rations.

MATRIARCH—mother who rules a family or clan. All important decisions were referred to the *matriarch* of the tribe.

MATRIX—something which gives form; e.g., a mold. The linotype machine is equipped with a brass *matrix* for each letter so that a line can be assembled and cast in lead.

MAWKISH—slightly nauseating, insipidly sentimental. Her constant display of fawning affection was *mawkish*.

MAXIMUM—most. In this course the *maximum* number of cuts allowed is six.

MEDIAN—middle, middle item in a series. In a series of seven items, the fourth is the *median*.

MEDICINAL—having the property of healing. The plants had a high *medicinal* value.

MEDIOCRE—of middle quality. A *mediocre* student in high school will rank low among candidates for college.

MEDLEY—mixture, often of musical selections. The magazine was a *medley* of humor, verse, and short stories.

MELANGE—mixture. The room was decorated in a *melange* of styles ranging from Jacobean to Louis XVI.

MELLIFLUENT—sweetly flowing. The soprano had an extremely *mellifluent* voice.

MEMORANDUM—written reminder, informal written interoffice communication. The office manager circulated a *memorandum* outlining the procedures to be followed in the fire drill. Plural: memoranda.

MENACE—threaten, express an intention to inflict injury. The periodic floods *menaced* the city with destruction.

MENDACIOUS—lying. Baron Munchausen was humorously *mendacious*.

MENDICANT—beggar, begging. Visitors to impoverished countries are often shocked at the number of *mendicants* in the streets.

MENISCUS—a crescent. The *meniscus* of the cow's horns in the painting reminded one of the crescent moon.

MERETRICIOUS—superficially attractive, enticing by false charms. Her heavy makeup and the dim light combined to giver her a *meretricious* allure.

MERITORIOUS—deserving reward. Medals were awarded for *meritorious* service.

METAMORPHOSE—transform. Two months abroad *metamorphosed* him into a man of the world.

METICULOUS—showing careful attention to detail, very precise. The sewing in the jacket was so *meticulous* that one could hardly see the stitches.

MILITATE—operate against, work against. A poor appearance at the interview will *militate* against your being hired.

MINISTRATIVE—serving helpfully. Nurses are *ministrative* toward their patients.

MINUSCULE—tiny, minute (after a small cursive script). Such *minuscule* particles cannot be viewed with the usual classroom microscope.

MINUTE—tiny, very precise. The device records the presence of even *minute* amounts of radiation. The writer's *minute* attention to the refinements of style resulted in an elegantly worded essay.

MISANTHROPY—dislike or distrust of mankind. The *misanthropy* of the hermit was known to all.

MISAPPROPRIATION—the act of using for a wrong purpose. The *misappropriation* of the funds caused much misery.

MISCALCULATE—to calculate erroneously. He failed because of his *miscalculations*.

MISCEGENATION—interbreeding of races. *Miscegenation* is illegal in areas where racial prejudice is strongest.

MISCELLANY—collection of various or unlike things. The old steamer trunk contained a *miscellany* of papers, clothes, and assorted junk.

MISCONCEIVE—to have an erroneous understanding of. The judge *misconceived* the nature of the testimony.

MISCONSTRUCTION—wrong interpretation of words or things, a mistaking of the true meaning. His *misconstruction* of the facts causes him to act unjustly.

MISCREANT—villain, villainous. The *miscreant* kidnapper was caught and jailed.

MISDEMEANOR—a misbehaving, a minor legal offense. His offense made him guilty of a *misdemeanor*.

MISNOMER—wrong or inaccurate name. At this season Muddy River is a *misnomer;* the waters are sweet and crystalline.

MISSAL—prayer book. He opened the *missal* to follow the service.

MISTRAL—cold, dry, north wind common in southern Europe. The *mistral* has been known to blow 175 days a year at Marseilles.

MITIGATE—lessen, make milder. He sought to *mitigate* the evil he had done.

MNEMONICS—art of memory development. Picture association is one of the keys to *mnemonics*.

MODICUM—a little, a small quantity. The boy only had a *modicum* of learning.

MODULATE—tone down. *Modulate* your television set after 10 p.m.

MOLEST—disturb, annoy, bother. The children were warned not to *molest* the bulldog.

MOLLIFY—to soothe, placate. The irate customer was *mollified* by the manager's prompt action and apology.

MONETARY—pertaining to money or consisting of money, financial. A penny is a *monetary* unit in this country.

MONITOR—to watch over, check on. An office was set up to *monitor* all radio broadcasts originating within the country.

MONOLITH—large piece of stone. The obelisk in Central Park, New York, is a *monolith* brought here as a gift of the King of Egypt.

MONTAGE—picture made up of pictures or material from several sources. The illustration was a *montage* of various European scenes.

MORALE—level of spirits, mental or emotional condition. After a landslide victory at the polls, *morale* in the party was at a peak.

MORASS—swamp, bog, messy or troublesome state. The application became mired in a *morass* of paperwork; there was no response for several weeks.

MORDANT—biting, sarcastic. His *mordant* remarks hurt her vanity.

MORES—customs, principles of conduct of a culture.

The *mores* of any group are enforced by indoctrination and social pressure to conform.

MORIBUND—dying. The *moribund* king called for the prime minister.

MOROSE—gloomy, sulking, unreasonably unhappy. The boy was *morose* for days over his failure to get tickets for the concert.

MORTGAGE—a pledge of property as security for a loan. Few people can afford to buy a house without taking a *mortgage* on it.

MOTIVATION—reason for doing something. The *motivation* for her questions was not mere curiosity but a genuine desire to help.

MOTLEY—variegated, composed of clashing elements. A *motley* crowd attacked the consulate.

MUDDLE—confuse or stupefy. He was badly *muddled* because of the liquor he had drunk.

MUFTI—civilian dress. Naval officers must wear a hat even when in *mufti*.

MUNDANE—worldly, humdrum, unexciting. The film was undistinguished, a *mundane* exercise in horror movie clichés.

MUTATION—change. He deplored the *mutations* of fortune.

MUTILATE—to cut up, damage severely. The computer cannot read a *mutilated* card.

MYOPIA—nearsightedness. The optometrist prescribed glasses for his *myopia*.

NADIR—lowest point. Enrollment hit its *nadir* last year and has been rising slowly since.

NAIVE—unsophisticated, artless. He was *naive* as the result of a sheltered life in the country.

NAPE—back of neck. The collar chafed his *nape*.

NARCISSISM—love of one's own body. The word *narcissism* is derived from the mythical *Narcissus* who fell in love with his reflection in a stream.

NATANT—swimming or floating. The *natant* leaves of the waterlilies covered the surface of the pond.

NAUSEATE—cause disgust and nausea to. Food *nauseates* the patient.

NEBULOUS—hazy, indistinct. He had a *nebulous* theory about memorizing key words as an aid to study.

NECESSITATE—render unavoidable, compel. Sickness *necessitated* his stay in the hospital.

NEFARIOUS—abominable, wicked in the extreme. He was expelled because of his *nefarious* activities.

NEGATE—to make nothing, undo or make ineffective. The witness's full confession *negated* the need for further questions.

NEGATIVE—implying or expressing refusal. I received a *negative* answer to my request.

NEGLIGIBLE—too small or insignificant to be worthy of consideration. The difference in their ages is *negligible*.

NEGOTIABILITY—the quality of being transferable by endorsement. The *negotiability* of the check made it acceptable payment for the articles.

NEGOTIATE—to bargain, confer with the intent of reaching an agreement. As long as both sides are willing to *negotiate* in good faith, a strike can be avoided.

NEOPHYTE—new convert. He gave lessons each night to the *neophytes*.

NEURALGIA—pain along the course of a nerve. *Neuralgic* pains are often confused with rheumatism.

NEUROTIC—suffering from or typical of neurosis, a range of mental disorders less severe than psychosis. Hysterical pain—physical discomfort without organic cause—is a common *neurotic* symptom.

NEUTRALIZE—to reduce to a state of indifference between different parties. The sea was *neutralized* by the nations through a treaty.

NIGGARDLY—stingy. She was too *niggardly* to buy an appropriate gift.

NIHILISM—disbelief in religion or moral principles. War fosters a spirit of *nihilism*, particularly among the defeated.

NIMBUS—bright cloud around the head of a deity, represented in art as a bright disk. The *nimbus* was common in Renaissance art.

NIRVANA—in Buddhism, the state of perfect blessedness. The peace of *nirvana* is said to be marked by the complete extinction of all desires.

NOCTAMBULIST—one who walks in his sleep. The *noctambulist* had to be watched carefully.

NOCTURNE—a piece of music designed to be played at night. The *nocturne* was particularly dreamy and expressive.

NODE—knot or protuberance. A *node* appears at the joints of a plant.

NOMENCLATURE—the names of things in any art or science, the whole vocabulary of technical terms that are appropriate to any particular branch of science. The *nomenclature* of botany had to be studied carefully.

NONAGENARIAN—a person in his 90s. The *nonagenarian* looks forward to a century mark.

NONCHALANT—indifferent, cool, unconcerned. The woman acted in a *nonchalant* manner, pretending not to notice the stars.

NONCOMPLIANCE—failure to comply. His *noncompliance* with the terms of the contract forced them to sue.

NONPAREIL—without equal. His achievements were *nonpareil*.

NONSENSICAL—absurd, foolish. The actions of the children were *nonsensical*.

NON SEQUITUR—Latin phrase meaning "it does not follow"; a statement or conclusion that does not follow logically from what has gone before. His speech was a tissue of *non sequiturs* that appealed to his audience's emotions at the expense of their intelligence.

NOTARY—person empowered to attest signatures, certify documents, etc. The signature is valid if witnessed by a *notary* public.

NOTORIOUS—famous in an unfavorable way. The official was *notorious* among his associates for failing to keep appointments.

NOVICE—person new to a job or activity, someone inexperienced. A *novice* in the job, she needed more time than an experienced worker to complete the same tasks.

NOXIOUS—harmful, injurious, unwholesome. The *noxious* fumes from the refinery poisoned the air.

NULL AND VOID—legal expression for not valid, without legal force. If it is not properly signed, the will may be declared *null and void*.

NULLIFY—to make void or without effect. The new contract *nullifies* their previous agreement.

NUZZLE—rub or push with the nose, nestle, snuggle. The horse *nuzzled* her gently, looking for a lump of sugar.

OBDURATE—callous, hardened. He was *obdurate* and resisted the pleadings of his friends.

OBEISANCE—gesture of respect, such as bowing. They made an *obeisance* to the king.

OBELISK—a slender, four-sided pillar, gradually tapering as it rises, having the top in the form of a pyramid. Cleopatra's Needle is an *obelisk* that may be seen in Central Park, New York City.

OBESITY—excessive fatness. Her *obesity* was due to her love of rich foods.

OBFUSCATE—confuse, make obscure. Do not *obfuscate* the facts with irrelevant issues.

OBITUARY—an account of the decease of a person or persons. His *obituary* was written by those who loved him.

OBJECTIVE—(adj.) unbiased, not influenced by personal involvement, detached. It is extremely difficult to be *objective* about one's own weaknesses. (n.) aim, goal. Our *objective* is greater efficiency; we must study the possible means to that goal.

OBLIGATORY—required, morally or legally binding. He feels nothing in common with his family, yet he makes an *obligatory* visit to them once or twice a year.

OBLITERATE—demolish, destroy all trace of. The building had been completely *obliterated*.

OBLIVIOUS—so preoccupied as not to notice. The absentminded professor was *oblivious* of the fire caused by his experiment.

OBLOQUY—public disgrace; ill repute. He faced *obloquy* as a result of his ignoble actions.

OBNOXIOUS—odious, hateful, offensive, repugnant. They left because of the *obnoxious* odors.

OBSCENE—foul, offensive, disgusting, indecent. His language was *obscene;* it offended everyone.

OBSCURE—dim, murky, not easily seen or understood, abstruse. His message was *obscure*.

OBSEQUIOUS—servile, overly willing to obey. His *obsequious* obedience to the conquerors turned our stomachs.

OBSESS—beset, haunt the mind. He was *obsessed* with the idea he was important.

OBSOLETE—outmoded, no longer in use or appropriate. Since several offices have been relocated, the old directory is *obsolete*.

OBSTACLE—hindrance, something that bars a path or prevents progress. She refused to think of her handicap as an *obstacle* to a fulfilling career.

OBSTREPEROUS—noisy, boisterous. The *obstreperous* customer was asked to leave.

OBTRUDE—to enter when not invited. It was unfair to *obtrude* upon their privacy.

OBTUSE—dull, not having acute sensibility. The man did not understand because of his *obtuse* wit.

OBVIATE—meet and dispose of, make unnecessary. *Obviate* the necessity for earning money, and all your time is your own.

OBVIOUS—self-evident. The truth is *obvious* to the well-informed.

OCCIDENTAL—pertaining to the part of the earth west of Asia. The finest gems come from *occidental* countries, according to some experts.

OCCIPITAL—pertaining to the back of the head. An *occipital* pain may be the result of overwork or the symptom of a serious ailment.

OCULAR—of the eye. An *ocular* injury impaired her vision temporarily.

OLEAGINOUS—oily. Margarine, butter, and other *oleaginous* products often contain some cholesterol.

OMIT—leave, pass by, or neglect; leave out. He *omitted* an important passage when he read his speech.

OMNIPOTENT—all-powerful. By the end of the third match, he felt *omnipotent*.

ONEROUS—difficult and unpleasant, burdensome. His work was *onerous*.

ONUS—burden, responsibility. The *onus* of proof is on the accuser; the defendant is presumed innocent until proved guilty.

OPPROBRIUM—reproach for disgraceful conduct, infamy. He deserved all the *opprobrium* he received for turning his back on a friend.

OPTIMUM—best for a purpose, most favorable. Under *optimum* conditions of light and moisture, the plant will grow to over three feet.

OPTION—(v.) to purchase the right to buy or sell something within a specified time. For a thousand dollars she *optioned* the novel for one year, wrote a script, and sold it to the movies. (n.) choice, power or right to choose. Before acting, consider your *options*.

OPTIONAL—not required, open to choice. Air conditioning is *optional;* its cost is not included in the sticker price.

ORBICULAR—circular, orb-shaped. The boomerang made an *orbicular* path back to the sender.

ORDINANCE—a city statute. The city council passed an *ordinance* prohibiting the wearing of shorts in the streets.

ORDNANCE—military weapons. He was quartermaster in charge of *ordnance.*

ORDURE—filth, excrement. As soon as he entered the hovel, he could smell the stench of *ordure.*

ORIFICE—opening into a cavity. The surgeon worked through an *orifice* below the ribs.

OSCILLATE—swing in a regular motion. The pendulum continued to *oscillate,* but the clock hands did not move.

OSTENSIBLE—avowed, apparent. The *ostensible* purpose of the withdrawal was to pay a debt, but actually the money was used for entertainment.

OSTENTATIOUS—pretentious, showy. Some people abhor large diamonds as being too *ostentatious.*

PACIFIC—calm, tranquil, placid. The *Pacific* Ocean was so named by its discoverer because it was free from storms and tempests.

PACT—an agreement or covenant. A Faustian bargain is a *pact* with the devil.

PAEAN—a song of praise. He sang a *paean* for Apollo.

PAINSTAKING—very careful or diligent. The search for the lost ring was long and *painstaking.*

PAISLEY—a soft fabric woven in a detailed, colorful pattern used originally for shawls. She wore a *paisley* shawl.

PALAVER—talk smoothly or flatteringly. The explorers had to *palaver* with the natives.

PALLIATE—make an offense seem less grave. He attempted to *palliate* his error by explaining the extenuating circumstances.

PALPITATE—beat rapidly, flutter, or move with slight throbs. The *palpitation* of her heart was due to fright.

PAMPER—gratify to the fullest, coddle, spoil. She *pampered* her pet dog in every possible manner.

PANACEA—a remedy for all ills. Even money is no *panacea.*

PANEGYRIC—a discourse in praise of a person. He delivered a *panegyric* on his patron.

PANIC—sudden and overwhelming terror, exaggerated alarm. When the children heard the noise, they fled in a *panic.*

PANOPLY—a complete set of armor. The knights marched into the tourney grounds in full *panoply.*

PANORAMIC—offering a broad or unlimited view. From the summit of the mountain one has a *panoramic* view of the whole range.

PANTHEISM—any religion that identifies the universe with God. Monism is an essential element of *pantheism.*

PANTOSCOPIC—affording a wide scope of vision, seeing everything. *Pantoscopic* spectacles are spectacles that are divided into two segments, of which the upper is for distant vision and the lower is for reading or viewing near objects.

PARADIGM—model, pattern to be copied. The teacher handed out a sample letter as a *paradigm* of the correct form.

PARADOX—internal contradiction, a statement that appears to contradict itself. "This sentence is false" is an example of a *paradox.*

PARALYZE—to unnerve or render ineffective. The catastrophe *paralyzed* the community.

PARAPET—wall on the edge of a roof. The soldiers fired from behind the castle's *parapet.*

PARAPHRASE—a rewording, repetition of the meaning of something in different words. To *paraphrase* someone's work without acknowledging the source of one's information is a form of plagiarism.

PARASITE—person or creature who lives at the expense of another without giving anything in return. The members of the ruling class were for the most part *parasites* who enjoyed wealth produced by others and contributed nothing of value to the economic or cultural life of their nation.

PAREGORIC—camphorated tincture of opium. The *paregoric* was well worth its high cost to the bedridden patient.

PARIAH—outcast. When he began to associate with Communists, he became a *pariah* among his old friends.

PARIETAL—of any wall-like structure in the body; e.g., the side of the skull. The head blow resulted in a *parietal* injury.

PARITY—comparative equality. Congress aims to keep farm prices at 80 percent of a *parity* with prices of manufactured goods.

PAROCHIAL—narrow in viewpoint; pertaining to a parish. His views were strictly *parochial,* but his tastes were quite sophisticated.

PAROLE—conditional release, release from prison before full sentence is served. Freed on *parole,* the convict was required to report periodically to an officer assigned to his case.

PAROXYSM—spasmodic pain. You could sense the *paroxysm* that accompanied the birth of the foal.

PARSIMONIOUS—frugal, stingy. Although she lived in prosperous comfort, she seemed *parsimonious* to her more extravagant relatives.

PARTISAN—devoted or committed to a party or cause, especially blindly or unreasonably so. *Partisan* loyalty can no longer be taken for granted; voters are now attracted to individuals more than to parties.

PARTITION—division into parts. The present *partition* of

Germany followed from the occupation of the country by the Allied forces in World War II.

PATENT—(adj.) obvious, easily seen. The promise of tax relief was a *patent* attempt to win last-minute support from the farmers. (n.) exclusive right, as to a product or invention. The company's *patent* on the formula expires after a certain number of years.

PATRON—a supporter or defender. For donating her time and energy to the museum, she was honored as a *patron* of the arts.

PECCADILLO—a small fault. He insisted on cavilling over *peccadillos*.

PECTORAL—pertaining to the chest. The surgeon made a *pectoral* incision to reach the heart.

PECULATE—embezzle. Bonding companies have learned that a bookkeeper's speculation often leads to *peculation*.

PECULIAR—odd, special, unique, not ordinary. The fragrance is *peculiar* to violets; no other flower smells the same.

PECUNIARY—financial. He had no *pecuniary* interest in the project.

PEDANTIC—making a needless display of learning. The *pedantic* pedagogue pedaled to the palace spouting Platonic principles.

PEEVISH—fretful, hard to please. The girl was unpopular because she was so *peevish*.

PEJORATIVE—disparaging. Calling a man a skunk is *pejorative*.

PENAL—concerning legal punishment. The *penal* code defines crimes and their legal penalties.

PENCHANT—a strong inclination. He has a *penchant* for making friends.

PENDING—waiting to be decided. It required much patience to wait while the petition was *pending*.

PENSILE—changing. The nests of some birds are *pensile*.

PENSION—regular payments to someone who has fulfilled certain requirements. After twenty years of service she retired on a full *pension*.

PENULT—the next to the last syllable in a word. In the word "evolution," the accent is on the *penult*.

PENURIOUS—stingy. A poor man is *penurious* by necessity.

PERAMBULATE—walk about. We *perambulated* over the grounds for several hours.

PER CAPITA—for each person. The country has a *per capita* income of under $800.

PERCEIVE—feel, comprehend, note, understand. I *perceived* that the beast was harmless.

PERCEPTION—the act of receiving impressions by the senses. *Perception* is that act of the mind whereby the mind becomes conscious of anything, including hunger, thirst, cold, or heat.

PERCUSSION—violent striking of one thing against another. The drum is a *percussion* instrument.

PEREGRINATION—the act of passing through any space,

journeying. The astronomer studied the *peregrination* of the moon in its monthly revolution.

PEREMPTORY—imperative. The captain gave a *peremptory* command for a major advance.

PERFORATE—to make holes in. The top of the box had been *perforated* to allow the air to circulate.

PERIGEE—the point in an orbit nearest the earth. Tomorrow the moon will be at its *perigee*.

PERIPHERAL—of an edge or boundary. The man who notices people almost behind him has excellent *peripheral* vision.

PERISTALTIC—alternate constriction and dilation of a tube. Food moves through the intestines as a result of *peristaltic* action.

PERMEABLE—capable of having fluids pass through. Most clay dishes are *permeable*.

PERMUTATION—rearrangement of the order of a group of items. The sequences CBA and BCA are *permutations* of ABC.

PERNICIOUS—causing much harm. Excessive drinking is a *pernicious* habit.

PERORATION—the last part of a speech. From the exordium through the *peroration*, the speaker used four glasses of water and 92 minutes.

PERPENDICULAR—in an up-and-down direction, vertical, upright, at a right angle. The lamppost, having been grazed by the truck, was no longer *perpendicular*.

PERPETRATE—to do something evil, to commit, as a crime. The committee *perpetrated* the hoax in an attempt to defame the rival candidate.

PERQUISITE—an incidental compensation. A chauffeured car is one of the *perquisites* of a commissioner's position.

PERSIST—to continue, especially against opposition. Despite the rebuffs, he *persisted* in his efforts to befriend the disturbed youngster.

PERSONNEL—employees. The company's *personnel* enjoyed generous health benefits and vacation time.

PERSPICUITY—clearness in expression. His *perspicuity* made him an excellent teacher.

PERTINENT—relevant, concerning the matter at hand. Since those circumstances were vastly different, that example is not *pertinent* to this case.

PERUSE—to read carefully, study. She *perused* the text, absorbing as much information as she could.

PERVIOUS—admitting of passage, open to influence. The man was *pervious* to criticism and often benefited from the constructive advice of his colleagues.

PETTY—small, trivial, unimportant, small-minded. Don't bother the supervisor with *petty* problems but try to handle them yourself.

PETULANCE—petty fretfulness. *Petulance* is a vestige of childhood desire for more parental attention.

PICTURESQUE—having a rough, unfamiliar, or quaint natural beauty. The mountains with their rugged crags and steep ravines present a *picturesque* landscape.

PILASTER—an architectural support designed to resemble a column. He found the child leaning against a *pilaster* on the facade of the church.

PINNACLE—peak, acme. She had reached such a *pinnacle* of fame that everywhere in the country her name was a household word.

PIQUANT—stimulating taste, agreeably pungent. Mustard and chutney are *piquant* in different ways.

PIQUE—a fit of resentment. His *pique* at the scolding lasted all day.

PISCATORIAL—pertaining to fishing. His *piscatorial* penchant kept him afloat most of the weekend.

PLACATE—to soothe the anger of, pacify. A quick temper is often easily *placated*.

PLACID—peaceful, undisturbed. The drug had relieved her anxiety, leaving her in a *placid* and jovial mood.

PLATITUDE—trite remark. He spouts *platitudes* all day but can't solve a practical problem.

PLAUSIBLE—seeming credible, likely, trustworthy. Since his clothes were soaked, his story of falling into the creek seemed *plausible*.

PLENARY—full, fully attended. The issue was so serious that the committee called a *plenary* meeting of the board to decide on a course of action.

PLETHORA—oversupply. There is a *plethora* of bad news and a paucity of good news.

PLIABLE—flexible, able to bend, readily influenced, yielding. Having no preconceived opinion on the matter, we were *pliable*, ready to be swayed by a forceful speech.

PLURALITY—the difference between the highest total and the next highest total. With 437 votes, Slater had a *plurality* of 42 over Merrick's 395.

PODIUM—raised platform, as for use by speakers or musical conductors. The poet stepped to the *podium* to address the audience.

POGROM—an organized massacre of a certain class of people. The Russian *pogroms* in the 1880s forced a huge exodus of Jews.

POIGNANT—with sharp emotional appeal. He read the *poignant* passage and began to cry.

POLEMICS—art of disputing. He is an expert at *polemics* and is studying for a career in law.

POLITY—organization or constitution of a government. The American *polity* of representational democracy derives mainly from a British model.

POLYMER—a compound of high molecular weight. *Polymers* are basic to the creation of plastics.

PONTIFICATE—speak pompously. He would rise slowly, *pontificate* for half an hour, and sit down without having said a thing we didn't know before.

PORRINGER—soup plate. Eat a *porringer* of cereal every morning.

PORTENTOUS—foreshadowing future events, especially somber ones. The thunderstorm that broke as we were leaving seemed *portentous* but in fact the weather was lovely for the rest of the trip.

POSTERITY—succeeding generations. Many things we build today are for *posterity*.

POTENTIAL—possible, not yet realized. If she qualifies for the promotion, her *potential* earnings for the next year might be close to $20,000.

POULTICE—a soft moist mass applied to the body for medical purposes. A *poultice* of bread was applied to draw out the poison.

PRAGMATIC—concerned with practical values. He has a *pragmatic* outlook on all economic theory.

PRECARIOUS—insecure. His position on the ledge was *precarious*.

PRECEDENT—similar earlier event, especially one used as a model or justification for present action. The lawyer's brief argued that the legal *precedents* cited by the opposition were not relevant because of subsequent changes in the law.

PRECIPITOUS—steep like a precipice. The road had a *precipitous* drop on the south side.

PRECISE—exact. The coroner determined the *precise* time of murder by examining the victim.

PRECLUDE—make impossible. Obeying the law would *preclude* my getting home in five minutes.

PRECOCIOUS—advanced in development. *Precocious* children should be given enriched programs of study.

PRECURSOR—predecessor, forerunner. The Continental Congress was the *precursor* of our bicameral Congress of today.

PREDATOR—pertaining to plundering. The hawk is a *predatory* bird.

PREDECESSOR—one who has preceded or gone before another in a position or office. In his inaugural address the new president of the association praised the work done by his *predecessor*.

PREDICAMENT—troublesome or perplexing situation from which escape seems difficult. Having promised to balance the budget, to cut taxes, and to increase defense spending, the newly-elected president found himself in a hopeless *predicament*.

PREDILECTION—preference, liking. He had a *predilection* for good food at any price.

PREDOMINANTLY—for the most part. Although there are a few older students, the class is *predominantly* made up of eighteen-year-olds.

PREEMINENT—most outstanding. He is the *preeminent* doctor in his field.

PREEMPT—to exclude others by taking first. Regularly scheduled programs were *preempted* by convention coverage.

PREJUDICED—biased, judging in advance without adequate evidence. Since I have never liked westerns, I was *prejudiced* against the film before I ever saw it.

PRELIMINARY—going before the main event or business,

introductory. A few easy *preliminary* questions put the applicant at ease.

PREMEDITATION—the act of meditating beforehand, previous deliberation. The *premeditation* of the crime was what made it so heinous.

PREMISE—proposition or idea on which an argument or action is based. I waited to call, on the *premise* that they would not be home until evening.

PREOCCUPIED—having one's thoughts elsewhere, inattentive. *Preoccupied* by her dilemma, she missed her stop on the train.

PREPOSTEROUS—very absurd. The idea of the President's coming to our class was *preposterous*.

PREROGATIVE—privilege or right. Going home after school is your *prerogative*.

PRESCRIBE—to recommend, especially in a professional capacity. For the headache the physician *prescribed* aspirin.

PRESUME—to accept as true without proof; to anticipate or take for granted, overstep bounds. An accused person is *presumed* innocent until proved guilty. I was furious that she had *presumed* to take the car without permission.

PRETERNATURAL—supernatural. He believed in the *preternatural* powers of the self-declared witch.

PREVALENT—current, widely found, common. Feelings of anger and helplessness are *prevalent* among the voters in that district.

PREVARICATE—be evasive. When questioned directly, the suspect was forced to *prevaricate*.

PREVENTIVE—aiming to prevent or keep from happening. *Preventive* measures must be taken to guard against malaria.

PRIMARY—first, most important. Our *primary* goal is to train people for jobs that are actually available; other aspects of the program are secondary.

PRIMORDIAL—first in order of a series. The *primordial* world had no human beings.

PRINCIPAL—main, most important. The *principal* city economically is also the most populous in the state.

PRINCIPLE—a fundamental truth or role. A man of *principle* never goes back on his word.

PRIOR—earlier, and therefore usually taking precedence. The director will not be able to meet with you today due to a *prior* engagement.

PRIVET—a type of evergreen shrub. The house was surrounded by *privet* hedges.

PRIVILEGED—exempt from usual conditions, receiving special benefit; not to be made known, confidential. Only a few *privileged* outsiders have been permitted to observe the ceremony. Since communications between spouses are *privileged*, a man cannot be compelled to testify against his wife.

PROBABILITY—likelihood. The *probability* that your plane will crash is practically nil.

PROBATION—period of testing or evaluation. After a week's *probation*, the employee was hired permanently.

PROBITY—complete honesty, trustworthiness. The *probity* of the witness was placed in doubt.

PROCEED—to go forward, continue. Because of numerous interruptions, the work *proceeded* slowly.

PROCLAIM—to announce loudly, publicly, and with conviction. When the victory was announced, a holiday was *proclaimed* and all work ground to a halt.

PROCLIVITY—tendency. He had a *proclivity* for getting into trouble.

PROCRASTINATE—delay doing something, put off without reason. Since you will have to get it done eventually, you might as well stop *procrastinating* and get started.

PROCURE—to get, obtain, cause to occur. At the last minute the convict's attorney *procured* a stay of execution.

PRODIGAL—extravagant, spending freely. She is more *prodigal* with her advice than with more concrete assistance.

PRODIGIOUS—large. He had a *prodigious* nose and a tiny mouth.

PROFLIGATE—utterly immoral. The *profligate* son was a regular source of income for his father's attorney.

PROLIX—long-winded. *Prolix* lectures are most boring.

PROLONG—to draw out to greater length. The treatment *prolongs* life but cannot cure the disease, which is terminal.

PROMISCUOUS—without discrimination or selection. *Promiscuous* sex seems common today.

PROMULGATE—to announce publicly as a law or doctrine. The revolutionary government *promulgated* some of the promised reforms.

PROPINQUITY—nearness. The *propinquity* of gas stations decreased the value of the property.

PROPORTIONATE—in correct proportion or relation of amount, fairly distributed. An area's representation in the House of Representatives is *proportionate* to its population.

PROSCRIBE—to outlaw, forbid by law. Theft is *proscribed* mostly by state law.

PROSECUTE—to carry on legal proceedings against. In return for information, the attorney general has agreed not to *prosecute* your client.

PROSELYTE—convert won over from another belief. The *proselyte* often is the most fanatic believer.

PROSPECTUS—booklet describing a business enterprise, investment, or forthcoming publication distributed to prospective buyers. The *prospectus* for the real estate development was mailed to potential investors.

PROSPER—to thrive, do well, grow richer. An expensive suit and a new car suggested that the man's business was *prospering*.

PROTAGONIST—leading character. Mike Hammer is the *protagonist* of a whole series of detective stories.

PROTOCOL—rigid code of correct procedure, especially in diplomacy. *Protocol* demands that we introduce the ambassador before the special envoy; to fail to do so would be interpreted as an affront.

PROTOTYPE—original model, first example. Homer's *Iliad* became the *prototype* for much of the later epic poetry of Europe.

PROTRACT—to draw out in time or space, lengthen. The jury's deliberations were *protracted* by confusion over a point of law.

PROTUBERANCE—something that juts out, bulge. Jimmy Durante was proud of his facial *protuberance*.

PROVENDER—dry food for animals. They stored the alfalfa for winter *provender*.

PROVIDENTIAL—fortunate, lucky. It was a *providential* rain that came last Saturday.

PROVISIONAL—temporary, for the time being only. The *provisional* government stepped down after the general elections.

PROVOCATION—a provoking, a cause for resentment or attack. The attack, coming without *provocation*, took them by surprise.

PROXIMITY—nearness. The *proximity* of the shopping mall is a great advantage to those residents who do not drive.

PSYCHIC—of the mind, acting outside of known physical laws. He claimed special *psychic* powers, including the ability to foresee the future.

PUNCTILIOUS—exact in formalities and details. Be *punctilious* in obeying your doctor.

PUNCTUALITY—being on time. The train had an excellent record for *punctuality;* it almost always arrived precisely at 8:15.

PURLOIN—carry away dishonestly, steal. "The *Purloined* Letter" is a famous mystery story.

PURULENT—discharging pus. The *purulent* sore requires a doctor's care.

PUSILLANIMOUS—faint-hearted. A young *pusillanimous* infantryman is a danger to an entire company.

PUTATIVE—supposed, reputed. His *putative* wealth was exaggerated by his ostentation.

PUTREFY—to decay, decompose. A compost heap is made of *putrefied* organic matter.

PYRRHIC VICTORY—victory gained at too great cost. An atomic war can provide only a *Pyrrhic victory* to any party.

QUADRENNIAL—lasting four years, occurring once in four years. The *quadrennial* games were anticipated eagerly.

QUANDARY—doubt, uncertainty, a state of difficulty or perplexity. He was in a *quandary* because the problem was so complex.

QUENCH—extinguish, put out, slake. She *quenched* the flames with water.

QUERY—question. He *queried* the witness about his alibi.

QUIESCENT—not aroused, inactive. The eternal problem of juvenile delinquency becomes *quiescent* during the excitement of war.

QUINTESSENCE—concentrated essence. It is the *quintessence* of coffee flavor.

QUIRK—a turn, a twist, a caprice. A sudden *quirk* of fancy caused her to change her mind.

QUIVER—to shake or tremble, to shudder. The dog *quivered* with excitement.

QUIXOTIC—extravagantly chivalrous, impractical. His actions were *quixotic* and thoroughly useless.

QUORUM—the minimum number of members that must be present for an assembly to conduct business. No votes may be taken until there are enough representatives present to constitute a *quorum*.

QUOTA—proportional share. The school had an unwritten *quota* system that set limits on the proportion of applicants from different geographical areas.

QUOTE—to cite, as a passage from some author; to name or repeat. He *quoted* the words of Woodrow Wilson in his speech.

QUOTIDIAN—daily, recurring daily. He had a *quotidian* fever.

QUOTIENT—in arithmetic, the number resulting from the division of one number by another. The *quotient* of ten divided by five is two.

RABBLE—a tumultous throng of vulgar, noisy people. The *rabble* assaulted the man violently.

RABID—furious, raging; suffering from rabies. The children were frightened by the *rabid* dog.

RADIATION—divergence in all directions from a point. Solar *radiation* is the *radiation* of the sun as estimated by the amount of energy that reaches the earth.

RAILLERY—banter, jesting language, good-humored pleasantry or slight satire. We imitated his actions because we knew he would not object to a little *raillery*.

RAMIFICATION—a division into subdivisions, a branching out. The *ramifications* of the subject were complex.

RAMPANT—springing or climbing unchecked, rank in growth. The *rampant* growth of weeds made the lawn look extremely unsightly.

RAMSHACKLE—tumbling down, shaky, out of repair. It was impossible to live in such a *ramshackle* house.

RANCOR—malice, ill will, anger. In spite of the insults of his opponent, the man remained calm and spoke without *rancor*.

RAPIDITY—speed. The *rapidity* with which her hands flew over the piano keys was too great to follow with the eye.

RATIFY—to give formal approval to. The proposed

amendment must be *ratified* by the states before it can become law.

RATIO—proportion, fixed relation of number or amount between two things. The *ratio* of women to men in middle-level positions in the firm is only one to seven.

RATIONALE—rational basis, explanation or justification supposedly based on reason. They defended their discrimination with the *rationale* that women were incompetent physically to handle the job.

RAZE—to destroy down to the ground, as a building. Buildings in the path of the highway construction will be *razed*.

REACTIONARY—extremely conservative, marked by opposition to present tendencies and advocating a return to some previous or simpler condition. The pamphlet expressed a *reactionary* hatred of innovation and a nostalgia for "the good old days."

REBUFF—a snub, repulse, blunt or impolite refusal. When overtures of friendship are met with *rebuff*, they are not likely to be renewed.

REBUKE—to reprimand, criticize sharply. He *rebuked* the puppy in stern tones for chewing the carpet.

REBUTTAL—contradiction, reply to a charge or argument. Each side was allowed five minutes for *rebuttal* of the other side's arguments.

RECALCITRANT—stubborn, refusing to obey. A *recalcitrant* child is a difficult pupil.

RECAPITULATE—mention or relate in brief, summarize. It is not my purpose to *recapitulate* all the topics that should find a place in democracy's message to the people.

RECEDE—to go back or away. The waters *receded* and left the beach covered with seaweed.

RECEPTIVE—able and tending to receive and accept, open to influence. The manager, unsatisfied with the store's appearance, was *receptive* to the idea of a major remodeling.

RECESSIVE—tending to recede or not make itself felt. The characteristic encoded in a *recessive* gene may be passed on to an individual's offspring even though it is not apparent in the individual.

RECIPIENT—one who receives. The *recipient* of the award had been chosen from among 200 candidates.

RECIPROCAL—done in return, affecting both sides, mutual. The United States has *reciprocal* trade agreements with many countries.

RECKLESS—not thinking of consequences, heedless, causing danger. People who feel they have nothing to lose often become *reckless*.

RECOLLECT—recall to memory, bring to mind. He could not *recollect* having made the appointment.

RECONCILE—to bring to agreement. After hours of recalculating the incorrect figures, we were able to *reconcile* the two accounts.

RECONSIDER—to think over again. When he refused the appointment, the committee asked whether he would *reconsider* his decision if more money were offered.

RECOURSE—seeking of aid or remedy in response to some action or situation. Unless you correct this error immediately, I will have no *recourse* but to complain to the manager.

RECRIMINATE—to return accusation for accusation. They *recriminated* constantly over the most trivial setbacks, each blaming the other whenever anything went wrong.

RECTITUDE—honesty, integrity, strict observance of what is right. Her unfailing *rectitude* in business dealings made her well trusted among her associates.

RECUMBENT—lying down. The painting depicted the goddess *recumbent* on a sumptuous couch.

RECUR—to happen again. Unless social conditions are improved, the riots are bound to *recur*.

REDEEM—to save, ransom, free by buying back. Though the film is boring in parts, it is *redeemed* by a gripping finale.

REDRESS—compensation for a wrong done. The petitioners asked the state for a *redress* of grievances for which they had no legal recourse.

REDUNDANT—wordy, repeating unnecessarily. The expressions "more preferably" and "continue to remain" are *redundant*.

REFINEMENT—the act of clearing from extraneous matter, purification. The *refinement* of the metals was necessary in order to free them from the impurities that made them unfit for commercial uses.

REFRAIN—to keep from doing something, to not do. Considerate parents *refrain* from criticizing their children in front of others.

REGAL—pertaining to a monarch. He had a *regal* air that impressed even those who knew he was an imposter.

REGIMEN—regular manner of living. The *regimen* of army life bored him.

REHABILITATE—restore to a former capacity, to reinstate. It was impossible to *rehabilitate* the delinquent.

REIMBURSE—refund, pay back. The company found it difficult to *reimburse* the salesman for all his expenses.

REITERATE—to repeat. The instructions were *reiterated* before each new section of the test.

RELEGATE—transfer to get rid of, assign to an inferior position. He *relegated* the policeman to a suburban beat.

RELEVANT—concerning the matter at hand, to the point, related. Her experience in government is *relevant* to her candidacy; her devotion to her family is not.

RELINQUISH—to give up, hand over. The aunt *relinquished* custody of the child to its mother.

REMINISCE—remember, talk about the past. When old friends get together, they love to *reminisce*.

REMIT—to pay, to send payment. The invoice was *remitted* by check; you should be receiving it shortly.

REMUNERATION—reward, payment, as for work done. Health benefits are part of the *remuneration* that goes with the position.

RENASCENT—being reborn. The *renascent* spirit of the 15th century fostered a new way of thinking.

RENEGE—to go back on a promise or agreement. Their assurances of good faith were hollow; they *reneged* on the agreement almost at once.

RENOUNCE—to give up or disown, usually by formal statement. The nation was urged to *renounce* its dependence on imports and to buy more American cars.

REPINE—complain, fret. The child *repined* for days at the loss of the puppy.

REPLENISH—to supply again, to make full or complete again something that has been depleted. Some natural resources, such as lumber, can be *replenished.*

REPREHEND—rebuke, reprimand, blame. He was *reprehended* for his rudeness and sent to his room.

REPRESS—to subdue, hold back, keep down, keep from expression or consciousness. We could not *repress* a certain nervousness as the plane bumped along the runway.

REPRIEVE—postponement of some evil, such as punishment. You have a *reprieve;* the test has been put off for a week.

REPRIMAND—severe criticism, especially a formal rebuke by someone in authority. Since it was a first offense, the judge let the teenager off with a *reprimand.*

REPRISAL—injury in return for injury. The Israelis launched a raid in *reprisal* for the night attack.

REPROVE—to censure, rebuke, find fault with. The instructor *reproved* the student for failing to hand in the assignments on time.

REPUDIATE—refuse to accept. The candidate *repudiated* the endorsement of the Communist party.

REQUISITE—required, necessary. No matter when he starts work, an employee may take vacation time as soon as he has worked the *requisite* number of weeks.

REQUISITION—formal written order or request. The office manager sent in a *requisition* for another desk and chair.

REQUITAL—thing given or done in return, repayment. He brought four chickens in *requital* for their kindness.

RESCIND—to cancel formally or take back. They *rescinded* their offer of aid when they became disillusioned with the project.

RESIDUE—something left over, remainder. A *residue* of coffee grounds was left at the bottom of the cup.

RESILIENT—able to spring back. The spring was still *resilient* after years of use.

RESPLENDENT—very bright, shining. She was *resplendent* with much jewelry.

RESPONDENT—person who responds or answers. Several *respondents* refused to answer most of the questions in the survey.

RESTITUTION—restoration to a rightful owner, reparation for an injury. He agreed to make *restitution* for the money he had stolen.

RESTRICT—to confine, keep within limits. Use of the computer room is *restricted* to authorized personnel.

RESUME—to begin again after an interruption. The courtroom proceedings *resumed* after an hour's recess for lunch.

RESURGENT—rising again. The *resurgent* spirit of nationalism caused riots in Cyprus.

RESUSCITATE—bring back to life. Artificial respiration was used to *resuscitate* the swimmer.

RETAIN—to keep. Throughout the grueling day she had managed somehow to *retain* her sense of humor.

RETALIATE—give evil for evil. The boxer *retaliated* with a stunning blow to the head.

RETARD—to slow. Drugs were successfully used to *retard* the progress of the disease.

RETICENT—restrained in speech, unwilling to talk. His *reticence* kept him from offering answers.

RETICULATION—netlike formation. He examined the *reticulation* of the coral.

RETROACTIVE—applying to what is past. A law may not apply *retroactively.*

RETROGRESS—go backward, lose ground. Because of the devastation of the recent earthquakes, living conditions in the region have *retrogressed.*

REVEAL—to make known, display. His dishonesty was *revealed* during the trial.

REVERENCE—feeling of deep respect or awe, as for something sacred. The great novelist was disconcerted by the *reverence* with which her students greeted her most casual remark.

REVIVE—to come or bring back to life. A cool drink and a bath *revived* her spirits.

RHEOSTAT—electrical resistor with changeable resistance. A *rheostat* is used to make lights dimmer.

RIFE—widespread, prevalent, filled with. The city was *rife* with rumors that a coup was imminent.

RISIBILITY—disposition to laugh. His *risibility* increased with each act of the play.

ROBUST—hardy, strong, healthy. Her *robust* health was apparent in her springy walk and glowing skin.

RUBICUND—red, ruddy. A *rubicund* nose was once the symbol of a drunkard.

RUBRIC—title, heading, or note in a book, originally printed in red. The *rubric* of the law tells the essence of what follows.

RUE—be sorry for, regret. He will *rue* the day he insulted me.

RUMINATE—chew the cud; think over at leisure. A cow

ruminates after it eats. I will *ruminate* on your proposal and let you know my decision later this week.

RUPTURE—a breaking off, breach. The bungling of the rescue operation, which resulted in the death of the ambassador, led to a *rupture* of diplomatic relations between the two nations.

SACCHARINE—pertaining to sugar, having the qualities of sugar, a chemical used as sugar. Diabetics substitute *saccharine* for sugar.

SAGACIOUS—wise, discerning. Teachers have more *sagacity* than students give them credit for.

SALACIOUS—obscene. Do not use *salacious* language in public.

SALIENT—conspicuous, noticeable, prominent. The *salient* points of the speech could not be forgotten by the audience.

SALUBRIOUS—healthful. The *salubrious* climate of Arizona cured his asthma.

SALUTARY—promoting health, conducive to good. The preacher's anecdotes provided a *salutary* lesson.

SALVAGE—to save or recover from disaster, such as shipwreck or fire. Divers *salvaged* gold coins and precious artifacts from the sunken Spanish galleon.

SALVATION—the act of preserving from destruction, danger, or great calamity. The governor's policy of delay proved to be the *salvation* of the state.

SANCTIMONY—assumed manner of holiness, pretense of piety. His *sanctimony* served to hide the fact that he indulged in the very vices he publicly condemned.

SANCTION—to authorize, approve, support. The parent organization refused to *sanction* the illegal demonstration staged by the splinter group.

SANCTITY—holiness, purity, godliness. The *sanctity* of the priest's oath could not be questioned.

SANGUINE—ardent and confident. The leader was *sanguine* of success.

SARDONIC—ironical. His *sardonic* smile irritated the guests.

SATIATE—gratify completely, surfeit. Employees at candy factories soon get so *satiated* that they never eat the stuff.

SATURATE—fill fully, soak, cause to become completely penetrated. The cloth was thoroughly *saturated* with the soapy water.

SATURNALIA—wild carousal. The victory was followed by a *saturnalia,* in which the entire company lost consciousness.

SCARAB—an ornament or amulet in the form of a beetle. In Egypt, it was customary to wear ornamental *scarabs* as charms.

SCARIFY—make scratches. Children *scarify* the furniture.

SCHEMATIC—in the form of an outline or diagram. A *schematic* drawing of the circuitry illustrated how the radio worked.

SCHISM—a split, break-up. The Great *Schism* created two Christian churches, the Eastern and the Western.

SCHIST—a type of crystalline rock. The island of Manhattan is made up largely of *schist.*

SCHIZOID—disposed to schizophrenia. He has a *schizoid* personality.

SCIATIC—pertaining to the hip. Pains in the *sciatic* nerves are not uncommon.

SCINTILLA—barely perceptible amount. There was not one *scintilla* of evidence of his guilt.

SCINTILLATING—sparkling, brilliant, witty. Absorbed in the *scintillating* conversation, the guests lost track of the time.

SCRUPLE—reluctance to act because of questions of conscience. The man was without *scruples.*

SECULAR—not religious. The *secular* authorities often have differences with the church in Italy.

SECURE—(adj.) safe, reliable, free from fear or danger. Her *secure* job assured her of a steady income for as long as she chose to work. (v.) to make safe, to obtain. I have *secured* two tickets for tonight's performance.

SEDITION—incitement to rebel against the government. *Sedition* is a major offense but is punishable under state laws.

SEDULOUS—painstaking and persevering. He was a *sedulous* worker.

SEISMIC—caused by earthquake. A seismograph measures the strength of *seismic* tremors in the earth.

SEMANTICS—a system or theory of meaning. In English *semantics,* many synonyms have quite different connotations.

SENTENTIOUS—containing striking sentences. It was a *sententious* speech that all will remember.

SENTIENT—capable of feeling. Even a dog is *sentient.*

SEQUESTER—seize by authority, set apart in seclusion. The jury was *sequestered* until the members could reach a verdict.

SERAGLIO—harem. A *seraglio* is permitted by the customs of Islamic countries.

SHIBBOLETH—password, identifying phrase of a group or movement. "Power to the people" was a popular *shibboleth* of the 1960s.

SIMIAN—pertaining to a monkey. *Simian* Hall is the most popular section of the zoo.

SIMONY—making profit from sacred things. Church law is much stricter than secular law regarding *simony.*

SIMULATE—to pretend, feign, give a false appearance of. Although she had guessed what the gift would be, she *simulated* surprise when she unwrapped the package.

SIMULTANEOUS—happening or existing at the same time. There were *simultaneous* broadcasts of the game on local television and radio stations.

SINECURE—job requiring little work. The man who is looking for a *sinecure* should avoid working here.

SINUOUS—with many curves. The *sinuous* stick turned out to be a snake.

SITE—piece of land considered as a location for something, such as a city. The archeologists began excavations at the *site* of the ancient city.

SKEPTICISM—doubt, partial disbelief. He accepted the answers to his political questions with a good deal of *skepticism*. Also: scepticism.

SLANDER—spoken false statement damaging to a person's reputation. The witness was guilty of *slander* when he falsely testified that his partner had connived in the tax fraud scheme.

SLATE—to put on a list, to schedule. The meeting is *slated* for next Tuesday.

SLATTERN—slovenly woman. The mendicant was a *slattern* who could not be expected to know what cleanliness was.

SLOUGH—soft, muddy ground, swamp. They put on high boots to get through the *slough*.

SMIRK—annoyingly smug or conceited smile. His arrogant behavior and *smirk* of satisfaction whenever he won made him unpopular with the fans.

SOLICITUDE—concern, anxiety, uneasiness of mind occasioned by the fear of evil or the desire for good. The teacher had a great *solicitude* for the welfare of her students.

SOMATIC—bodily. Psychological disturbances often result in *somatic* symptoms.

SONOROUS—resonant. His *sonorous* voice helped make him a famous orator.

SOPORIFIC—causing sleep. Because of the drug's *soporific* effect, you should not try to drive after taking it.

SPARTAN—very simple, frugal, hardy, disciplined, or self-denying. In addition to the usual classes, the military school imposed a *spartan* regimen of physical training.

SPATULA—a flat, broad instrument. He picked up the griddle cake with the *spatula*.

SPECIFIC—precise, well-defined, not general. The patron was not looking for any *specific* book but had just come in to browse.

SPECIOUS—deceptively plausible. He advanced his cause with *specious* arguments.

SPECULUM—mirror, instrument for dilating a cavity to aid seeing. The surgeon inserted a *speculum* into the orifice in order to see better.

SPLENETIC—fretfully spiteful, peevish. The heat, the cranky children, the pressure of a heavy workload—all contributed to her *splenetic* outburst.

SPONTANEOUS—coming from natural impulse, having no external cause. *Spontaneous* combustion causes oily rags to burst into flames.

SPORADIC—occasional. He made *sporadic* attempts to see his estranged wife.

SPURIOUS—false, counterfeit, phony. The junta's promise of free elections was *spurious,* a mere sop to world opinion.

SQUALID—wretched, filthy, miserable. The *squalid* shantytown was infested with vermin and rife with disease.

STALACTITE—calcium deposit hanging from cave root. Great caverns abound with *stalactites* hanging from the ceiling.

STALEMATE—deadlock, situation in which neither side in a game or contest can make a move. Talks have reached a *stalemate;* neither side is authorized to make the necessary concessions.

STAMINA—power of endurance, physical resistance to fatigue or stress. While younger swimmers tend to be faster over short distances, older swimmers often have more *stamina*.

STATURE—height, elevation (often used figuratively). His work in physics was widely admired in the profession and his *stature* as an expert in his field unquestioned.

STATUS—position, rank, present condition. Her *status* as vice president allows her to take such action without prior approval by the board of directors.

STATUTE—a formal regulation. As the *statute* of limitations had expired, he was not arrested for the crime he had committed long ago.

STEALTHY—furtive, secret. While their grandfather was distracted by the phone, the children made a *stealthy* raid on the refrigerator.

STENTORIAN—loud. His *stentorian* voice carried across the auditorium without aid.

STIGMA—distinguishing blemish inflicted by others. The *stigma* caused by gossip lasted long after the accusation was disproved.

STIPULATE—make an express demand or agreement. The lawyers *stipulated* that the case should be adjourned.

STOICAL—showing calm fortitude. He was *stoical* in the face of great misfortunes.

STRATAGEM—a scheme that outwits by trickery. He presented another *stratagem* to overcome the lead of the opposition.

STRENUOUS—rugged, vigorous, marked by great energy or effort. Climbing the volcano was *strenuous* exercise even for the physically fit.

STRIDENT—harsh-sounding. She had a *strident* voice that sent shivers down my back.

STRINGENT—severe, strict, compelling. The speaker presented *stringent* arguments for the unwelcome cutbacks.

SUAVE—smoothly polite. His *suave* manners reflected great confidence and poise.

SUBCUTANEOUS—beneath the skin. Injections of most vaccines are made *subcutaneously*.

SUBDUE—overcome, calm, render less intense or less

harsh. The understanding actions of the nurse helped to *subdue* the stubborn and unruly child.

SUBJOIN—to add something in writing. A codicil was *subjoined* to the will.

SUBMIT—to give in, surrender, yield; to give, hand in. Although the doctors were dubious of his full recovery, the patient refused to *submit* to despair. The couple *submitted* their application to the loan officer.

SUBPOENA—writ summoning a witness. They issued *subpoenas* to all necessary witnesses.

SUBSIDY—financial aid granted by the government. Shippers and airlines receive a federal *subsidy* in the form of mail delivery contracts.

SUBSTITUTE—person or thing put in place of something else. A temporary worker filled in as a *substitute* for personnel on vacation.

SUBTERFUGE—deceitful means of escaping something unpleasant. The lie about a previous engagement was a *subterfuge* by which they avoided a distasteful duty.

SUBVENTION—a grant of financial aid. Road building is sped by federal *subvention*.

SUBVERSIVE—tending to undermine or destroy secretly. The editor was accused of disseminating propaganda *subversive* to the national security.

SUCCESSIVE—following one after another without interruption. Last week it rained on four *successive* days.

SUCCESSOR—one who follows another, as in an office or job. Retiring from office, the mayor left a budget crisis and a transit strike to his *successor*.

SUCCINCT—to the point, terse. A *succinct* communiqué summed up the situation in four words.

SUCCOR—aid, help in distress. Despite the threat of harsh reprisals, many townspeople gave *succor* to the refugees.

SUFFICIENCY—abundance, ampleness, adequate substance or means. They accumulated a *sufficiency* of wealth for their needs.

SUFFUSE—to overspread. The floor was *suffused* with a disinfectant wax.

SUMMARIZE—to cover the main points. The newscaster *summarized* the content of the President's speech.

SUNDRY—miscellaneous, various. *Sundry* errands can be consolidated into a single trip in order to save gas.

SUPERCILIOUS—proud and haughty. The *supercilious* attitude of wealthy families has been a cause of many social upheavals.

SUPERFICIAL—on or concerned with the surface only, shallow. The *superficial* review merely gave a synopsis of the movie's plot.

SUPERFLUOUS—extra, beyond what is necessary. It was clear from the scene what had happened; his lengthy explanations were *superfluous*.

SUPERSEDE—take the place of. The administration appointed new department heads to *supersede* the old.

SUPERVISE—to oversee, direct work, superintend. A new employee must be carefully *supervised* to insure that he learns the routine correctly and thoroughly.

SUPINE—lying on the back, passive, inactive. The girls were *supine* on the beach, roasting in the sun.

SUPPLANT—to take the place of, especially unfairly. The mother claimed that her sister had deliberately tried to *supplant* her in the daughter's affections.

SUPPLEMENT—to add to, especially in order to make up for a lack. The dietician recommended that she *supplement* her regular meals with iron pills.

SUPPLICATE—beg. He *supplicated* for a pardon.

SURFEIT—excess. There was a *surfeit* of food at the table, and no one could finish the meal.

SURPASS—to excel, go beyond. The success of our program *surpassed* even our high expectations.

SURREPTITIOUS—unauthorized, clandestine. They met *surreptitiously* in the night to exchange information.

SURROGATE—official in charge of probate of wills. The *surrogate* ruled that the guardians might receive a fee.

SURVEILLANCE—watching. The suspect was kept under *surveillance*.

SUSCEPTIBLE—easily affected, liable. He is *susceptible* to colds because of his recent illness.

SUSPEND—to stop or cause to be inactive temporarily; to hang. Service on the line was *suspended* while the tracks were being repaired. The light fixture was *suspended* from the beam by a chain.

SUTURE—stitch on a wound. The surgeon made several *sutures* to close the wound.

SYBARITE—person devoted to luxury. A *sybarite* requires a good income in modern times.

SYCOPHANT—self-serving flatterer. A wise ruler pays no attention to *sycophants*.

SYLLOGISM—logical argument in which a conclusion is drawn from two premises; e.g., All cats have fur. Ralph is a cat. Therefore, Ralph has fur.

SYLVAN—pertaining to the woods. The *sylvan* atmosphere of her backyard was inviting.

SYMPOSIUM—meeting for discussion of a subject. They listened to a television *symposium* on the subject of better schools.

SYNCOPATE—to accent musical beats not normally accented. Jazz music is often *syncopated*.

SYNTHESIS—combination of parts into a whole. Photo*synthesis* is the process of making plant food from air and water, with the aid of sunlight.

SYSTEMATIC—orderly, following a system. A *systematic* review of hiring in the past two years revealed discrepancies between official policy and actual practice.

TABULATE—to arrange data in some order. The election results were *tabulated* by township.

TACHOMETER—instrument for measuring rotational speed. They watched the *tachometer* closely, keeping an eye on the engine's rpms.

TACITLY—silently, by implication, without words. He *tacitly* assented to the arguments of his wife.

TAINT—to be infected or corrupted, to be affected with incipient putrefaction. Hot weather *taints* unrefrigerated meat.

TANGENTIAL—digressing, off the point, not central. Facts about the author's life, while they may be fascinating, are *tangential* to an evaluation of her works.

TANGIBLE—capable of being touched, having objective reality and value. The new position offered an opportunity for creativity as well as the more *tangible* reward of a higher salary.

TARDINESS—lateness. His *tardiness* was habitual; he was late getting to class most mornings.

TAUTOLOGY—useless repetition without the addition of new ideas; e.g., The modern car of today is a contemporary product.

TAWDRY—showy and cheap. She wore *tawdry* jewelry that marked her bad taste.

TAXONOMY—science of classification. The *taxonomy* of law first separates the civil from the criminal.

TEDIOUS—boring, long and tiresome. The film was so *tedious* that we walked out in disgust before it was half over.

TEMPORIZE—delay immediate action in order to gain time. He *temporized* until he knew what they wanted from him.

TENABLE—capable of being held or defended. The club had no *tenable* reasons for the exclusion; it was purely a case of prejudice.

TENACITY—persistence, quality of holding firmly. His *tenacity* as an investigator earned him the nickname "Bulldog."

TENANCY—state or time of being a tenant. We observed nothing during the first few weeks of our *tenancy*.

TENDON—in anatomy, a hard, insensible cord or bundle of connective tissue by which a muscle is attached to a bone. The Achilles *tendon* connects the heel with the calf of the leg.

TENEMENT—dwelling place, apartment, especially a building that is run-down, dirty, etc. Rows of dilapidated *tenements* lined the streets of the impoverished neighborhood.

TENET—a doctrine or belief. Muslims follow the *tenets* of Mohammed.

TENSILE—pertaining to tension. The *tensile* strength of steel is greater than that of plastic.

TENTATIVE—done as a test, experiment, or trial. The negotiators have reached a *tentative* agreement, the details of which have yet to be worked out.

TENUOUS—held by a thread, flimsy. The business survived on a *tenuous* relationship with one customer.

TERMINATE—to end. She *terminated* the interview by standing up and thanking us for coming.

TERMINOLOGY—special vocabulary used in a field of study. Use proper *terminology* in technical writing so that your meaning will not be ambiguous.

TERSE—to the point, using few words. The official's *terse* replies to our questions indicated that he did not welcome being interrupted.

TEXTILE—cloth, woven material. New England in the nineteenth century was dotted with *textile* mills operated by water power.

THEOREM—a speculative truth, a proposition to be proved by a chain of reasoning. The professor emphasized the fact that a *theorem* is something to be proved.

THERAPEUTIC—pertaining to curing disease. Some *therapeutic* drugs can be poisonous if taken in excess.

THERMODYNAMIC—using force created by conversion of heat into mechanical energy. The development of the steam engine was the major step in *thermodynamics* that ushered in the Industrial Revolution.

THESAURUS—dictionary of synonyms. A good *thesaurus* distinguishes the shades of meaning among words with similar definitions.

THESIS—essay, proposition to be debated. He completed his doctoral *thesis*.

TILDE—diacritical mark (~) used in Spanish to indicate a certain pronunciation of the letter *n*; e.g., señor, cañon.

TIRADE—a vehement speech. He shouted a long *tirade* at the man who had hit his car from behind.

TITHE—tax of one tenth. Many churches expect their members to give a *tithe* to charity.

TOCCATA—piano or organ composition designed to show player's technique. Bach, Schumann, and Debussy created some of the great *toccatas*.

TOCSIN—alarm bell. The church bell served as a *tocsin*.

TOLERATE—permit, put up with. We *tolerate* ignorance in ourselves because we are too indolent to study.

TORPIDITY—dullness, inactivity, sluggishness. His *torpidity* amounted to a total loss of sensation.

TORTILLA—a large, round, thin cake prepared from a paste made of the soaked grains of corn, baked on a heated stone slab. The *tortilla* is the substitute for bread in Mexico.

TRACHEA—windpipe. A fish bone caught in his *trachea*.

TRACTABLE—easily led. A *tractable* worker is a boon to the supervisor but is not always a good leader.

TRADUCE—slander, publicly defame. Her reputation was *traduced* by malicious innuendo.

TRANQUILITY—peacefulness. Complete *tranquility* comes only with death.

TRANSCENDENT—excelling, surpassing others. The high cost of the house was due to its obviously *transcendent* worth.

TRANSCRIBE—to make a written copy of. These almost

illegible notes must be *transcribed* before anyone else will be able to use them.

TRANSCRIPT—written copy. The court reporter read from the *transcript* of the witness's testimony.

TRANSFUSE—pour from one container to another. They gave the victim a blood *transfusion*.

TRANSGRESSION—the breaking of a law or commandment. We ask God to forgive our *transgressions*.

TRANSITION—change, passage from one place or state to another. The *transition* of the weather from hot to cold took a surprisingly short time.

TRANSITORY—fleeting, passing, not permanent. It is normal to feel a *transitory* depression over life's setbacks.

TRANSLATE—to change from one medium to another, especially from one language or code to another. The flight attendant *translated* the announcement into Spanish for the benefit of two of the passengers.

TRANSLITERATE—change letters or words into a different alphabet. Prayer books written in Hebrew often contain *transliterations* of Hebrew words written in Latin script.

TRANSMUTE—change from one form or substance to another. Water power can be *transmuted* into electricity.

TRANSVERSE—lying across. They placed the ties *transversely* on the tracks and waited for the train to crash.

TRAUMA—wound. Many ailments in adults are related to psychic *traumas* in childhood.

TRAVAIL—difficult labor. Years of *travail* were required before the pioneers could reap a living from their lands.

TRAVESTY—imitation of a serious work so as to make it seem ridiculous. His production of Shakespeare in modern style was a *travesty*.

TREATY—formal agreement between nations. An economic alliance between the governments was established by *treaty*.

TRENCHANT—sharp, penetrating, forceful. His *trenchant* remarks were more dangerous than his sword.

TREPIDATION—an involuntary trembling, particularly from fear or terror. The stories they had heard caused them much *trepidation*.

TRIBULATION—great trouble. The Pilgrims faced many *tribulations* before the first colonies were firmly established.

TRIBUNAL—court of justice. The decision was left to an international *tribunal*.

TRIBUTARY—serving to make up a greater object of the same kind, contributing. The *tributaries* of the Amazon River can be found on the map.

TROGLODYTE—cave man. The *troglodyte* had the same emotions as modern man, but not the same needs.

TRUCULENT—ferocious, savage, harsh. The champion affected a *truculent* manner to intimidate the young challenger.

TRUMPERY—worthless ornaments. Tawdry *trumpery* is a mark of frumpery.

TRUNCATE—to shorten by cutting. The shrubs were uniformly *truncated* to form a neat hedge.

TRUNCHEON—club. British police carry *truncheons*.

TRUSS—support, tie up in a bundle. The chicken was *trussed* with string before roasting.

TUMID—swollen, inflated, pompous. The *tumid* river was fed by melting snow.

TURBULENT—violent, in wild motion, agitated. The *turbulent* stream claimed many lives.

TURGID—swollen. The man was in constant pain because his limbs were *turgid* as the result of an incurable disease.

TURPITUDE—depravity. A person convicted of moral *turpitude* may not be permitted entry into the United States.

TUTELAGE—guardianship. He grew up under his cousin's *tutelage*.

TYKE—mischievous child. The little *tyke* would not leave me alone.

TYRO—novice, beginner. He is a *tyro* in finance.

UBIQUITY—existence everywhere at the same time, omnipresence. The *ubiquity* of God has often been denied.

ULTIMATELY—as a final result, at last. Afflictions may *ultimately* prove to be blessings.

ULULATION—a howling, wailing. The *ululation* of the wolf caused the tourists much terror.

UMBILICAL—navel. The doctor cut the *umbilical* cord to free the newborn infant from its mother.

UMBRAGE—suspicion of being slighted. He takes *umbrage* if you look at him sideways.

UNACCOUNTABLE—mysterious, not able to be explained. The *unaccountable* disappearance of the family led to wild stories of flying saucers.

UNCANNY—weird, so acute as to appear mysterious. After a lifetime of fishing those waters, the old man was able to predict weather changes with *uncanny* precision.

UNCOUTH—unrefined, awkward. His *uncouth* behavior was marked by a simple inability to handle a knife and fork.

UNDULATING—waving, vibrating, having a form or outline resembling that of a series of waves. A stretch of country is said to be *undulating* when it presents a succession of elevation and depressions resembling waves of the sea.

UNETHICAL—without or not according to moral principles. Although he did not break any law, the man's conduct in taking advantage of credulous clients was certainly *unethical*.

UNGAINLY—not expert or dexterous, clumsy, awkward. He walked in an *ungainly* manner as the result of the accident.

UNGUENT—ointment for burns. He poured a greasy *unguent* over his shoulders to alleviate the pain.

UNGULATE—having hoofs. Horses and cows are both *ungulate,* but bears are not.

UNIFORM—not varying in degree or rate, consistent at all times. Most countries do not have a *uniform* temperature.

UNILATERAL—one-sided, pertaining to one side. A *unilateral* bond is one that binds one party only.

UNIQUE—without a like or equal, unmatched, single in its kind. The statue was priceless because it was truly *unique.*

UNKEMPT—uncombed, not cared for, disorderly. He was recognized by his *unkempt* beard.

UNMITIGATED—not lessened, not softened in severity or harshness, not toned down. According to President Eliot of Harvard, inherited wealth is an *unmitigated* curse when divorced from culture.

UNOSTENTATIOUS—not given to showy display. Despite their wealth, they lived simply and *unostentatiously.*

UNPERCEIVED—not heeded, not observed, not noticed. The thief escaped because his actions were *unperceived* by the policeman.

UNPRECEDENTED—never before done, without precedent. Sputnik I accomplished *unprecedented* feats.

UNRAVEL—untangle, explain, clear from complication. The detective was able to *unravel* the mystery.

UNRELIABLE—not dependable. Because of his *unreliable* attendance at conferences, the professor was not asked to prepare a speech.

UNSCRUPULOUS—unprincipled, not constrained by moral feelings. The *unscrupulous* landlord refused to return the security deposit, claiming falsely that the tenant had damaged the apartment.

UNWIELDY—ponderous, too bulky and clumsy to be moved easily. Four men were required to move the *unwieldy* rock.

UPBRAID—charge with something disgraceful, reproach, reprove with severity. The husband *upbraided* his wife for her extravagances.

UPROARIOUS—making a great tumult, noisy. The laughter of the drunken men was *uproarious.*

URBANE—smoothly polite. He travels in *urbane* circles and is as suave as any of his friends.

URCHIN—mischievous child. He needed no urging to help the *urchin.*

URGENT—pressing, having the nature of an emergency. We received an *urgent* message to call the hospital.

URN—vase with a foot or pedestal. His ashes were placed in an *urn* that stayed on the mantel for a month.

URSINE—pertaining to bears. *Ursine* neighbors are common in western national park campsites.

USURPATION—act of seizing and enjoying the power or property of another without right. The *usurpation* of the kingdom by the conquerors caused much misery.

UTENSIL—implement, tool. Forks and other *utensils* are in the silverware drawer.

UTILIZE—to use, put to use. We will *utilize* all the resources of the department in the search for the missing child.

UXORIOUS—excessively or foolishly fond of one's wife. He was described as an *uxorious* husband.

VACANT—empty, unoccupied. The *vacant* lot was overgrown with weeds.

VACATE—to leave empty. The court ordered the demonstrators to *vacate* the premises.

VACILLATION—fluctuation of mind, unsteadiness of character, change from one purpose to another, inconstancy. His *vacillation* in giving orders made him difficult to work for.

VACUITY—dullness of comprehension, lack of intelligence, stupidity. The *vacuity* of her mind was apparent to all who knew her.

VACUOUS—empty. His *vacuous* speeches won him no converts.

VAIN—unsuccessful. They tried *vainly* to win the game.

VALIDITY—being supported by fact, proof, or law. The bill was never paid because its *validity* could not be substantiated.

VALOR—worthiness, courage, strength of mind in regard to danger. His *valor* enabled him to encounter the enemy bravely.

VANDAL—one who deliberately disfigures or destroys property. The *vandals* burned the paintings.

VANGUARD—the troops who march in front of any army, the advance guard. The uniforms of the *vanguard* were the most colorful of all.

VANQUISH—conquer, overcome, overpower. Napoleon *vanquished* the Austrian army.

VAPID—dull, flat, insipid. The time was passed in *vapid* conversation about the weather.

VARIABLE—changing, fluctuating. The weather report stated that the winds would be *variable.*

VARIEGATE—diversify in external appearance, mark with different colors. The builder created a *variegated* pattern with marble of different hues.

VELLUM—a fine parchment made of calfskin, which has been limed, shaved, washed, stretched, scraped, and rubbed down with pumice stone. The manuscript was written on the finest quality *vellum.*

VENAL—able to be corrupted or bribed. The *venal* judge privately offered to hand down the desired verdict for a price.

VENDETTA—blood feud. The two families carried on a *vendetta* through three generations.

VENERATE—respect. I *venerate* the memory of Dr. Schweitzer, although I did not agree with him entirely.

VENOUS—pertaining to a vein or veins. *Venous* blood is carried by the veins to the right side of the heart.

VENTRICLE—the name given to various cavities in the body that are smaller than the stomach. The cerebrum has several *ventricles* and the cerebellum one.

VERBATIM—word for word, in the same words. The lawyer requested the defendant to repeat the speech *verbatim*.

VERBOSE—using more words than are necessary, tedious from a multiplicity of words. The audience was bored by the *verbose* politician.

VERDANT—green, fresh. The *verdant* lawn made the old house look beautiful.

VERDICT—decision, especially a legal judgment of guilt or innocence. In our legal system, the *verdict* of a jury in convicting a defendant must be unanimous.

VERGE—be on the border or edge of something. Their behavior was *verging* on hysteria.

VERIFY—prove to be true, establish the proof of. The principal expected the student to *verify* his statements.

VERISIMILITUDE—appearance of truth. There is a great *verisimilitude* here, but I still do not believe this is conclusive evidence.

VERITY—truthfulness, honesty, the quality of being real or actual. The *verity* of the document could not be questioned.

VERNACULAR—native language. He spoke in the *vernacular* of southern Germany.

VERNAL—pertaining to spring. The *vernal* influence was everywhere apparent, particularly in the park, where young couples strolled hand in hand.

VERTEX—top, highest point, apex. The view was breathtaking from the *vertex* of the hill.

VERTICAL—upright, in an up-and-down position. A graph is constructed around a *vertical* and a horizontal axis.

VERTIGO—dizziness, giddiness, a sense of apparent rotary movement of the body. The physician explained that the *vertigo* was due to some chronic disease of the heart.

VESTIGE—remnant, remainder, trace. The artifacts were the last *vestiges* of an earlier civilization.

VETERINARY—concerning the medical treatment of animals. Reliable *veterinary* services are indispensable in areas where people raise animals for their livelihood.

VEX—to irritate, distress, cause disquiet. She was periodically *vexed* by anonymous phone calls.

VEXATIOUS—irritating, distressing, causing disquiet. The *vexatious* suit was brought to court for the sole purpose of harassing those concerned.

VIABILITY—capacity to live. The statistician compiled a chart that indicated the *viability* of male infants as compared with that of female infants.

VIBRATE—swing, oscillate, move one way and then the other. The strings of the instrument *vibrate* when they are touched.

VICARIOUS—experienced secondhand through imagining another's experience. She enjoyed *vicariously* the achievements of her daughter.

VICISSITUDE—regular change or succession of one thing to another, a passing from one condition to another. The *vicissitude* of fortune made him a poor man.

VIGILANT—watchful, on guard. As a Supreme Court Justice he had always been *vigilant* against any attempt to encroach on the freedoms guaranteed by the Bill of Rights.

VILIFY—defame, attempt to degrade by slander. He was sued for attempting to *vilify* the physician.

VINDICATE—uphold. The judgment of the author was *vindicated* by the phenomenal sale of the text.

VINDICTIVE—unforgiving, showing a desire for revenge. Stung by the negative reviews of his film, the director made *vindictive* personal remarks about critics.

VISCOSITY—in physics, the resistance to flow of a fluid. Motor oil has a greater *viscosity* than water.

VITALITY—life, energy, liveliness, power to survive. She had been physically active all her life and at the age of eighty still possessed great *vitality*.

VITUPERATE—abuse verbally. The convicted prisoner began to *vituperate* the judge.

VOCIFEROUS—making a noisy outcry. There are some who come to meetings merely to add to the *vociferous* din.

VOLATILE—changing to vapor, quickly changeable, fickle. She had a *volatile* temper—easily angered and easily appeased.

VOLITION—deliberate will. He performed the act of his own *volition*.

VORACIOUS—ravenous, very hungry, eager to devour. The *voracious* appetite of the man startled the other guests.

WADI—Arabian watercourse. The arroyo in America is similar to the *wadi* in Arabia; they both carry water only in season.

WAFT—to pass by as if on a buoyant medium. The scent of lilacs *wafted* in through the window.

WAGGERY—mischievous merriment, sportive trick, sarcasm in good humor. The *waggery* of the schoolboy was not appreciated by the teacher.

WAINSCOT—wood panels for a room. The mahogany *wainscot* and the high ceiling were all that remained to mark the former luxury of the room.

WAIVE—to forego, give up voluntarily something to which one is entitled. In cases of unusual hardship, the normal fee may be *waived*.

WARP—bend slightly throughout. The board *warped* in the sun. His ideas were *warped* by a bad environment.

WARRANT—to deserve, justify. The infraction was too minor to *warrant* a formal reprimand.

WASSAIL—a toast, a drinking party. The Christmas *wassail* is part of the tradition of the day.

WATERLOGGED—soaked with water. The ship was at the mercy of the waves because of its *waterlogged* condition.

WATERMARK—any distinguishing device that is indelibly stamped in the substance of a sheet of paper during the process of manufacture. The *watermarks* used by the earlier paper makers have given names to several of the present standard sizes of paper, such as pot, foolscap, crown, and elephant.

WAYWARD—perverse, capricious, willful, erratic, fluctuating. The *wayward* flight of the bat was difficult to trace.

WEAN—detach or alienate, disengage from any former pursuit. He found it difficult to *wean* his heart from its temporal enjoyments.

WELD—join pieces of metal by compression and great heat. Steel bars were *welded* to make a frame.

WELTER—to wallow, roll like a wave; a commotion. He took the *welter* of the crowds in stride, slipping down the street as quickly as he could.

WHEEDLE—coax, cajole. The woman knew exactly how to *wheedle* what she wanted from the man.

WHEY—milky water left after curds of milk have been removed. Miss Muffet ate her curds and *whey*.

WHIMSICAL—fantastic, quaint. The children enjoyed the fairy tale because it was so *whimsical*.

WHINE—express distress or complaint by a plaintive, drawling cry. The dog *whined* pitifully

WHISK—to wipe, sweep, or brush with a light, rapid, motion. She *whisked* the dust from the table.

WICKED—evil in principle and practice. The *wicked* law separated the woman from her child.

WIELD—to use with full command or power. The soldier was skilled at *wielding* his sword.

WILY—artful, cunning. He was *wily* enough to avoid detection.

WIMPLE—a covering of material over the head and around the chin, still worn as a conventional dress for nuns. The fashion editor reported that *wimples* were going to be stylish.

WINCE—to shrink, as from a blow or from pain, flinch. He *winced* under her sarcasm.

WINCH—crank with a handle that is turned, usually for hoisting or hauling. They couldn't hoist the cargo onto the deck because the *winch* was too rusty to turn.

WINNOW—examine, sift for the purpose of separating the bad from the good. His statement was so garbled that it was impossible to *winnow* the falsehoods from the truth.

WINSOME—delightful, attractive, charming. The girl's face was *winsome*.

WIZARDRY—magic, sorcery. The *wizardry* of the magician left the audience breathless.

WIZENED—shrivelled up, withered. The *wizened* old ladies looked like evil witches.

WONT—accustomed. He was *wont* to stroll about the grounds before breakfast.

WORLDLY—secular, engrossed in unspiritual customs and habits. The priest was far too engrossed in *worldly* matters.

WRAITH—ghost. When the children entered the haunted house, they fully expected to encounter *wraiths*.

WREST—take by violence. It was impossible for the child to *wrest* his toy from the bigger boy.

WRIT—in law, a mandatory precept under seal in the name of the highest authority of the state. The *writ* of account was given to the lawyer.

WRY—produced by distortion of features. He made a *wry* face when I suggested castor oil.

XENOPHOBIA—fear and hatred of strangers or foreigners. The *xenophobia* of the candidate expressed itself in his extreme and unrealistic isolationism.

XYLEM—woody tissue of plants. Cellulose is derived from the *xylem* of spruce trees and other plants.

XYLOGRAPHY—a process of decorative engraving on wood. The furniture was valuable because of the beauty of its *xylography*.

YAMMER—whine, complain, shriek, yell. The nurse declared that the children had *yammered* without reason.

YARDSTICK—a three-foot measure; a standard of measurement. A test serves as a *yardstick* of academic achievement for your teachers or professors.

YEARN—to feel longing or desire. The parents *yearned* for their recently deceased child.

YEOMAN—a freeholder who works his own land. A *yeoman* usually occupies a position in the social scale between a gentleman and a laborer.

YODEL—a vocalization in which the singer changes suddenly from the natural voice to a falsetto and back. The *yodel* is peculiar to the Swiss and Tyrolese mountaineers.

YOGA—one of the branches of Hindu philosophy. *Yoga* explains how the human soul may obtain emancipation by concentration of the mind on some grand, central truth.

YOWL—a protracted, wailing cry. The dog's *yowls* went on all night.

ZANY—like a buffoon, clownish. The *zany* guide made awkward attempts at mimicking the tricks of the professional clown.

ZEAL—ardor, fervor, enthusiasm, earnestness. He left a record for *zeal* that cannot fail to be an inspiration.

ZENITH—point directly overhead. The sun reaches its *zenith* at noon.

HOW TO ANSWER SYNONYM AND ANTONYM QUESTIONS

Two words are **synonyms** if they mean the same thing. In a synonym question you must pick the word or phrase closest in meaning to the given word. This is the simplest kind of vocabulary question.

Two words are **antonyms** if they have opposite meanings. In an antonym question, you must pick the word or phrase most nearly opposite in meaning to the given word.

1. Read each question carefully.

2. If you know that some of the answer choices are wrong, eliminate them.

3. In a synonym test, from the answer choices that seem possible, select the one that *most nearly* means the same as the given word, even if it is a word you yourself don't normally use. The correct answer may not be a perfect synonym, but of the choices offered it is the *closest* in meaning to the given word. Make up a sentence using the given word. Then test your answer by putting it in the place of the given word in your sentence. The meaning of the sentence should be unchanged.

4. In an antonym test, from the answer choices that seem possible, select the one *most nearly* opposite in meaning to the given word.

5. First answer the questions you know. You can come back to the others later.

SAMPLE SYNONYM QUESTION

Before doing the practice tests, study the following synonym and antonym examples.

We had to *terminate* the meeting because a fire broke out in the hall. *Terminate* most nearly means

(A) continue   (C) end
(B) postpone   (D) extinguish

Some actual tests will give you the word in a sentence. You must then make sure that your answer (1) makes sense in the given sentence, and (2) does not change the meaning of the sentence.

The correct answer is (C) *end*. Even if you don't know what *terminate* means, you can eliminate choice (A) *continue* because it doesn't make much sense to say, "We had to continue the meeting because a fire broke out in the hall." Choice (B) *postpone* means "to put off until another time." It makes sense in the given sentence but it also changes the meaning of the sentence. Choice (D) *extinguish* is similar in meaning to *terminate* but not as close as *end*. One can *extinguish* (put an end to) a fire but not a meeting.

SAMPLE ANTONYM QUESTION

2. RURAL
   (A) bucolic   (B) farms
   (C) urban   (D) country

The correct answer is (C) *urban*. Even if you don't know what *urban* means, you can eliminate choices (A), (B), and (D) if you know they are synonymous with or pertain to the word *rural*.

HOW TO ANSWER SENTENCE COMPLETION QUESTIONS

In a sentence completion question you are given a sentence or longer passage in which something has been left blank. A number of words or phrases are suggested to fill that blank. You must select the word or phrase that will *best* complete the meaning of the passage as a whole.

Sentence completion questions are more complex than synonym or antonym questions. They test not only your knowledge of basic vocabulary but also your ability to understand what you read. While studying individual words may be helpful, the best way to prepare for this type of question is to read a lot. A dictionary will tell you what a word means; reading will teach you how it is actually used.

1. Read each question carefully, looking at all the answer choices.

2. Eliminate any answer choices that seem obviously wrong.

3. Of the remaining choices, select the one that *best* completes the meaning of the sentence or passage given. Although more than one answer may make sense, the best choice will be the one that is most exact, appropriate, or likely, considering the information given in the sentence or passage.

4. To check yourself, read the sentence or passage through again, putting your answer in the blank.

5. First answer the questions you know. If you have trouble with a question, leave it and come back to it later.

SAMPLE SENTENCE COMPLETION QUESTION

Before doing the practice tests, study the following example.

Trespassing on private property is _____ by law.
(A) proscribed   (C) prescribed
(B) warranted   (D) eliminated

The most likely and therefore correct answer is (A) *proscribed,* which means "forbidden" or "outlawed." *Warranted* (B) may remind you of a *warrant* for arrest, which might be a result of trespassing. *Warranted,* however, means "justified," which would make the given sentence obviously untrue. Choice (C) *prescribed* looks similar to the correct answer but means "recommended." Like *warranted,* it makes nonsense out of the given sentence. Choice (D) *eliminated* is also less likely than (A). The law may be intended to eliminate trespassing but it can never be completely successful in doing so.

HOW TO ANSWER TRUE-FALSE QUESTIONS

True-false questions can be deceptively easy or very confusing. Always read the statements carefully before you choose your answer, and remember the following rules:

1. Suspect the truth of broad statements containing all-or-nothing words such as *never, always, absolutely,* or *impossible.*

2. Watch out for simple words or phrases which negate an otherwise obvious statement. If any part of a statement is false, even a simple word or phrase, then the entire statement is false.

3. In a composite true-false question, which contains more than one complete statement, all parts must be true in order for the answer to be *true.*

SAMPLE TRUE-FALSE QUESTIONS

Before doing the practice tests, study the following examples.

Vegetation is sparse in the Sahara where the climate is hot and humid.   T   F

The Statue of Liberty is in New York and Chicago is not in Illinois.   T   F

In the first example, the answer is false. Vegetation is indeed sparse in the Sahara, but the climate is dry, not humid. Therefore, the entire question is false. In the second example, the answer is also false. While the first part of this composite question is true, the second part is false, and therefore the entire question must be considered false.

HOW TO ANSWER MATCHING QUESTIONS

Because matching questions are complex, you need to be particularly careful about reading the instructions thoroughly. Generally, this type of question consists of two columns. The elements in the first column are then matched according to the directions with the elements in the second column.

1. Read instructions carefully to make sure you understand exactly what you are supposed to do before you attempt to match elements in the columns.

2. Work with one column at a time, matching each item in that column with items in the second column.

3. To avoid confusion, lightly pencil out items in the second column as you match them up with items in the first column.

SAMPLE MATCHING QUESTION

Before doing the practice tests, study the following example.

DIRECTIONS: Below are ten words numbered 1 through 10, and ten other words lettered (A) to (J). For each of the numbered words, select the lettered word which is most nearly the same in meaning.

1. fiscal		(A)	ambiguous
2. deletion		(B)	preference
3. equivocal		(C)	financial
4. corroboration		(D)	winding
5. predeliction		(E)	erasure
6. sallow		(F)	skill
7. tortuous		(G)	yellowish
8. virtuosity		(H)	thin
9. scion		(I)	confirmation
10. tenuous		(J)	heir

Correct Answers

1. (C)	3. (A)	5. (B)	7. (D)	9. (J)
2. (E)	4. (I)	6. (G)	8. (F)	10. (H)

HOW TO ANSWER VERBAL ANALOGY QUESTIONS

Verbal analogies test your understanding of word meanings and your ability to grasp relationships between words and ideas. There are various classifications of relationships, such as similarity (synonym), opposition (antonym), cause and effect, and sequence. A verbal analogy may be written in mathematical form (CLOCK : TIME :: THERMOMETER : TEMPERATURE) or expressed in words (CLOCK is to TIME as THERMOMETER is to TEMPERATURE).

A verbal analogy has four terms in two pairs. You may be presented with the first complete pair, which establishes the relationship, and the first half of the second pair followed by a list of possible matches. Or you may just be given the first pair, and then a selection of paired terms from which you must find the pair that implies the same relationship as the first pair.

1. Read each question carefully.

2. Establish what the exact relationship is between the two terms in the sample pair.

3. Study the selection of possible answers carefully and eliminate any pairs which do not share the same relationship as the sample pair.

4. Read the remaining choices through again, this time substituting the key relationship word from the sample pair (e.g., CLOCK *measures* TIME; THERMOMETER *measures* TEMPERATURE).

5. Answer the easy questions first. You can come back to the others later.

SAMPLE VERBAL ANALOGY QUESTIONS

WINTER : SUMMER :: COLD : (A) wet (B) future (C) warm (D) freezing

Winter and summer are opposites. Cold and warm are also opposites. Therefore (C) is correct.

SPELLING : PUNCTUATION :: (A) pajamas : fatigue (B) powder : shaving (C) bandage : cut (D) biology : physics

Spelling and punctuation are parts of the mechanics of English. Biology and physics are parts of the field of science. Therefore, (D) is correct.

PART III
TESTING YOUR
VOCABULARY SKILLS

SYNONYM TEST ANSWER SHEET

TEST 1

1. Ⓐ Ⓑ Ⓒ Ⓓ	5. Ⓐ Ⓑ Ⓒ Ⓓ	9. Ⓐ Ⓑ Ⓒ Ⓓ	13. Ⓐ Ⓑ Ⓒ Ⓓ	17. Ⓐ Ⓑ Ⓒ Ⓓ
2. Ⓐ Ⓑ Ⓒ Ⓓ	6. Ⓐ Ⓑ Ⓒ Ⓓ	10. Ⓐ Ⓑ Ⓒ Ⓓ	14. Ⓐ Ⓑ Ⓒ Ⓓ	18. Ⓐ Ⓑ Ⓒ Ⓓ
3. Ⓐ Ⓑ Ⓒ Ⓓ	7. Ⓐ Ⓑ Ⓒ Ⓓ	11. Ⓐ Ⓑ Ⓒ Ⓓ	15. Ⓐ Ⓑ Ⓒ Ⓓ	
4. Ⓐ Ⓑ Ⓒ Ⓓ	8. Ⓐ Ⓑ Ⓒ Ⓓ	12. Ⓐ Ⓑ Ⓒ Ⓓ	16. Ⓐ Ⓑ Ⓒ Ⓓ	

TEST 2

1. Ⓐ Ⓑ Ⓒ Ⓓ	3. Ⓐ Ⓑ Ⓒ Ⓓ	5. Ⓐ Ⓑ Ⓒ Ⓓ	7. Ⓐ Ⓑ Ⓒ Ⓓ	9. Ⓐ Ⓑ Ⓒ Ⓓ
2. Ⓐ Ⓑ Ⓒ Ⓓ	4. Ⓐ Ⓑ Ⓒ Ⓓ	6. Ⓐ Ⓑ Ⓒ Ⓓ	8. Ⓐ Ⓑ Ⓒ Ⓓ	10. Ⓐ Ⓑ Ⓒ Ⓓ

TEST 3

1. Ⓣ Ⓕ	5. Ⓣ Ⓕ	9. Ⓣ Ⓕ	13. Ⓣ Ⓕ	17. Ⓣ Ⓕ
2. Ⓣ Ⓕ	6. Ⓣ Ⓕ	10. Ⓣ Ⓕ	14. Ⓣ Ⓕ	18. Ⓣ Ⓕ
3. Ⓣ Ⓕ	7. Ⓣ Ⓕ	11. Ⓣ Ⓕ	15. Ⓣ Ⓕ	19 Ⓣ Ⓕ
4. Ⓣ Ⓕ	8. Ⓣ Ⓕ	12. Ⓣ Ⓕ	16. Ⓣ Ⓕ	20. Ⓣ Ⓕ

TEST 4

1. Ⓐ Ⓑ Ⓒ Ⓓ	5. Ⓐ Ⓑ Ⓒ Ⓓ	9. Ⓐ Ⓑ Ⓒ Ⓓ	13. Ⓐ Ⓑ Ⓒ Ⓓ	17. Ⓐ Ⓑ Ⓒ Ⓓ
2. Ⓐ Ⓑ Ⓒ Ⓓ	6. Ⓐ Ⓑ Ⓒ Ⓓ	10 Ⓐ Ⓑ Ⓒ Ⓓ	14. Ⓐ Ⓑ Ⓒ Ⓓ	18. Ⓐ Ⓑ Ⓒ Ⓓ
3. Ⓐ Ⓑ Ⓒ Ⓓ	7. Ⓐ Ⓑ Ⓒ Ⓓ	11. Ⓐ Ⓑ Ⓒ Ⓓ	15. Ⓐ Ⓑ Ⓒ Ⓓ	
4. Ⓐ Ⓑ Ⓒ Ⓓ	8. Ⓐ Ⓑ Ⓒ Ⓓ	12. Ⓐ Ⓑ Ⓒ Ⓓ	16. Ⓐ Ⓑ Ⓒ Ⓓ	

TEST 5

1. Ⓐ Ⓑ Ⓒ Ⓓ	3. Ⓐ Ⓑ Ⓒ Ⓓ	5. Ⓐ Ⓑ Ⓒ Ⓓ	7. Ⓐ Ⓑ Ⓒ Ⓓ	9. Ⓐ Ⓑ Ⓒ Ⓓ
2. Ⓐ Ⓑ Ⓒ Ⓓ	4. Ⓐ Ⓑ Ⓒ Ⓓ	6. Ⓐ Ⓑ Ⓒ Ⓓ	8. Ⓐ Ⓑ Ⓒ Ⓓ	10. Ⓐ Ⓑ Ⓒ Ⓓ

TEST 6

1. Ⓐ Ⓑ Ⓒ Ⓓ	5. Ⓐ Ⓑ Ⓒ Ⓓ	9. Ⓐ Ⓑ Ⓒ Ⓓ	13. Ⓐ Ⓑ Ⓒ Ⓓ	17. Ⓐ Ⓑ Ⓒ Ⓓ
2. Ⓐ Ⓑ Ⓒ Ⓓ	6. Ⓐ Ⓑ Ⓒ Ⓓ	10. Ⓐ Ⓑ Ⓒ Ⓓ	14. Ⓐ Ⓑ Ⓒ Ⓓ	18. Ⓐ Ⓑ Ⓒ Ⓓ
3. Ⓐ Ⓑ Ⓒ Ⓓ	7. Ⓐ Ⓑ Ⓒ Ⓓ	11. Ⓐ Ⓑ Ⓒ Ⓓ	15. Ⓐ Ⓑ Ⓒ Ⓓ	19. Ⓐ Ⓑ Ⓒ Ⓓ
4. Ⓐ Ⓑ Ⓒ Ⓓ	8. Ⓐ Ⓑ Ⓒ Ⓓ	12. Ⓐ Ⓑ Ⓒ Ⓓ	16. Ⓐ Ⓑ Ⓒ Ⓓ	20. Ⓐ Ⓑ Ⓒ Ⓓ

TEST 7

1. Ⓐ Ⓑ Ⓒ Ⓓ	5. Ⓐ Ⓑ Ⓒ Ⓓ	9. Ⓐ Ⓑ Ⓒ Ⓓ	13. Ⓐ Ⓑ Ⓒ Ⓓ	17. Ⓐ Ⓑ Ⓒ Ⓓ
2. Ⓐ Ⓑ Ⓒ Ⓓ	6. Ⓐ Ⓑ Ⓒ Ⓓ	10. Ⓐ Ⓑ Ⓒ Ⓓ	14. Ⓐ Ⓑ Ⓒ Ⓓ	18. Ⓐ Ⓑ Ⓒ Ⓓ
3. Ⓐ Ⓑ Ⓒ Ⓓ	7. Ⓐ Ⓑ Ⓒ Ⓓ	11. Ⓐ Ⓑ Ⓒ Ⓓ	15. Ⓐ Ⓑ Ⓒ Ⓓ	19. Ⓐ Ⓑ Ⓒ Ⓓ
4. Ⓐ Ⓑ Ⓒ Ⓓ	8. Ⓐ Ⓑ Ⓒ Ⓓ	12. Ⓐ Ⓑ Ⓒ Ⓓ	16. Ⓐ Ⓑ Ⓒ Ⓓ	20. Ⓐ Ⓑ Ⓒ Ⓓ

SYNONYM TEST ANSWER SHEET

TEST 8

1. Ⓐ Ⓑ Ⓒ Ⓓ	5. Ⓐ Ⓑ Ⓒ Ⓓ	9. Ⓐ Ⓑ Ⓒ Ⓓ	13. Ⓐ Ⓑ Ⓒ Ⓓ	17. Ⓐ Ⓑ Ⓒ Ⓓ
2. Ⓐ Ⓑ Ⓒ Ⓓ	6. Ⓐ Ⓑ Ⓒ Ⓓ	10. Ⓐ Ⓑ Ⓒ Ⓓ	14. Ⓐ Ⓑ Ⓒ Ⓓ	18. Ⓐ Ⓑ Ⓒ Ⓓ
3. Ⓐ Ⓑ Ⓒ Ⓓ	7. Ⓐ Ⓑ Ⓒ Ⓓ	11. Ⓐ Ⓑ Ⓒ Ⓓ	15. Ⓐ Ⓑ Ⓒ Ⓓ	19. Ⓐ Ⓑ Ⓒ Ⓓ
4. Ⓐ Ⓑ Ⓒ Ⓓ	8. Ⓐ Ⓑ Ⓒ Ⓓ	12. Ⓐ Ⓑ Ⓒ Ⓓ	16. Ⓐ Ⓑ Ⓒ Ⓓ	20. Ⓐ Ⓑ Ⓒ Ⓓ

TEST 9

1. Ⓐ Ⓑ Ⓒ Ⓓ	5. Ⓐ Ⓑ Ⓒ Ⓓ	9. Ⓐ Ⓑ Ⓒ Ⓓ	13. Ⓐ Ⓑ Ⓒ Ⓓ	17. Ⓐ Ⓑ Ⓒ Ⓓ
2. Ⓐ Ⓑ Ⓒ Ⓓ	6. Ⓐ Ⓑ Ⓒ Ⓓ	10. Ⓐ Ⓑ Ⓒ Ⓓ	14. Ⓐ Ⓑ Ⓒ Ⓓ	18. Ⓐ Ⓑ Ⓒ Ⓓ
3. Ⓐ Ⓑ Ⓒ Ⓓ	7. Ⓐ Ⓑ Ⓒ Ⓓ	11. Ⓐ Ⓑ Ⓒ Ⓓ	15. Ⓐ Ⓑ Ⓒ Ⓓ	19. Ⓐ Ⓑ Ⓒ Ⓓ
4. Ⓐ Ⓑ Ⓒ Ⓓ	8. Ⓐ Ⓑ Ⓒ Ⓓ	12. Ⓐ Ⓑ Ⓒ Ⓓ	16. Ⓐ Ⓑ Ⓒ Ⓓ	20. Ⓐ Ⓑ Ⓒ Ⓓ

TEST 10

1. Ⓐ Ⓑ Ⓒ Ⓓ	5. Ⓐ Ⓑ Ⓒ Ⓓ	9. Ⓐ Ⓑ Ⓒ Ⓓ	13. Ⓐ Ⓑ Ⓒ Ⓓ	17. Ⓐ Ⓑ Ⓒ Ⓓ
2. Ⓐ Ⓑ Ⓒ Ⓓ	6. Ⓐ Ⓑ Ⓒ Ⓓ	10. Ⓐ Ⓑ Ⓒ Ⓓ	14. Ⓐ Ⓑ Ⓒ Ⓓ	18. Ⓐ Ⓑ Ⓒ Ⓓ
3. Ⓐ Ⓑ Ⓒ Ⓓ	7. Ⓐ Ⓑ Ⓒ Ⓓ	11. Ⓐ Ⓑ Ⓒ Ⓓ	15. Ⓐ Ⓑ Ⓒ Ⓓ	19. Ⓐ Ⓑ Ⓒ Ⓓ
4. Ⓐ Ⓑ Ⓒ Ⓓ	8. Ⓐ Ⓑ Ⓒ Ⓓ	12. Ⓐ Ⓑ Ⓒ Ⓓ	16. Ⓐ Ⓑ Ⓒ Ⓓ	20. Ⓐ Ⓑ Ⓒ Ⓓ

TEST 11

1. Ⓐ Ⓑ Ⓒ Ⓓ	5. Ⓐ Ⓑ Ⓒ Ⓓ	9. Ⓐ Ⓑ Ⓒ Ⓓ	13. Ⓐ Ⓑ Ⓒ Ⓓ	17. Ⓐ Ⓑ Ⓒ Ⓓ
2. Ⓐ Ⓑ Ⓒ Ⓓ	6. Ⓐ Ⓑ Ⓒ Ⓓ	10. Ⓐ Ⓑ Ⓒ Ⓓ	14. Ⓐ Ⓑ Ⓒ Ⓓ	18. Ⓐ Ⓑ Ⓒ Ⓓ
3. Ⓐ Ⓑ Ⓒ Ⓓ	7. Ⓐ Ⓑ Ⓒ Ⓓ	11. Ⓐ Ⓑ Ⓒ Ⓓ	15. Ⓐ Ⓑ Ⓒ Ⓓ	19. Ⓐ Ⓑ Ⓒ Ⓓ
4. Ⓐ Ⓑ Ⓒ Ⓓ	8. Ⓐ Ⓑ Ⓒ Ⓓ	12. Ⓐ Ⓑ Ⓒ Ⓓ	16. Ⓐ Ⓑ Ⓒ Ⓓ	

Total Number of Questions   195
Total Incorrect −
_____
Total Correct =   × .51= _____%
                              Score

SYNONYM TEST ONE

DIRECTIONS: *For each question in this test, select the appropriate letter preceding the word which is most nearly the same in meaning as the italicized word in each sentence. Correct answers to these test questions will be found at the end of the chapter.*

1. An *amendment* is a
   (A) civic center   (B) charter
   (C) penalty   (D) change

2. A *quorum* is a
   (A) minority   (B) committee
   (C) majority   (D) bicameral system

3. *Clearance* refers to a
   (A) weight   (B) hoistway
   (C) distance   (D) cleaning process

4. *Pasteurized* milk is milk that has been
   (A) watered   (B) condemned
   (C) embargoed   (D) purified

5. *Antitoxin* is used in cases of
   (A) corrupt governmental officials
   (B) sanitary inspection
   (C) disease
   (D) elevator construction

6. *Libel* refers to the
   (A) process of incurring financial liability
   (B) publication of a false statement which injures others
   (C) deportation of aliens
   (D) necessity for compulsory schooling

7. *Naturalization* refers to the process of
   (A) becoming a civil service employee
   (B) being summoned to court
   (C) becoming a citizen
   (D) pledging allegiance to the American flag

8. To *comply* with a rule means to
   (A) abide by a rule   (B) abrogate a rule
   (C) dislike a rule   (D) ignore a rule

9. A *budget* is a
   (A) financial statement
   (B) method for training operators

   (C) device for insuring courtesy
   (D) means for selecting judges

10. A *fulcrum* is part of a
    (A) typewriter   (B) lever
    (C) radio   (D) lamp

11. The word *irate* means most nearly
    (A) irresponsible   (B) untidy
    (C) insubordinate   (D) angry

12. An *ambiguous* statement is one which is
    (A) forceful and convincing
    (B) capable of being understood in more than one sense
    (C) based upon good judgment and sound reasoning processes
    (D) uninteresting and too lengthy

13. To *extol* means most nearly to
    (A) summon   (B) praise
    (C) reject   (D) withdraw

14. The word *proximity* means most nearly
    (A) similarity   (B) exactness
    (C) harmony   (D) nearness

15. The word *detrimental* means most nearly
    (A) favorable   (B) lasting
    (C) harmful   (D) short-lived

16. The word *veracity* means most nearly
    (A) speed   (B) assistance
    (C) shrewdness   (D) truthfulness

17. The word *diversity* means most nearly
    (A) similarity   (B) value
    (C) triviality   (D) variety

18. The word *indigence* means most nearly
    (A) poverty   (B) corruption
    (C) intolerance   (D) morale

SYNONYM TEST TWO

DIRECTIONS: *Each question in this test consists of pairs of words. Each pair of words is preceded by a letter. For each question, select the one pair of words that are most nearly synonyms. Mark the letter of that pair on your answer sheet. Correct answers to these test questions will be found at the end of the chapter.*

1. (A) transitory—permanent
   (B) prohibit—allow
   (C) beautiful—ugly
   (D) broken—disunited

2. (A) elucidate—clarify
   (B) recent—ancient
   (C) enthusiasm—apathy
   (D) equivocal—indubitable

3. (A) extricate—imprison
   (B) concur—endorse
   (C) intimidate—assure
   (D) lucid—obscure

4. (A) abandon—hold
   (B) tedious—tiresome
   (C) consistent—varying
   (D) constrain—beseech

5. (A) deficient—ample
   (B) waste—conserve
   (C) compromise—quarrel
   (D) sanguine—optimistic

6. (A) monotony—variety
   (B) remote—near
   (C) propitiate—appease
   (D) many—few

7. (A) fraud—honesty
   (B) important—significant
   (C) mollify—vex
   (D) abate—maintain

8. (A) eradicate—destroy
   (B) barbarous—humane
   (C) compulsion—freedom
   (D) concur—differ

9. (A) morose—cheerful
   (B) munificent—penurious
   (C) censorious—fault-finding
   (D) predominate—subordinate

10. (A) gratify—displease
    (B) augment—increase
    (C) interpose—withdraw
    (D) irresponsible—accountable

SYNONYM TEST THREE

DIRECTIONS: For each of the following statements, mark T if the statement is true and F if it is false. Correct answers to these test questions will be found at the end of the chapter.

1. A *competent* employee is one who is slow and inefficient.　　T　F

2. A person who commits *perjury* does not tell the truth.　　T　F

3. The *prosecutor* in a criminal case is the lawyer who presents evidence against the defendant.　　T　F

4. A *destitute* person has a large amount of money.　　T　F

5. A person with a *florid* complexion has a pale face.　　T　F

6. A noise that is *audible* is capable of being heard.　　T　F

7. Anyone who is *agile* is quick and nimble.　　T　F

8. An employee who gives information in a *curt* manner is sympathetic and courteous.　　T　F

9. A person who is *prudent* is careless in his attention to duty.　　T　F

10. If a person pays an *exorbitant* amount of money for an article, he is paying a fair price.　　T　F

11. A *versatile* worker is one who is capable of doing many different things.　　T　F

12. *Transitory* benefits are likely to last for many years.　　T　F

13. A clergyman who follows a traditional doctrine is said to be *unorthodox*.　　T　F

14. A *circuitous* response to a question is direct and to the point.　　T　F

15. An *ambulatory* patient is one who is able to walk on his own.　　T　F

16. *Proponents* of the bill are likely to vote against it.　　T　F

17. A person who is *intractable* is easily swayed.　　T　F

18. A child who *feigns* illness is merely pretending to be sick.　　T　F

19. *Manual* controls are hand-operated.　T　F

20. Something *obsolete* is out of date.　　T　F

SYNONYM TEST FOUR

DIRECTIONS: For each question in this test, select the letter preceding the word which is most nearly the same in meaning as the italicized word in each sentence. Correct answers to these test questions will be found at the end of the chapter.

1. The person who is *diplomatic* in his relations with others is, most nearly,
   (A) well dressed
   (B) very tactful
   (C) somewhat domineering
   (D) deceitful and tricky

2. Action at this time would be *inopportune*. The word *inopportune* means most nearly
   (A) untimely (B) premeditated
   (C) sporadic (D) commendable

3. The word *appraise* means most nearly
   (A) consult (B) attribute
   (C) manage (D) judge

4. The word *cognizant* means most nearly
   (A) rare (B) reluctant
   (C) aware (D) haphazard

5. *Probity* is an important requirement of many positions. The word *probity* means most nearly
   (A) analytical ability (B) vision
   (C) tried integrity (D) perseverence

6. The word *denote* means most nearly
   (A) encumber (B) evade
   (C) furnish (D) indicate

7. The competent employee should know that a method of procedure which is *expedient* is most nearly
   (A) unchangeable
   (B) based upon a false assumption
   (C) suitable to the end in view
   (D) difficult to work out

8. An incentive which is *potent* is most nearly
   (A) impossible
   (B) highly effective
   (C) not immediately practicable
   (D) a remote possibility

9. An employer who is *judicious* is most nearly
   (A) domineering (B) argumentative
   (C) sincere (D) wise

10. He presented a *controversial* plan. The word *controversial* means most nearly
    (A) subject to debate (B) unreasonable
    (C) complex (D) comparable

11. *Rudiments* most nearly means
    (A) promotion opportunities
    (B) politics
    (C) basic methods and procedures
    (D) minute details

12. A *vivacious* person is one who is
    (A) kind (B) talkative
    (C) lively (D) well dressed

13. An *innocuous* statement is one which is
    (A) forceful (B) harmless
    (C) offensive (D) brief

14. To say that the order was *rescinded* means, most nearly, that the order was
    (A) revised (B) canceled
    (C) misinterpreted (D) confirmed

15. To say that the administrator *amplified* his remarks means, most nearly, that the remarks were
    (A) shouted (B) expanded
    (C) carefully analyzed (D) summarized briefly

16. *Peremptory* commands will be resented in any organization. The word *peremptory* means most nearly
    (A) unexpected (B) unreasonable
    (C) military (D) dictatorial

17. A person should know the word *sporadic* means, most nearly,
    (A) occurring regularly
    (B) sudden
    (C) scattered
    (D) disturbing

18. To *oscillate* means, most nearly, to
    (A) lubricate (B) waver
    (C) decide (D) investigate

SYNONYM TEST FIVE

DIRECTIONS: In each of the sentences below, one word is in italics. Following each sentence are four lettered words or phrases. For each sentence, choose the letter preceding the word or phrase which most nearly corresponds in meaning with the italicized word. Correct answers to these test questions will be found at the end of the chapter.

1. The change in procedure *stimulated* the men.
   (A) rewarded
   (B) antagonized
   (C) gave an incentive to
   (D) restricted the activities of

2. Courage is a trait difficult to *instill*.
   (A) measure exactly
   (B) impart gradually
   (C) predict accurately
   (D) restrain effectively

3. The vehicle was left *intact*.
   (A) a total loss
   (B) unattended
   (C) where it could be noticed
   (D) undamaged

4. The witness was *recalcitrant*.
   (A) cooperative
   (B) stubbornly resistant
   (C) highly excited
   (D) accustomed to hard work

5. A *conscientious* person is one who
   (A) feels obligated to do what he believes right
   (B) rarely makes errors

   (C) frequently makes suggestions for procedural improvements
   (D) has good personal relationships with others

6. It was reported that *noxious* fumes were escaping.
   (A) concentrated   (B) harmful
   (C) greenish-colored (D) heavy

7. A person with a *sallow* complexion was seen near the scene.
   (A) ruddy
   (B) dark
   (C) pale and yellowish
   (D) highly freckled

8. The word *cogent* means most nearly
   (A) confused   (B) opposite
   (C) unintentional (D) convincing

9. The word *divergent* means most nearly
   (A) simultaneous (B) differing
   (C) approaching   (D) parallel

10. The word *ostensibly* means most nearly
    (A) undoubtedly (B) infrequently
    (C) powerfully   (D) apparently

SYNONYM TEST SIX

DIRECTIONS: *Each of the numbered words given below is followed by four lettered words. For each numbered word, select the lettered word which most nearly defines it. Correct answers to these test questions will be found at the end of the chapter.*

1. corroboration
   (A) expenditure
   (B) compilation
   (C) confirmation
   (D) reduction

2. imperative
   (A) impending
   (B) impossible
   (C) compulsory
   (D) logical

3. feasible
   (A) simple
   (B) practicable
   (C) visible
   (D) lenient

4. salutary
   (A) popular
   (B) urgent
   (C) beneficial
   (D) forceful

5. acquiesce
   (A) endeavor
   (B) discharge
   (C) agree
   (D) inquire

6. diffidence
   (A) shyness
   (B) distinction
   (C) interval
   (D) discordance

7. heinous
   (A) atrocious
   (B) habitual
   (C) insulting
   (D) Hellenic

8. access
   (A) too much
   (B) extra
   (C) admittance
   (D) arrival

9. subsequent
   (A) preceding
   (B) early
   (C) following
   (D) winning

10. heritage
    (A) will
    (B) unbeliever
    (C) legend
    (D) inheritance

11. captious
    (A) headstrong
    (B) grasping
    (C) enchanting
    (D) critical

12. chagrin
    (A) enjoyment
    (B) smirk
    (C) humiliation
    (D) glumness

13. charlatan
    (A) quack
    (B) monster
    (C) genius
    (D) tyrant

14. chary
    (A) burned
    (B) intuitive
    (C) cautious
    (D) brazen

15. colloquial
    (A) illiterate
    (B) pertaining to oratory
    (C) pertaining to common speech
    (D) not acceptable

16. congenital
    (A) harmonious
    (B) sympathetic
    (C) inherent
    (D) fringed

17. congruent
    (A) noisy
    (B) agreeing
    (C) quarrelsome
    (D) sticky

18. sluice
    (A) drainpipe
    (B) pupil
    (C) tree
    (D) detective

19. crypt
    (A) vault
    (B) message
    (C) puzzle
    (D) ancient ruins

20. culpable
    (A) dangerous
    (B) soft
    (C) blameworthy
    (D) easily perceived

SYNONYM TEST SEVEN

DIRECTIONS: Each of the numbered words given below is followed by four lettered words. For each numbered word, select the lettered word which most nearly defines it. Correct answers to these test questions will be found at the end of the chapter.

1. acclimate
   (A) predict weather
   (B) become accustomed to
   (C) enjoy good climate
   (D) drill thoroughly

2. affable
   (A) friendly   (B) silly
   (C) legendary   (D) dismayed

3. affluence
   (A) persuasion   (B) power
   (C) inspiration   (D) wealth

4. analogous
   (A) alike   (B) hidden
   (C) metallic   (D) unreasonable

5. aspersion
   (A) offense   (B) scattering
   (C) dullness   (D) slander

6. astigmatism
   (A) disgrace
   (B) visual defect
   (C) miserliness
   (D) purity of character

7. bellicose
   (A) amusing   (B) pugnacious
   (C) resounding   (D) obese

8. blanch
   (A) frighten   (B) decompose
   (C) scold   (D) whiten

9. broach
   (A) make gaudy
   (B) begin discussion
   (C) fancy carriage
   (D) piece of jewelry

10. carillon
    (A) stately dance   (B) hilarity
    (C) bells   (D) folk song

11. degraded
    (A) unassorted   (B) declassified
    (C) receded   (D) debased

12. delectable
    (A) ripe   (B) easily found
    (C) unwanted   (D) delicious

13. derelict
    (A) filthy   (B) abandoned
    (C) beggarly   (D) antiquated

14. dilatory
    (A) slow   (B) enlarged
    (C) aimless   (D) expansive

15. doddering
    (A) overindulgent   (B) prattling
    (C) infirm   (D) scribbling

16. dynamic
    (A) noisy   (B) static
    (C) forceful   (D) magnetic

17. edify
    (A) proclaim   (B) revise
    (C) whirl   (D) enlighten

18. enervated
    (A) neurotic   (B) weakened
    (C) cowardly   (D) strengthened

19. engender
    (A) make inanimate
    (B) imperil
    (C) manage skillfully
    (D) produce

20. equanimity
    (A) composure   (B) uniformity
    (C) equal justice   (D) indifference

SYNONYM TEST EIGHT

DIRECTIONS: *Each of the numbered words given below is followed by four lettered words. For each numbered word, select the lettered word which most nearly defines it. Correct answers to these test questions will be found at the end of the chapter.*

1. erudition
   (A) coarseness   (B) scholarship
   (C) pompousness   (D) elimination

2. extraneous
   (A) foreign   (B) lavish
   (C) preposterous   (D) superior

3. facetious
   (A) effortless   (B) congratulatory
   (C) droll   (D) supercilious

4. fiasco
   (A) failure   (B) holiday
   (C) confection   (D) dilemma

5. flagrant
   (A) homeless
   (B) purposefully conspicuous
   (C) emblematic
   (D) aromatic

6. flotilla
   (A) small fleet   (B) procession
   (C) fluctuation   (D) wreckage

7. garrulous
   (A) fretful   (B) artistic
   (C) murderous   (D) talkative

8. genial
   (A) wise   (B) magic
   (C) customary   (D) cheerful

9. gibberish
   (A) small monkey
   (B) incoherent talk
   (C) contemptuous retort
   (D) foolish laughter

10. hiatus
    (A) link   (B) gap
    (C) peak   (D) team

11. hoax
    (A) practical joke
    (B) flagrant lie
    (C) spiteful remark
    (D) unsuccessful plot

12. hypothetical
    (A) irrefutable   (B) conditional
    (C) triangular   (D) spellbound

13. ideology
    (A) subversive philosophy
    (B) body of opinions
    (C) science of thought processes
    (D) belief in perfection

14. impotent
    (A) worthless   (B) meaningless
    (C) powerless   (D) fearless

15. indigenous
    (A) angry   (B) impoverished
    (C) native   (D) insulting

16. indolence
    (A) audacity   (B) arrogance
    (C) laziness   (D) poverty

17. pedestrian
    (A) passenger   (B) walker
    (C) street-crosser   (D) traffic light

18. integrity
    (A) competence   (B) renown
    (C) consolidation   (D) honesty

19. lampoon
    (A) satire   (B) lake
    (C) torch   (D) reflection

20. laudatory
    (A) arrogant   (B) clean
    (C) boisterous   (D) praiseworthy

SYNONYM TEST NINE

DIRECTIONS: *Select the word or phrase closest in meaning to the given word.*
Mark its letter on the answer sheet. Correct answers to these questions will be found
at the end of the chapter.

1. supervise
    (A) acquire   (B) oppress
    (C) oversee   (D) restrain

2. mitigate
    (A) lessen   (B) incite
    (C) measure   (D) prosecute

3. logical
    (A) reasoned   (B) calm
    (C) fixed   (D) cold

4. peculiar
    (A) sensitive   (B) special
    (C) arbitrary   (D) indefensible

5. effect
    (A) raise   (B) put on
    (C) bring about   (D) pass

6. utilize
    (A) offer   (B) employ
    (C) ponder   (D) enjoy

7. adroit
    (A) clever   (B) moist
    (C) aimless   (D) artistic

8. uniformity
    (A) costume   (B) sameness
    (C) custom   (D) boredom

9. legible
    (A) printed   (B) allowed
    (C) typed   (D) readable

10. augment
    (A) adopt   (B) increase
    (C) modify   (D) predict

11. complex
    (A) group of buildings
    (B) tower
    (C) neighborhood
    (D) corporation

12. request
    (A) tell   (B) ask
    (C) suspect   (D) complain

13. courteous
    (A) fast   (B) polite
    (C) impersonal   (D) royal

14. tenacity
    (A) firmness   (B) temerity
    (C) sagacity   (D) discourage-
    ment

15. insignificant
    (A) useless   (B) unrewarding
    (C) low   (D) unimportant

16. execute
    (A) resign   (B) affect
    (C) carry out   (D) harm

17. unique
    (A) sole   (B) odd
    (C) certain   (D) valuable

18. utensil
    (A) machine   (B) fork
    (C) tool   (D) object

19. outcome
    (A) result   (B) aim
    (C) premise   (D) statistic

20. dogmatic
    (A) manual   (B) doctrinaire
    (C) canine   (D) unprincipled

SYNONYM TEST TEN

DIRECTIONS: *Each of the numbered words given below is followed by four lettered words. For each numbered word, select the lettered word which most nearly defines it. Correct answers are at the end of the chapter.*

1. abnegation
   (A) provocation   (B) annulment
   (C) declaration   (D) renunciation

2. acerbic
   (A) harsh   (B) abstemious
   (C) mocking   (D) aggressive

3. adventitious
   (A) exciting   (B) hazardous
   (C) accidental   (D) presumptuous

4. ambiance
   (A) duplicity   (B) environment
   (C) zeal   (D) reverie

5. amorphous
   (A) vase-shaped   (B) dusky
   (C) formless   (D) pain-assuaging

6. aplomb
   (A) sinecure   (B) haughtiness
   (C) poise   (D) inflexibility

7. argot
   (A) mass of metal   (B) sea voyage
   (C) wrath   (D) class jargon

8. baroque
   (A) elaborate   (B) beaded
   (C) gruff   (D) sarcastic

9. succulent
   (A) juicy   (B) arid
   (C) burdensome   (D) prolific

10. surname
    (A) last name   (B) first name
    (C) nickname   (D) alias

11. carafe
    (A) covered vehicle
    (B) outdoor restaurant
    (C) water bottle
    (D) Arabic headgear

12. claque
    (A) exclusive set
    (B) demagogic appeal
    (C) conductor's baton
    (D) paid applauders

13. crass
    (A) naive   (B) coarse
    (C) frank   (D) remorseful

14. nebulous
    (A) cloudy   (B) subdued
    (C) awkward   (D) careless

15. culpable
    (A) bearable   (B) untenable
    (C) censurable   (D) vulnerable

16. dalliance
    (A) espionage   (B) trifling
    (C) procrastination   (D) diplomacy

17. deprecate
    (A) lower the worth
    (B) express disapproval
    (C) apologize for
    (D) applaud

18. desiccate
    (A) raze   (B) defile
    (C) dry up   (D) destroy

19. diatribe
    (A) bitter harangue
    (B) prescribed regimen
    (C) relief map
    (D) outline

20. ensconce
    (A) inscribe
    (B) illuminate by torchlight
    (C) settle comfortably
    (D) devour

SYNONYM TEST ELEVEN

DIRECTIONS: *For each question in this test select the letter preceding the word which is most nearly the same in meaning as the given word. Correct answers to these test questions will be found at the end of the chapter.*

1. eschew
   (A) digest
   (B) shun
   (C) exterminate
   (D) name of beneficiary

2. exceptionable
   (A) rare
   (B) liable to prosecution
   (C) of fine quality
   (D) objectionable

3. visceral
   (A) sticky   (B) swollen
   (C) phlegmatic   (D) intestinal

4. flout
   (A) mock   (B) whip
   (C) stumble (D) display

5. insidious
   (A) insincere (B) vapid
   (C) subtle   (D) insignificant

6. gaffer
   (A) old man
   (B) social blunder
   (C) joke
   (D) laudatory review

7. gauche
   (A) pertaining to South American ranches
   (B) awkward
   (C) drowsy
   (D) reddish yellow

8. sachet
   (A) dance step   (B) hiding place
   (C) official seal (D) small bag

9. slake
   (A) smear   (B) arouse
   (C) debate hotly (D) quench

10. imprecation
    (A) extemporaneous musical composition
    (B) prodigality
    (C) hint
    (D) curse

11. inure
    (A) swear falsely (B) accustom
    (C) imprison   (D) begin

12. laminated
    (A) layered   (B) decorated
    (C) illumined (D) ordained

13. legate
    (A) ambassador (B) sponsor
    (C) bequest   (D) commission

14. vouchsafe
    (A) protect (B) set aside
    (C) support (D) grant

15. limpid
    (A) deep   (B) still
    (C) musical (D) clear

16. mandible
    (A) steward (B) insect
    (C) shackle (D) jaw

17. obloquy
    (A) abuse (B) forgetfulness
    (C) angle (D) ranting oration

18. acumen
    (A) intensity (B) accuracy
    (C) insight   (D) instinct

19. peccadillo
    (A) wild pig
    (B) burrowing mammal
    (C) petty fault
    (D) bric-a-brac

ANTONYM TEST ANSWER SHEET

TEST 1

1. Ⓐ Ⓑ Ⓒ Ⓓ 3. Ⓐ Ⓑ Ⓒ Ⓓ 5. Ⓐ Ⓑ Ⓒ Ⓓ 7. Ⓐ Ⓑ Ⓒ Ⓓ 9. Ⓐ Ⓑ Ⓒ Ⓓ
2. Ⓐ Ⓑ Ⓒ Ⓓ 4. Ⓐ Ⓑ Ⓒ Ⓓ 6. Ⓐ Ⓑ Ⓒ Ⓓ 8. Ⓐ Ⓑ Ⓒ Ⓓ 10. Ⓐ Ⓑ Ⓒ Ⓓ

TEST 2

1. Ⓐ Ⓑ Ⓒ Ⓓ 3. Ⓐ Ⓑ Ⓒ Ⓓ 5. Ⓐ Ⓑ Ⓒ Ⓓ 7. Ⓐ Ⓑ Ⓒ Ⓓ 9. Ⓐ Ⓑ Ⓒ Ⓓ
2. Ⓐ Ⓑ Ⓒ Ⓓ 4. Ⓐ Ⓑ Ⓒ Ⓓ 6. Ⓐ Ⓑ Ⓒ Ⓓ 8. Ⓐ Ⓑ Ⓒ Ⓓ 10. Ⓐ Ⓑ Ⓒ Ⓓ

TEST 3

1. Ⓐ Ⓑ Ⓒ Ⓓ 3. Ⓐ Ⓑ Ⓒ Ⓓ 5. Ⓐ Ⓑ Ⓒ Ⓓ 7. Ⓐ Ⓑ Ⓒ Ⓓ 9. Ⓐ Ⓑ Ⓒ Ⓓ
2. Ⓐ Ⓑ Ⓒ Ⓓ 4. Ⓐ Ⓑ Ⓒ Ⓓ 6. Ⓐ Ⓑ Ⓒ Ⓓ 8. Ⓐ Ⓑ Ⓒ Ⓓ 10. Ⓐ Ⓑ Ⓒ Ⓓ

TEST 4

1. Ⓐ Ⓑ Ⓒ Ⓓ 3. Ⓐ Ⓑ Ⓒ Ⓓ 5. Ⓐ Ⓑ Ⓒ Ⓓ 7. Ⓐ Ⓑ Ⓒ Ⓓ 9. Ⓐ Ⓑ Ⓒ Ⓓ
2. Ⓐ Ⓑ Ⓒ Ⓓ 4. Ⓐ Ⓑ Ⓒ Ⓓ 6. Ⓐ Ⓑ Ⓒ Ⓓ 8. Ⓐ Ⓑ Ⓒ Ⓓ 10. Ⓐ Ⓑ Ⓒ Ⓓ

TEST 5

1. Ⓐ Ⓑ Ⓒ Ⓓ 3. Ⓐ Ⓑ Ⓒ Ⓓ 5. Ⓐ Ⓑ Ⓒ Ⓓ 7. Ⓐ Ⓑ Ⓒ Ⓓ 9. Ⓐ Ⓑ Ⓒ Ⓓ
2. Ⓐ Ⓑ Ⓒ Ⓓ 4. Ⓐ Ⓑ Ⓒ Ⓓ 6. Ⓐ Ⓑ Ⓒ Ⓓ 8. Ⓐ Ⓑ Ⓒ Ⓓ 10. Ⓐ Ⓑ Ⓒ Ⓓ

TEST 6

1. Ⓐ Ⓑ Ⓒ Ⓓ 3. Ⓐ Ⓑ Ⓒ Ⓓ 5. Ⓐ Ⓑ Ⓒ Ⓓ 7. Ⓐ Ⓑ Ⓒ Ⓓ 9. Ⓐ Ⓑ Ⓒ Ⓓ
2. Ⓐ Ⓑ Ⓒ Ⓓ 4. Ⓐ Ⓑ Ⓒ Ⓓ 6. Ⓐ Ⓑ Ⓒ Ⓓ 8. Ⓐ Ⓑ Ⓒ Ⓓ 10. Ⓐ Ⓑ Ⓒ Ⓓ

TEST 7

1. Ⓐ Ⓑ Ⓒ Ⓓ 3. Ⓐ Ⓑ Ⓒ Ⓓ 5. Ⓐ Ⓑ Ⓒ Ⓓ 7. Ⓐ Ⓑ Ⓒ Ⓓ 9. Ⓐ Ⓑ Ⓒ Ⓓ
2. Ⓐ Ⓑ Ⓒ Ⓓ 4. Ⓐ Ⓑ Ⓒ Ⓓ 6. Ⓐ Ⓑ Ⓒ Ⓓ 8. Ⓐ Ⓑ Ⓒ Ⓓ 10. Ⓐ Ⓑ Ⓒ Ⓓ

TEST 8

1. Ⓐ Ⓑ Ⓒ Ⓓ 3. Ⓐ Ⓑ Ⓒ Ⓓ 5. Ⓐ Ⓑ Ⓒ Ⓓ 7. Ⓐ Ⓑ Ⓒ Ⓓ 9. Ⓐ Ⓑ Ⓒ Ⓓ
2. Ⓐ Ⓑ Ⓒ Ⓓ 4. Ⓐ Ⓑ Ⓒ Ⓓ 6. Ⓐ Ⓑ Ⓒ Ⓓ 8. Ⓐ Ⓑ Ⓒ Ⓓ 10. Ⓐ Ⓑ Ⓒ Ⓓ

ANTONYM TEST ANSWER SHEET

TEST 9

1. Ⓐ Ⓑ Ⓒ Ⓓ   3. Ⓐ Ⓑ Ⓒ Ⓓ   5. Ⓐ Ⓑ Ⓒ Ⓓ   7. Ⓐ Ⓑ Ⓒ Ⓓ   9. Ⓐ Ⓑ Ⓒ Ⓓ
2. Ⓐ Ⓑ Ⓒ Ⓓ   4. Ⓐ Ⓑ Ⓒ Ⓓ   6. Ⓐ Ⓑ Ⓒ Ⓓ   8. Ⓐ Ⓑ Ⓒ Ⓓ   10. Ⓐ Ⓑ Ⓒ Ⓓ

TEST 10

1. Ⓐ Ⓑ Ⓒ Ⓓ   3. Ⓐ Ⓑ Ⓒ Ⓓ   5. Ⓐ Ⓑ Ⓒ Ⓓ   7. Ⓐ Ⓑ Ⓒ Ⓓ   9. Ⓐ Ⓑ Ⓒ Ⓓ
2. Ⓐ Ⓑ Ⓒ Ⓓ   4. Ⓐ Ⓑ Ⓒ Ⓓ   6. Ⓐ Ⓑ Ⓒ Ⓓ   8. Ⓐ Ⓑ Ⓒ Ⓓ   10. Ⓐ Ⓑ Ⓒ Ⓓ

Total Number of Questions   100
Total Incorrect −
Total Correct =   × 1 = _____%
Score

ANTONYM TEST ONE

DIRECTIONS: *For each question in this test, choose the word or expression that has most nearly the opposite meaning of the numbered word. Mark the letter preceding that word on your answer sheet. Correct answers for all antonym tests will be found at the end of the chapter.*

1. CONCLUSION
   (A) limit   (B) hurry
   (C) beginning (D) evil

2. HUMBLE
   (A) simple (B) hurt
   (C) proud   (D) just

3. BLUNT
   (A) dull (B) brown
   (C) keen (D) large

4. VAGUE
   (A) conceited (B) sick
   (C) distinct   (D) costly

5. REPROACH
   (A) arrive (B) commend
   (C) carry   (D) remember

6. DOMINATE
   (A) polish (B) obey
   (C) occur   (D) open

7. BEWILDERED
   (A) confused   (B) healthy
   (C) delicious (D) sure

8. HEED
   (A) watch   (B) fear
   (C) disregard (D) listen

9. LOYAL
   (A) lovely   (B) unfaithful
   (C) unlucky (D) usual

10. COMPLICATED
    (A) intelligent (B) rude
    (C) stupid   (D) simple

ANTONYM TEST TWO

DIRECTIONS: For each question in this test, select the letter preceding the word that is opposite in meaning to the capitalized word. Correct answers for all antonym tests will be found at the end of the chapter.

1. ANIMOSITY
   (A) thoughtfulness (B) friendliness
   (C) reliability   (D) anxiety

2. ACRIMONIOUS
   (A) sprightly   (B) intelligent
   (C) soothing   (D) bitter

3. PHILANTHROPY
   (A) inhumanity   (B) beneficence
   (C) argument   (D) waste

4. BENEFACTOR
   (A) helper   (B) victor
   (C) enemy   (D) disciple

5. AVERT
   (A) hide   (B) cause
   (C) excuse   (D) deny

6. DEXTEROUS
   (A) clumsy   (B) helpful
   (C) composed   (D) independent

7. MAGNANIMOUS
   (A) generous   (B) conscious
   (C) petty   (D) reliable

8. INAUDIBLE
   (A) felt   (B) resonant
   (C) expansive   (D) opportune

9. AQUATIC
   (A) into the sea
   (B) of the land
   (C) in equal parts
   (D) beneath the water

10. UNANIMOUS
   (A) by a simple majority
   (B) by a small minority
   (C) without abstentions
   (D) in complete disagreement

ANTONYM TEST THREE

DIRECTIONS: *For each question in this test, select the letter preceding the word that is opposite in meaning to the capitalized word. Correct answers for all antonym tests will be found at the end of the chapter.*

1. DECADENCE
   (A) death   (B) budding
   (C) rhythm   (D) ridicule

2. CONCLUDE
   (A) occupy   (B) open
   (C) treat   (D) describe

3. CORROBORATE
   (A) correct   (B) strengthen
   (C) broaden   (D) undermine

4. DYNAMIC
   (A) untimely   (B) orderly
   (C) passive   (D) peaceful

5. CYCLIC
   (A) revolving   (B) singular
   (C) unknown   (D) indistinct

6. PREDICTABLE
   (A) unplanned   (B) unrelated
   (C) undetected   (D) unexpected

7. DEHYDRATE
   (A) damage   (B) moisten
   (C) evaporate   (D) fuse

8. INCITE
   (A) violate   (B) regret
   (C) boast   (D) discourage

9. CURSORY
   (A) thorough   (B) impolite
   (C) honest   (D) quickly

10. DUPLICATE
    (A) copy   (B) multiply
    (C) originate   (D) purify

ANTONYM TEST FOUR

DIRECTIONS: For each question in this test, select the letter preceding the word that is opposite in meaning to the capitalized word. Correct answers for all antonym tests will be found at the end of the chapter.

1. EULOGIZE
   (A) attract
   (B) heed
   (C) defame
   (D) shun

2. FACSIMILE
   (A) restoration
   (B) replica
   (C) original
   (D) familiarity

3. FIDELITY
   (A) treason
   (B) obscurity
   (C) doubtfulness
   (D) dependability

4. FINITE
   (A) regulated
   (B) ending
   (C) selfish
   (D) limitless

5. FLEXIBLE
   (A) tough
   (B) rigid
   (C) flabby
   (D) breakable

6. FRAGILE
   (A) aggressive
   (B) sturdy
   (C) stubborn
   (D) acute

7. GRATITUDE
   (A) thankfulness
   (B) indifference
   (C) insolence
   (D) criticism

8. CONGREGATE
   (A) relax
   (B) disbelieve
   (C) scatter
   (D) relinquish

9. ERRATIC
   (A) reliable
   (B) cloudless
   (C) cunning
   (D) equalized

10. INFRACTION
    (A) discipline
    (B) observance
    (C) expenditure
    (D) experience

ANTONYM TEST FIVE

DIRECTIONS: *For each question in this test, select the letter preceding the word that is opposite in meaning to the capitalized word. Correct answers for all antonym tests will be found at the end of the chapter.*

1. ILLITERATE
   (A) legal   (B) wealthy
   (C) uneducated   (D) scholarly

2. IRRATIONAL
   (A) legal   (B) speculative
   (C) thoughtful   (D) plentiful

3. ITINERANT
   (A) legal   (B) permanent
   (C) defensive   (D) enchanted

4. HYPERACTIVE
   (A) enthused   (B) lethargic
   (C) surrounding   (D) cultured

5. INTROVERTED
   (A) eager to please
   (B) willing to help
   (C) trying to change
   (D) interested in others

6. LEGIBLE
   (A) impossible to write
   (B) impossible to read
   (C) impossible to understand
   (D) impossible to see

7. INTERCEDE
   (A) suspend   (B) antagonize
   (C) overthrow   (D) humiliate

8. IMPRACTICAL
   (A) trained   (B) recommended
   (C) worthless   (D) useful

9. HYPOCRITICAL
   (A) exempt   (B) candid
   (C) protective   (D) snobbish

10. HOMOGENEOUS
    (A) unequal   (B) opposite
    (C) miscellaneous   (D) regulated

ANTONYM TEST SIX

DIRECTIONS: For each question in this test, select the letter preceding the word that is opposite in meaning to the capitalized word. Correct answers for all antonym tests will be found at the end of the chapter.

1. MANUAL
   (A) physical   (B) difficult
   (C) mental   (D) worthy

2. MEGAPHONE
   (A) loudspeaker   (B) muffler
   (C) recorder   (D) microphone

3. MINIMIZE
   (A) endanger   (B) itemize
   (C) demolish   (D) expand

4. PREMONITION
   (A) dangerous action
   (B) complete surprise
   (C) later action
   (D) unusual suggestion

5. MONOTONOUS
   (A) incomprehensible
   (B) newly discovered
   (C) exciting
   (D) acceptable

6. MULTITUDE
   (A) handful   (B) majority
   (C) minority   (D) quorum

7. INNOVATE
   (A) sell   (B) buy
   (C) choose   (D) copy

8. NONCOMBATANT
   (A) fighter   (B) coward
   (C) judge   (D) loser

9. MINORITY
   (A) democratic victory
   (B) more than half
   (C) winning group
   (D) wisest men

10. MONOLOGUE
    (A) solo   (B) novel
    (C) pantomime   (D) conversation

ANTONYM TEST SEVEN

DIRECTIONS: *For each question in this test, select the letter preceding the word that is opposite in meaning to the capitalized word. Correct answers for all antonym tests will be found at the end of the chapter.*

1. PACIFY
   (A) end disagreement
   (B) begin new methods
   (C) stir up anger
   (D) try quietly

2. PENSIVE
   (A) thoughtless   (B) careless
   (C) eager   (D) penitent

3. DISPOSSESS
   (A) remove completely
   (B) try saving
   (C) help inhabit
   (D) give generously

4. DEPORT
   (A) bring in   (B) try out
   (C) secure   (D) give in

5. POTENT
   (A) prepared   (B) weak
   (C) qualify   (D) ready

6. APATHY
   (A) sleep   (B) temptation
   (C) zeal   (D) hospitality

7. PARAPHRASE
   (A) act   (B) sing
   (C) quote   (D) demand

8. COMPULSION
   (A) illegitimacy   (B) improvement
   (C) significance   (D) freedom

9. COMPONENT
   (A) hoard   (B) total
   (C) foundation   (D) legend

10. PROPEL
    (A) dispel   (B) anchor
    (C) breathe in   (D) release

ANTONYM TEST EIGHT

DIRECTIONS: *For each question in this test, select the letter preceding the word that is opposite in meaning to the capitalized word. Correct answers for all antonym tests will be found at the end of the chapter.*

1. QUERY
   (A) commend   (B) search
   (C) answer   (D) comply

2. RESPLENDENT
   (A) cherished   (B) lackluster
   (C) abominable   (D) folding

3. DERIDE
   (A) fly   (B) praise
   (C) amend   (D) admit

4. RUPTURE
   (A) explode   (B) employ
   (C) believe   (D) seal

5. TRANSCRIPT
   (A) completion   (B) original
   (C) authority   (D) usefulness

6. SENTIMENTAL
   (A) unwilling   (B) unequal
   (C) unreliable   (D) unresponsive

7. ABSOLVE
   (A) free   (B) struggle
   (C) accuse   (D) cheat

8. INSPIRE
   (A) intend   (B) discourage
   (C) exchange   (D) outline

9. CONSTRICT
   (A) loosen   (B) repeat
   (C) inspect   (D) destroy

10. DEROGATORY
    (A) uneven   (B) equal
    (C) opposite   (D) flattering

ANTONYM TEST NINE

DIRECTIONS: *For each question in this test, select the letter preceding the word that is opposite in meaning to the capitalized word. Correct answers for all antonym tests will be found at the end of the chapter.*

1. TANGIBLE
   - (A) required
   - (B) untouchable
   - (C) presentable
   - (D) illegal

2. TENACITY
   - (A) safety
   - (B) individual
   - (C) smallness
   - (D) cowardice

3. ATHEIST
   - (A) agnostic
   - (B) heathen
   - (C) worshipper
   - (D) godlessness

4. URBANE
   - (A) crude
   - (B) polite
   - (C) educated
   - (D) sophisticated

5. VITALITY
   - (A) praise
   - (B) anger
   - (C) death
   - (D) survival

6. PROVOCATION
   - (A) explanation
   - (B) pacification
   - (C) condemnation
   - (D) exaltation

7. DIVULGE
   - (A) expel
   - (B) invade
   - (C) hide
   - (D) demand

8. TRANSIENT
   - (A) effective
   - (B) prosperous
   - (C) stationary
   - (D) well-traveled

9. UNISON
   - (A) combination
   - (B) completeness
   - (C) expulsion
   - (D) disagreement

10. EVADE
    - (A) gamble
    - (B) withdraw
    - (C) seek
    - (D) intend

ANTONYM TEST TEN

DIRECTIONS: *For each question in this test, select the letter preceding the word that is opposite in meaning to the capitalized word. Correct answers for all antonym tests will be found at the end of the chapter.*

1. PERIODIC
   (A) preventable (B) imperfect
   (C) constant (D) beginning

2. REPULSION
   (A) prevention (B) attraction
   (C) explanation (D) observation

3. IMPLANT
   (A) take in (B) take off
   (C) take out (D) take up

4. RAPPORT
   (A) hatred (B) courtesy
   (C) success (D) waste

5. MIGRATORY
   (A) wealthy (B) ungrateful
   (C) stationary (D) prejudiced

6. RECUPERATE
   (A) promote (B) worsen
   (C) delight (D) relieve

7. ARTICULATE
   (A) mumble (B) create
   (C) explain (D) impress

8. APPREHEND
   (A) remake (B) retain
   (C) revoke (D) release

9. FUGITIVE
   (A) hunter (B) traveler
   (C) explorer (D) sinner

10. DISCERN
    (A) misperceive (B) emit
    (C) expand (D) deploy

SENTENCE COMPLETION TEST
ANSWER SHEET

TEST 1

1. Ⓐ Ⓑ Ⓒ Ⓓ	4. Ⓐ Ⓑ Ⓒ Ⓓ	7. Ⓐ Ⓑ Ⓒ Ⓓ	10. Ⓐ Ⓑ Ⓒ Ⓓ
2. Ⓐ Ⓑ Ⓒ Ⓓ	5. Ⓐ Ⓑ Ⓒ Ⓓ	8. Ⓐ Ⓑ Ⓒ Ⓓ	11. Ⓐ Ⓑ Ⓒ Ⓓ
3. Ⓐ Ⓑ Ⓒ Ⓓ	6. Ⓐ Ⓑ Ⓒ Ⓓ	9. Ⓐ Ⓑ Ⓒ Ⓓ	12. Ⓐ Ⓑ Ⓒ Ⓓ

TEST 2

1. Ⓐ Ⓑ Ⓒ Ⓓ	4. Ⓐ Ⓑ Ⓒ Ⓓ	7. Ⓐ Ⓑ Ⓒ Ⓓ	10. Ⓐ Ⓑ Ⓒ Ⓓ
2. Ⓐ Ⓑ Ⓒ Ⓓ	5. Ⓐ Ⓑ Ⓒ Ⓓ	8. Ⓐ Ⓑ Ⓒ Ⓓ	11. Ⓐ Ⓑ Ⓒ Ⓓ
3. Ⓐ Ⓑ Ⓒ Ⓓ	6. Ⓐ Ⓑ Ⓒ Ⓓ	9. Ⓐ Ⓑ Ⓒ Ⓓ	12. Ⓐ Ⓑ Ⓒ Ⓓ

TEST 3

1. Ⓐ Ⓑ Ⓒ Ⓓ	4. Ⓐ Ⓑ Ⓒ Ⓓ	7. Ⓐ Ⓑ Ⓒ Ⓓ	10. Ⓐ Ⓑ Ⓒ Ⓓ
2. Ⓐ Ⓑ Ⓒ Ⓓ	5. Ⓐ Ⓑ Ⓒ Ⓓ	8. Ⓐ Ⓑ Ⓒ Ⓓ	11. Ⓐ Ⓑ Ⓒ Ⓓ
3. Ⓐ Ⓑ Ⓒ Ⓓ	6. Ⓐ Ⓑ Ⓒ Ⓓ	9. Ⓐ Ⓑ Ⓒ Ⓓ	12. Ⓐ Ⓑ Ⓒ Ⓓ

TEST 4

1. Ⓐ Ⓑ Ⓒ Ⓓ	4. Ⓐ Ⓑ Ⓒ Ⓓ	7. Ⓐ Ⓑ Ⓒ Ⓓ	10. Ⓐ Ⓑ Ⓒ Ⓓ
2. Ⓐ Ⓑ Ⓒ Ⓓ	5. Ⓐ Ⓑ Ⓒ Ⓓ	8. Ⓐ Ⓑ Ⓒ Ⓓ	11. Ⓐ Ⓑ Ⓒ Ⓓ
3. Ⓐ Ⓑ Ⓒ Ⓓ	6. Ⓐ Ⓑ Ⓒ Ⓓ	9. Ⓐ Ⓑ Ⓒ Ⓓ	12. Ⓐ Ⓑ Ⓒ Ⓓ

TEST 5

1. Ⓐ Ⓑ Ⓒ Ⓓ	4. Ⓐ Ⓑ Ⓒ Ⓓ	7. Ⓐ Ⓑ Ⓒ Ⓓ	10. Ⓐ Ⓑ Ⓒ Ⓓ
2. Ⓐ Ⓑ Ⓒ Ⓓ	5. Ⓐ Ⓑ Ⓒ Ⓓ	8. Ⓐ Ⓑ Ⓒ Ⓓ	11. Ⓐ Ⓑ Ⓒ Ⓓ
3. Ⓐ Ⓑ Ⓒ Ⓓ	6. Ⓐ Ⓑ Ⓒ Ⓓ	9. Ⓐ Ⓑ Ⓒ Ⓓ	12. Ⓐ Ⓑ Ⓒ Ⓓ

TEST 6

1. Ⓐ Ⓑ Ⓒ Ⓓ	4. Ⓐ Ⓑ Ⓒ Ⓓ	7. Ⓐ Ⓑ Ⓒ Ⓓ	10. Ⓐ Ⓑ Ⓒ Ⓓ
2. Ⓐ Ⓑ Ⓒ Ⓓ	5. Ⓐ Ⓑ Ⓒ Ⓓ	8. Ⓐ Ⓑ Ⓒ Ⓓ	11. Ⓐ Ⓑ Ⓒ Ⓓ
3. Ⓐ Ⓑ Ⓒ Ⓓ	6. Ⓐ Ⓑ Ⓒ Ⓓ	9. Ⓐ Ⓑ Ⓒ Ⓓ	12. Ⓐ Ⓑ Ⓒ Ⓓ

TEST 7

1. Ⓐ Ⓑ Ⓒ Ⓓ	4. Ⓐ Ⓑ Ⓒ Ⓓ	7. Ⓐ Ⓑ Ⓒ Ⓓ	10. Ⓐ Ⓑ Ⓒ Ⓓ
2. Ⓐ Ⓑ Ⓒ Ⓓ	5. Ⓐ Ⓑ Ⓒ Ⓓ	8. Ⓐ Ⓑ Ⓒ Ⓓ	11. Ⓐ Ⓑ Ⓒ Ⓓ
3. Ⓐ Ⓑ Ⓒ Ⓓ	6. Ⓐ Ⓑ Ⓒ Ⓓ	9. Ⓐ Ⓑ Ⓒ Ⓓ	12. Ⓐ Ⓑ Ⓒ Ⓓ

SENTENCE COMPLETION TEST
ANSWER SHEET

TEST 8

1. Ⓐ Ⓑ Ⓒ Ⓓ   4. Ⓐ Ⓑ Ⓒ Ⓓ   7. Ⓐ Ⓑ Ⓒ Ⓓ   10. Ⓐ Ⓑ Ⓒ Ⓓ
2. Ⓐ Ⓑ Ⓒ Ⓓ   5. Ⓐ Ⓑ Ⓒ Ⓓ   8. Ⓐ Ⓑ Ⓒ Ⓓ   11. Ⓐ Ⓑ Ⓒ Ⓓ
3. Ⓐ Ⓑ Ⓒ Ⓓ   6. Ⓐ Ⓑ Ⓒ Ⓓ   9. Ⓐ Ⓑ Ⓒ Ⓓ   12. Ⓐ Ⓑ Ⓒ Ⓓ

TEST 9

1. Ⓐ Ⓑ Ⓒ Ⓓ   4. Ⓐ Ⓑ Ⓒ Ⓓ   7. Ⓐ Ⓑ Ⓒ Ⓓ   10. Ⓐ Ⓑ Ⓒ Ⓓ
2. Ⓐ Ⓑ Ⓒ Ⓓ   5. Ⓐ Ⓑ Ⓒ Ⓓ   8. Ⓐ Ⓑ Ⓒ Ⓓ   11. Ⓐ Ⓑ Ⓒ Ⓓ
3. Ⓐ Ⓑ Ⓒ Ⓓ   6. Ⓐ Ⓑ Ⓒ Ⓓ   9. Ⓐ Ⓑ Ⓒ Ⓓ   12. Ⓐ Ⓑ Ⓒ Ⓓ

TEST 10

1. Ⓐ Ⓑ Ⓒ Ⓓ   4. Ⓐ Ⓑ Ⓒ Ⓓ   7. Ⓐ Ⓑ Ⓒ Ⓓ   10. Ⓐ Ⓑ Ⓒ Ⓓ
2. Ⓐ Ⓑ Ⓒ Ⓓ   5. Ⓐ Ⓑ Ⓒ Ⓓ   8. Ⓐ Ⓑ Ⓒ Ⓓ   11. Ⓐ Ⓑ Ⓒ Ⓓ
3. Ⓐ Ⓑ Ⓒ Ⓓ   6. Ⓐ Ⓑ Ⓒ Ⓓ   9. Ⓐ Ⓑ Ⓒ Ⓓ   12. Ⓐ Ⓑ Ⓒ Ⓓ

Total Number of Questions   120
Total Incorrect −
Total Correct =   × .83 = _____%
Score

SENTENCE COMPLETION
TEST ONE

DIRECTIONS: Each of the following sentences or passages contains a blank. Select the word or phrase that will best complete the meaning of the sentence or passage as a whole. Mark its letter on the answer sheet. Correct answers to this test will be found at the end of the chapter.

1. He was the chief _____ of his uncle's will. After taxes he was left with an inheritance worth close to twenty thousand dollars.
   (A) exemption   (B) pensioner
   (C) beneficiary   (D) contestant

2. In view of the extenuating circumstances and the defendant's youth, the judge recommended _____ .
   (A) conviction   (B) a defense
   (C) a mistrial   (D) leniency

3. The basic concept of civil service is that where a public job exists, all those who possess the _____ shall have an opportunity to compete for it.
   (A) potential   (B) contacts
   (C) qualifications (D) credits

4. They would prefer to hire someone fluent in Spanish since the neighborhood in which the clinic is located is _____ Hispanic.
   (A) imponderably   (B) sparsely
   (C) consistently   (D) predominantly

5. The candidate's _____ was carefully planned; she traveled to six cities and spoke at nine rallies.
   (A) pogrom   (B) itinerary
   (C) adjournment   (D) apparition

6. In the face of an uncooperative Congress, the Chief Executive may find himself _____ to accomplish the political program to which he is committed.
   (A) impotent   (B) equipped
   (C) neutral   (D) contingent

7. The authorities declared an _____ on incoming freight because of the trucking strike.
   (A) impression   (B) immolation
   (C) embargo   (D) opprobrium

8. The _____ on the letter indicated that it had been mailed in Minnesota three weeks previously.
   (A) address   (B) stamp
   (C) postmark   (D) envelope

9. The television ads _____ an unprecedented public response. Sales skyrocketed and within a few months the brand name had become a household word.
   (A) boosted   (B) promised
   (C) elicited   (D) favored

10. The chairman submitted a _____ for the new equipment but it won't be delivered for two weeks.
    (A) requisition   (B) reason
    (C) proposal   (D) plea

11. Although for years substantial resources had been devoted to alleviating the problem, a satisfactory solution remained _____ .
    (A) costly   (B) probable
    (C) elusive   (D) esoteric

12. The local police department will not accept for _____ a report of a person missing from his residence if such residence is located outside of the city.
    (A) foreclosure   (B) convenience
    (C) investigation (D) control

SENTENCE COMPLETION
TEST TWO

DIRECTIONS: Each of the following sentences or passages contains a blank. Select the word or phrase that will best complete the meaning of the sentence or passage as a whole. Mark its letter on the answer sheet. Correct answers to this test will be found at the end of the chapter.

1. The consumer group is optimistic about the
   _____ of the new regulations on the
   industry's safety standards.
   (A) incision (B) effect
   (C) affectation (D) input

2. The mayor sent a letter _____ our
   invitation and commending us on our work;
   she regrets that she will be unable to attend
   the opening ceremonies due to a prior
   commitment.
   (A) rebuffing (B) reconsidering
   (C) returning (D) acknowledging

3. His wealth of practical experience and his
   psychological acuity more than _____
   his lack of formal academic training.
   (A) concede to (B) comprise
   (C) compensate for (D) educate for

4. Suffering from _____, she was forced
   to spend almost all her time indoors.
   (A) claustrophobia (B) agoraphobia
   (C) anemia (D) ambivalence

5. The treaty cannot go into effect until it has
   been _____ by the Senate.
   (A) considered (B) debated
   (C) ratified (D) shelved

6. You will have to speak to the head of the
   agency; I am not _____ to give out that
   information.
   (A) willing (B) authorized
   (C) programmed (D) happy

7. When new individuals have proved their
   capability and reliability, they ought to

achieve journeyman status in the company
_____.
(A) intrinsically (B) permanently
(C) automatically (D) decisively

8. You must _____ a copy of your latest
   federal income tax return before your loan
   application can be considered.
   (A) surrender (B) replicate
   (C) supplement (D) submit

9. It is easy to see the difference between the
   two photographs when they are placed in
   _____.
   (A) disarray (B) juxtaposition
   (C) composition (D) collaboration

10. The criticism that supervisors are discrimi-
    natory in their treatment of subordinates is
    to some extent _____, for the subjec-
    tive nature of many supervisory decisions
    makes it probable that many employees who
    have not progressed will attribute their lack
    of success to supervisory favoritism.
    (A) knowledgeable (B) unavoidable
    (C) detrimental (D) deniable

11. Traditionally, the more _____ sectors
    of the population in the northern states tend
    to belong to the Republican Party.
    (A) democratic (B) radical
    (C) conciliatory (D) conservative

12. Short of a further major _____ of
    business conditions, it is difficult to see how
    inventory liquidation could continue at cur-
    rent rates much beyond mid-year.
    (A) infiltration (B) obliteration
    (C) deterioration (D) machination

SENTENCE COMPLETION
TEST THREE

DIRECTIONS: Each of the following sentences or passages contains a blank. Select the word or phrase that will best complete the meaning of the sentence or passage as a whole. Mark its letter on the answer sheet. Correct answers to this test will be found at the end of the chapter.

1. The Freedom of Information Act gives private citizens _____ government files.
(A) access to   (B) excess of
(C) redress of   (D) release from

2. Among the most serious emergencies for which first aid should be taught is _____ from asphyxiation, such as may result from drowning, electric shock, or exhaust-gas poisoning.
(A) salvation
(B) resuscitation
(C) humiliation
(D) overstimulation

3. It is wise to get a written _____ of the costs of labor and materials before commissioning someone to do the work.
(A) account   (B) promise
(C) estimate   (D) invoice

4. His remarks were so _____ that we could not decide which of the possible meanings was correct.
(A) ambiguous   (B) facetious
(C) impalpable   (D) congruent

5. With such controversial subjects there is always the risk that any standards set up will yield or be _____ in one way or another.
(A) dismantled   (B) intercepted
(C) enforced   (D) circumvented

6. Publication of the article was timed to _____ with the professor's fiftieth birthday.
(A) coincide   (B) harmonize
(C) amalgamate   (D) terminate

7. The effects of the drug can be _____ by drinking large quantities of water.
(A) reprimanded   (B) implemented
(C) neutralized   (D) admitted

8. When the desk was placed facing the window, he found himself _____ from his work by the activity in the street.
(A) distraught   (B) destroyed
(C) distracted   (D) decimated

9. Since she is not _____ to using this kind of copier, you had better instruct her on how to add paper.
(A) amenable   (B) accustomed
(C) adaptable   (D) impartial

10. Compulsory education was instituted for the purpose of preventing _____ of young children and of guaranteeing them a minimum of education.
(A) malnutrition   (B) usurpation
(C) homelessness   (D) exploitation

11. A man who commits a wrong may be required to _____ his property as a penalty.
(A) confiscate   (B) destroy
(C) forfeit   (D) assess

12. When human relationships are involved in a job, it is difficult to set precise _____ for judging how well the job is being done. Merely physical or monetary standards are inadequate.
(A) options   (B) criteria
(C) behavior   (D) reports

SENTENCE COMPLETION
TEST FOUR

DIRECTIONS: Each of the following sentences or passages contains a blank. Select the word or phrase that will best complete the meaning of the sentence or passage as a whole. Mark its letter on the answer sheet. Correct answers to this test will be found at the end of the chapter.

1. The assigned task _____ the ability to analyze the available data and to draw conclusions about their implications.
   (A) inculcates   (B) obtrudes
   (C) precludes   (D) entails

2. In his suit against the government the veteran claimed that he had been sent into an area _____ by the carcinogenic defoliant without being informed of the risk or being provided with adequate protective gear.
   (A) affected   (B) sterilized
   (C) irradiated   (D) contaminated

3. An accident report should be written as soon as possible after the necessary _____ has been obtained.
   (A) bystander   (B) formulation
   (C) information   (D) permission

4. To give in to the terrorists' demands would be a betrayal of our responsibilities; such _____ would only encourage others to adopt similar methods for gaining their ends.
   (A) defeats   (B) appeasement
   (C) appeals   (D) subterfuge

5. To protect the respondents' privacy, names and social security numbers are _____ the questionnaires before the results are tabulated.
   (A) referred to   (B) deleted from
   (C) retained in   (D) appended to

6. The cause of the child's death was _____ from the fire's thick smoke.
   (A) myopia   (B) asphyxiation
   (C) strangulation   (D) hemorrhage

7. It has come to the attention of the court that a newspaper recently published a series of photographs _____ taken during a court session.
   (A) surreptitiously (B) judiciously
   (C) patently   (D) patiently

8. The woman sued the magazine, claiming that the article _____ her character.
   (A) demoted   (B) deplored
   (C) denigrated   (D) implicated

9. He is studying the language _____ in preparation for the assignment; he spends several hours a day practicing with the tapes.
   (A) sporadically   (B) superficially
   (C) profoundly   (D) intensively

10. The arresting officer is expected to testify that he saw the _____ thief fleeing from the scene of the crime.
    (A) convicted   (B) delinquent
    (C) alleged   (D) offensive

11. While fewer documents are being kept, the usefulness of those _____ is now insured by an improved cataloguing system.
    (A) printed   (B) discarded
    (C) read   (D) retained

12. In a country where public offices are created solely for the benefit of the people, no one person has any more _____ right to official station than another.
    (A) intrinsic   (B) sincere
    (C) technical   (D) confidential

SENTENCE COMPLETION
TEST FIVE

DIRECTIONS: Each of the following sentences or passages contains a blank. Select the word or phrase that will best complete the meaning of the sentence or passage as a whole. Mark its letter on the answer sheet. Correct answers to this test will be found at the end of the chapter.

1. The _____, assumed for the sake of the discussion, was that business would get better for the next five years.
(A) labyrinth (B) hypothesis
(C) outlay (D) itinerary

2. The man _____ the speaker at the meeting by shouting false accusations.
(A) corrected (B) interfered
(C) disconcerted (D) acknowledged

3. The only fair way to choose who will have to work over the holiday is to pick someone _____ by drawing lots.
(A) covertly (B) conspicuously
(C) randomly (D) carefully

4. Although he has a reputation for aloofness, his manner on that occasion was so _____ that everyone felt perfectly at ease.
(A) reluctant (B) gracious
(C) malign (D) plausible

5. Do not undertake a daily program of _____ exercise such as jogging without first having a physical checkup.
(A) light (B) spurious
(C) hazardous (D) strenuous

6. The commissioner tolerates no _____ in the application of these procedures; the regulations of the agency must in all cases be followed to the letter.
(A) laxity (B) rupture
(C) censure (D) enthusiasm

7. Research in that field has become so _____ that researchers on different aspects of the same problem may be unfamiliar with each other's work.
(A) secure (B) specialized
(C) partial (D) departmental

8. A shift to greater use of renewable or inexhaustible resources in the production of power would slow the depletion of _____ fuel materials.
(A) regional (B) irradiated
(C) chemical (D) irreplaceable

9. The day will come when _____ will look back upon us and our time with a sense of superiority.
(A) teachers (B) posterity
(C) scientists (D) ancestors

10. A change in environment is very likely to _____ a change in one's work habits.
(A) affect (B) inflict
(C) effect (D) prosper

11. She revolutionized the way things were done, but many of the _____ for which she broke ground were left to be fully realized by others.
(A) innovations (B) initiations
(C) foundations (D) provocations

12. The overseer certified that the temporary _____ was the result of an injury incurred on the job. The employee was transferred to another position until he was able to resume his usual duties.
(A) disease (B) disability
(C) leave (D) condition

SENTENCE COMPLETION TEST SIX

DIRECTIONS: Each of the following sentences or passages contains a blank. Select the word or phrase that will best complete the meaning of the sentence or passage as a whole. Mark its letter on the answer sheet. Correct answers to this test will be found at the end of the chapter.

1. The _____ of such crimes between the hours of midnight and 6 a.m. has been reduced 30 percent since April.
   (A) threat   (B) circumstance
   (C) incidence   (D) graph

2. To arrest a person is to _____ his liberty by legal authority so that he may be held to answer for a crime.
   (A) confer on him (B) set bail for
   (C) deprive him of (D) dispel from him

3. In order to save time, the supervisor directed that some forms be consolidated and others _____ entirely.
   (A) eliminated   (B) incorporated
   (C) combined   (D) disconnected

4. For the sake of public confidence, public officials should avoid even the _____ of a conflict of interest.
   (A) appearance   (B) resistance
   (C) actuality   (D) apparition

5. A string of lies had landed her in such a hopeless _____ that she didn't know how to extricate herself.
   (A) status   (B) pinnacle
   (C) enigma   (D) predicament

6. Although she was otherwise efficient and responsible, _____ was not one of her virtues. She was rarely in the office by nine.
   (A) conscientiousness (B) tardiness
   (C) politeness   (D) punctuality

7. In developing photographic film, a highly concentrated _____ containing a caustic alkali such as sodium hydroxide is essential.
   (A) solution   (B) coalition
   (C) concoction   (D) cremation

8. A professional journalist will attempt to _____ the facts learned in an interview by an independent investigation.
   (A) retell   (B) endorse
   (C) query   (D) verify

9. Her transcript indicates that she has satisfactorily completed the _____ number of courses for an associate degree.
   (A) requited   (B) rescinded
   (C) requisite   (D) relative

10. The police received a(n) _____ call giving them valuable information which led to an arrest. The caller refused to give his name out of fear of reprisals.
    (A) anonymous   (B) asinine
    (C) private   (D) candid

11. In an attempt to _____ a strike, the parties agreed to negotiate through the night.
    (A) trigger   (B) avert
    (C) arbitrate   (D) herald

12. While lenses and frames form the focus of operations, the company also makes a host of other _____ products, such as artificial eyes and instruments used to correct vision defects, as well as eyeglass cases.
    (A) panoramic   (B) corporate
    (C) ocular   (D) optimistic

SENTENCE COMPLETION
TEST SEVEN

DIRECTIONS: Each of the following sentences or passages contains a blank. Select the word or phrase that will best complete the meaning of the sentence or passage as a whole. Mark its letter on the answer sheet. Correct answers to this test will be found at the end of the chapter.

1. More residents turned out for the town meeting than the board had anticipated. There were not enough seats to _____ them all.
   (A) count   (B) hear
   (C) ascertain (D) accommodate

2. Because of their previous exposure to this strain of influenza, they are fortunately _____ to the current outbreak.
   (A) immune   (B) adamant
   (C) oblivious (D) not liable

3. A majority of the membership constitutes a _____ to do business in the Senate.
   (A) forum   (B) quorum
   (C) podium (D) minority

4. The _____ of the award stopped by the financial aid office to pick up his check.
   (A) recipient (B) subject
   (C) donor   (D) sponsor

5. Her expertise is vital to our operation. We could not _____ her services.
   (A) redouble (B) dispense with
   (C) define   (D) invest in

6. The ability to grow or reproduce and to change or mutate has long been regarded as a special _____ of living agents.
   (A) evolution (B) detriment
   (C) vitality (D) characteristic

7. The study produced a _____ amount of data, so much in fact that it will take several weeks to prepare the report.
   (A) considerate (B) minuscule
   (C) considerable (D) constant

8. Since the evidence is incomplete, we will have to come to a decision based on what seem to be reasonable _____.
   (A) actions (B) operations
   (C) proofs (D) assumptions

9. At the outset, opposition to the planned highway seemed futile, but the neighborhood association _____ its campaign until the city agreed to reconsider the route.
   (A) proclaimed (B) persisted in
   (C) insisted on (D) refrained from

10. The field of _____ medicine concerns not the treatment but the avoidance of disease. Studies of diet, exercise, drinking habits, and other factors are contributing to a better understanding of what constitutes good health.
    (A) curative   (B) surgical
    (C) veterinary (D) preventive

11. Unfortunately these favorable influences can be expected to _____ or even disappear within the next few years.
    (A) defray (B) recur
    (C) abate (D) vanish

12. No one knows more about the special program than she does; she has been its director since its _____.
    (A) operation   (B) inception
    (C) culmination (D) fulfillment

SENTENCE COMPLETION
TEST EIGHT

DIRECTIONS: Each of the following sentences or passages contains a blank. Select the word or phrase that will best complete the meaning of the sentence or passage as a whole. Mark its letter on the answer sheet. Correct answers to this test will be found at the end of the chapter.

1. Repetition of words and ideas can confuse as well as emphasize a point, and may make your speech _____.
   (A) redundant   (B) concise
   (C) illiterate   (D) effective

2. The secretary was unfailingly _____ to the clients, no matter how demanding and unreasonable they were.
   (A) irksome   (B) courteous
   (C) superficial   (D) related

3. Supported by aid from the federal government, university research activity enjoyed a period of unprecedented _____.
   (A) expansion   (B) collapse
   (C) reprieve   (D) extenuation

4. An arithmetic average or mean is arrived at by adding up the value of all the items and then dividing the _____ by the number of items.
   (A) remainder   (B) quotient
   (C) value   (D) total

5. Though brilliantly presented, the report was _____ since the information on which it was based was erroneous.
   (A) informative   (B) verbose
   (C) worthless   (D) marred

6. Since every society produces cultural elements—customs, artifacts, and so forth—unique to itself, translation of terms from its language to that of another society must sometimes be _____.
   (A) wrong   (B) unnatural
   (C) rectified   (D) imprecise

7. He often, out of modesty, _____ his own contribution; without his efforts, however, the program would still be in the planning stage.
   (A) affirms   (B) represses
   (C) belittles   (D) rescinds

8. The pioneers did not settle in this area because the land was _____.
   (A) decimated   (B) robust
   (C) barren   (D) lucid

9. As citizens we would be _____ if we did not make these facts public.
   (A) nominative   (B) elective
   (C) private   (D) derelict

10. Given a clear knowledge of what is expected of him, the subordinate requires in addition the definite assurance that he will have the _____ of his superiors so long as his actions are consistent with established policies and are taken within the limits of his responsibility.
    (A) independence   (B) satisfaction
    (C) authority   (D) support

11. As the workload increased, she _____ responsibility for many routine tasks to an assistant.
    (A) preserved   (B) delegated
    (C) handled   (D) abased

12. The principal object of the _____ law is to define crime and prescribe punishments.
    (A) penal   (B) parole
    (C) state   (D) federal

SENTENCE COMPLETION
TEST NINE

DIRECTIONS: Each of the following sentences or passages contains a blank. Select the word or phrase that will best complete the meaning of the sentence or passage as a whole. Mark its letter on the answer sheet. Correct answers to this test will be found at the end of the chapter.

1. The use of a roadblock is simply an adaptation to police practices of the military _____ of encirclement.
   (A) aggression   (B) consequence
   (C) concept   (D) flanking

2. Monetary policy was _____ primarily through the flexible use of both open-market operations and adjustments in the discount rate.
   (A) implemented   (B) associated
   (C) unified   (D) deliberated

3. The Constitution provides that no person shall twice be put in _____ for the same offense.
   (A) prison   (B) jeopardy
   (C) the army   (D) court

4. A _____ in the diplomatic service, she had not yet encountered such a question of protocol.
   (A) success   (B) volunteer
   (C) veteran   (D) novice

5. News reports alleged that high officials had been aware of the _____, and even illegal, covert activities of the group.
   (A) open   (B) unethical
   (C) explicit   (D) administrative

6. Because of the fire hazard, regulations forbid the use of highly _____ materials in certain items, such as children's pajamas.
   (A) synthetic
   (B) flammable
   (C) inflammatory
   (D) flame-retardant

7. The new secretary has a more businesslike manner than her _____ in the job.
   (A) precedent   (B) ancestor
   (C) successor   (D) predecessor

8. The supervisor tried to be as _____ as possible when dealing with her subordinates. It was, she felt, more important to be fair than to be liked by everyone.
   (A) cheerful   (B) reticent
   (C) personal   (D) objective

9. The director did not have the time today to give the report more than a _____ reading.
   (A) peripheral   (B) concentrated
   (C) dubious   (D) cursory

10. _____ action on the part of the policeman revived the victim before brain damage could occur.
    (A) Prompt   (B) Fiscal
    (C) Violent   (D) Delayed

11. The gifted young man was soon _____ with local architects, helping with various minor civil commissions.
    (A) commiserating   (B) scintillating
    (C) collaborating   (D) directing

12. A(n) _____ budgetary review uncovered evidence of misappropriation of funds by agency officials.
    (A) extensive   (B) useless
    (C) insignificant   (D) obsolete

SENTENCE COMPLETION TEST TEN

DIRECTIONS: Each of the following sentences or passages contains a blank. Select the word or phrase that will best complete the meaning of the sentence or passage as a whole. Mark its letter on the answer sheet. Correct answers to this test will be found at the end of the chapter.

1. Because of her long experience in office management, it was _____ that she was the right person for the job.
   (A) absolute   (B) assigned
   (C) proved   (D) assumed

2. The determination of the value of the employees in an organization is fundamental not only as a guide to the administration of salary schedules, promotion, demotion, and transfer, but also as a means of checking the _____ of selection methods.
   (A) effectiveness   (B) initiation
   (C) evaluation   (D) system

3. The mayor, _____ the violence that had swept the city, imposed a curfew and called on the President to send the National Guard to restore order.
   (A) deploring   (B) placating
   (C) suspending   (D) commending

4. The value of the collection in the current market has been _____ at about twelve hundred dollars.
   (A) sold   (B) assessed
   (C) optioned   (D) auctioned

5. For many years slums have been recognized as breeding disease, juvenile delinquency, and crime, which not only threaten the health and welfare of people who live there, but also _____ the structure of society as a whole.
   (A) rebuild   (B) bolster
   (C) weaken   (D) disengage

6. An item cannot be sent by first class mail if it _____ 70 pounds.
   (A) exceeds   (B) is under
   (C) has over   (D) holds

7. Excessive fatigue can _____ be attributed to inadequate working conditions, for instance, poor lighting.
   (A) inevitably   (B) occasionally
   (C) ever   (D) never

8. Now, many years later, with the benefit of much _____, we see the activities in which these people engaged in a very unfavorable light.
   (A) foresight   (B) education
   (C) hindsight   (D) research

9. Ever since the conference yesterday the ambassador has been giving every spare moment to a _____ of the case.
   (A) prediction   (B) retarding
   (C) dismissal   (D) consideration

10. The company received a _____ from the government to develop new sources of energy.
    (A) reward   (B) compendium
    (C) subsidy   (D) memorandum

11. A police officer's _____ job is to prevent crime.
    (A) primary   (B) only
    (C) ostentatious   (D) infrequent

12. The _____ with which the agent calmed the anxieties and soothed the tempers of the travelers inconvenienced by the delay was a mark of frequent experience with similar crises.
    (A) evasiveness   (B) reverence
    (C) facility   (D) mannerism

VERBAL ANALOGY TEST
ANSWER SHEET

TEST 1

1. Ⓐ Ⓑ Ⓒ Ⓓ 3. Ⓐ Ⓑ Ⓒ Ⓓ 5. Ⓐ Ⓑ Ⓒ Ⓓ 7. Ⓐ Ⓑ Ⓒ Ⓓ 9. Ⓐ Ⓑ Ⓒ Ⓓ
2. Ⓐ Ⓑ Ⓒ Ⓓ 4. Ⓐ Ⓑ Ⓒ Ⓓ 6. Ⓐ Ⓑ Ⓒ Ⓓ 8. Ⓐ Ⓑ Ⓒ Ⓓ 10. Ⓐ Ⓑ Ⓒ Ⓓ

TEST 2

1. Ⓐ Ⓑ Ⓒ Ⓓ 3. Ⓐ Ⓑ Ⓒ Ⓓ 5. Ⓐ Ⓑ Ⓒ Ⓓ 7. Ⓐ Ⓑ Ⓒ Ⓓ 9. Ⓐ Ⓑ Ⓒ Ⓓ
2. Ⓐ Ⓑ Ⓒ Ⓓ 4. Ⓐ Ⓑ Ⓒ Ⓓ 6. Ⓐ Ⓑ Ⓒ Ⓓ 8. Ⓐ Ⓑ Ⓒ Ⓓ 10. Ⓐ Ⓑ Ⓒ Ⓓ

TEST 3

1. Ⓐ Ⓑ Ⓒ Ⓓ 3. Ⓐ Ⓑ Ⓒ Ⓓ 5. Ⓐ Ⓑ Ⓒ Ⓓ 7. Ⓐ Ⓑ Ⓒ Ⓓ 9. Ⓐ Ⓑ Ⓒ Ⓓ
2. Ⓐ Ⓑ Ⓒ Ⓓ 4. Ⓐ Ⓑ Ⓒ Ⓓ 6. Ⓐ Ⓑ Ⓒ Ⓓ 8. Ⓐ Ⓑ Ⓒ Ⓓ 10. Ⓐ Ⓑ Ⓒ Ⓓ

TEST 4

1. Ⓐ Ⓑ Ⓒ Ⓓ 3. Ⓐ Ⓑ Ⓒ Ⓓ 5. Ⓐ Ⓑ Ⓒ Ⓓ 7. Ⓐ Ⓑ Ⓒ Ⓓ 9. Ⓐ Ⓑ Ⓒ Ⓓ
2. Ⓐ Ⓑ Ⓒ Ⓓ 4. Ⓐ Ⓑ Ⓒ Ⓓ 6. Ⓐ Ⓑ Ⓒ Ⓓ 8. Ⓐ Ⓑ Ⓒ Ⓓ 10. Ⓐ Ⓑ Ⓒ Ⓓ

TEST 5

1. Ⓐ Ⓑ Ⓒ Ⓓ 3. Ⓐ Ⓑ Ⓒ Ⓓ 5. Ⓐ Ⓑ Ⓒ Ⓓ 7. Ⓐ Ⓑ Ⓒ Ⓓ 9. Ⓐ Ⓑ Ⓒ Ⓓ
2. Ⓐ Ⓑ Ⓒ Ⓓ 4. Ⓐ Ⓑ Ⓒ Ⓓ 6. Ⓐ Ⓑ Ⓒ Ⓓ 8. Ⓐ Ⓑ Ⓒ Ⓓ 10. Ⓐ Ⓑ Ⓒ Ⓓ

TEST 6

1. Ⓐ Ⓑ Ⓒ Ⓓ 3. Ⓐ Ⓑ Ⓒ Ⓓ 5. Ⓐ Ⓑ Ⓒ Ⓓ 7. Ⓐ Ⓑ Ⓒ Ⓓ 9. Ⓐ Ⓑ Ⓒ Ⓓ
2. Ⓐ Ⓑ Ⓒ Ⓓ 4. Ⓐ Ⓑ Ⓒ Ⓓ 6. Ⓐ Ⓑ Ⓒ Ⓓ 8. Ⓐ Ⓑ Ⓒ Ⓓ 10. Ⓐ Ⓑ Ⓒ Ⓓ

TEST 7

1. Ⓐ Ⓑ Ⓒ Ⓓ 3. Ⓐ Ⓑ Ⓒ Ⓓ 5. Ⓐ Ⓑ Ⓒ Ⓓ 7. Ⓐ Ⓑ Ⓒ Ⓓ 9. Ⓐ Ⓑ Ⓒ Ⓓ
2. Ⓐ Ⓑ Ⓒ Ⓓ 4. Ⓐ Ⓑ Ⓒ Ⓓ 6. Ⓐ Ⓑ Ⓒ Ⓓ 8. Ⓐ Ⓑ Ⓒ Ⓓ 10. Ⓐ Ⓑ Ⓒ Ⓓ

TEST 8

1. Ⓐ Ⓑ Ⓒ Ⓓ 3. Ⓐ Ⓑ Ⓒ Ⓓ 5. Ⓐ Ⓑ Ⓒ Ⓓ 7. Ⓐ Ⓑ Ⓒ Ⓓ 9. Ⓐ Ⓑ Ⓒ Ⓓ
2. Ⓐ Ⓑ Ⓒ Ⓓ 4. Ⓐ Ⓑ Ⓒ Ⓓ 6. Ⓐ Ⓑ Ⓒ Ⓓ 8. Ⓐ Ⓑ Ⓒ Ⓓ 10. Ⓐ Ⓑ Ⓒ Ⓓ

VERBAL ANALOGY TEST
ANSWER SHEET

TEST 9

1. Ⓐ Ⓑ Ⓒ Ⓓ   3. Ⓐ Ⓑ Ⓒ Ⓓ   5. Ⓐ Ⓑ Ⓒ Ⓓ   7. Ⓐ Ⓑ Ⓒ Ⓓ   9. Ⓐ Ⓑ Ⓒ Ⓓ
2. Ⓐ Ⓑ Ⓒ Ⓓ   4. Ⓐ Ⓑ Ⓒ Ⓓ   6. Ⓐ Ⓑ Ⓒ Ⓓ   8. Ⓐ Ⓑ Ⓒ Ⓓ   10. Ⓐ Ⓑ Ⓒ Ⓓ

TEST 10

1. Ⓐ Ⓑ Ⓒ Ⓓ   3. Ⓐ Ⓑ Ⓒ Ⓓ   5. Ⓐ Ⓑ Ⓒ Ⓓ   7. Ⓐ Ⓑ Ⓒ Ⓓ   9. Ⓐ Ⓑ Ⓒ Ⓓ
2. Ⓐ Ⓑ Ⓒ Ⓓ   4. Ⓐ Ⓑ Ⓒ Ⓓ   6. Ⓐ Ⓑ Ⓒ Ⓓ   8. Ⓐ Ⓑ Ⓒ Ⓓ   10. Ⓐ Ⓑ Ⓒ Ⓓ

TEST 11

1. Ⓐ Ⓑ Ⓒ Ⓓ   3. Ⓐ Ⓑ Ⓒ Ⓓ   5. Ⓐ Ⓑ Ⓒ Ⓓ   7. Ⓐ Ⓑ Ⓒ Ⓓ   9. Ⓐ Ⓑ Ⓒ Ⓓ
2. Ⓐ Ⓑ Ⓒ Ⓓ   4. Ⓐ Ⓑ Ⓒ Ⓓ   6. Ⓐ Ⓑ Ⓒ Ⓓ   8. Ⓐ Ⓑ Ⓒ Ⓓ   10. Ⓐ Ⓑ Ⓒ Ⓓ

TEST 12

1. Ⓐ Ⓑ Ⓒ Ⓓ   3. Ⓐ Ⓑ Ⓒ Ⓓ   5. Ⓐ Ⓑ Ⓒ Ⓓ   7. Ⓐ Ⓑ Ⓒ Ⓓ   9. Ⓐ Ⓑ Ⓒ Ⓓ
2. Ⓐ Ⓑ Ⓒ Ⓓ   4. Ⓐ Ⓑ Ⓒ Ⓓ   6. Ⓐ Ⓑ Ⓒ Ⓓ   8. Ⓐ Ⓑ Ⓒ Ⓓ   10. Ⓐ Ⓑ Ⓒ Ⓓ

Total Number of Questions   120
  Total Incorrect − _____
    Total Correct = _____ × .83 = ____%
                                      Score

VERBAL ANALOGY TEST ONE

DIRECTIONS: *In each question the two capitalized words have a certain relation-ship to each other. Select the letter of the pair of words which are related in the same way as the two capitalized words. Correct answers and explanations will be found at the end of the chapter.*

1. INTIMIDATE : FEAR ::
   (A) maintain : satisfaction
   (B) astonish : wonder
   (C) sooth : concern
   (D) feed : hunger

2. STOVE : KITCHEN ::
   (A) window : bedroom
   (B) sink : bathroom
   (C) television : living room
   (D) trunk : attic

3. CELEBRATE : MARRIAGE ::
   (A) announce : birthday
   (B) report : injury
   (C) lament : bereavement
   (D) face : penalty

4. MARGARINE : BUTTER ::
   (A) cream : milk
   (B) lace : cotton
   (C) nylon : silk
   (D) egg : chicken

5. NEGLIGENT : REQUIREMENT ::
   (A) careful : position
   (B) remiss : duty
   (C) cautious : injury
   (D) cogent : task

6. GAZELLE : SWIFT ::
   (A) horse : slow
   (B) wolf : sly
   (C) swan : graceful
   (D) elephant : gray

7. IGNOMINY : DISLOYALTY ::
   (A) fame : heroism
   (B) castigation : praise
   (C) death : victory
   (D) approbation : consecration

8. SATURNINE : MERCURIAL ::
   (A) Saturn : Venus
   (B) Apennines : Alps
   (C) redundant : wordy
   (D) allegro : adagio

9. ORANGE : MARMALADE ::
   (A) potato : vegetable
   (B) jelly : jam
   (C) tomato : ketchup
   (D) cake : picnic

10. BANISH : APOSTATE ::
    (A) reward : traitor
    (B) welcome : ally
    (C) remove : result
    (D) avoid : truce

VERBAL ANALOGY TEST TWO

DIRECTIONS: In each question the two capitalized words have a certain relationship to each other. Select the letter of the pair of words which are related in the same way as the two capitalized words. Correct answers and explanations will be found at the end of the chapter.

1. CIRCLE : SPHERE ::
   (A) square : triangle
   (B) balloon : jet plane
   (C) heaven : hell
   (D) wheel : orange

2. OPEN : SECRETIVE ::
   (A) mystery : detective
   (B) tunnel : toll
   (C) forthright : snide
   (D) better : best

3. AFFIRM : HINT ::
   (A) say : deny
   (B) assert : convince
   (C) confirm : reject
   (D) charge : insinuate

4. THROW : BALL ::
   (A) kill : bullet
   (B) shoot : gun
   (C) question : answer
   (D) hit : run

5. SPEEDY : GREYHOUND ::
   (A) innocent : lamb
   (B) animate : animal
   (C) voracious : tiger
   (D) sluggish : sloth

6. TRIANGLE : PYRAMID ::
   (A) cone : circle
   (B) corner : angle
   (C) square : box
   (D) pentagon : quadrilateral

7. IMPEACH : DISMISS ::
   (A) arraign : convict
   (B) exonerate : charge
   (C) imprison : jail
   (D) plant : reap

8. EMULATE : MIMIC ::
   (A) slander : defame
   (B) praise : flatter
   (C) aggravate : promote
   (D) complain : condemn

9. HAND : NAIL ::
   (A) paw : claw
   (B) foot : toe
   (C) head : hair
   (D) ear : nose

10. SQUARE : DIAMOND ::
    (A) cube : sugar
    (B) circle : ellipse
    (C) innocence : jewelry
    (D) pentangle : square

VERBAL ANALOGY TEST THREE

DIRECTIONS: In each question the two capitalized words have a certain relationship to each other. Select the letter of the pair of words which are related in the same way as the two capitalized words. Correct answers and explanations will be found at the end of the chapter.

1. WOODSMAN : AXE ::
    (A) mechanic : wrench
    (B) carpenter : saw
    (C) draftsman : ruler
    (D) doctor : prescription

2. BIGOTRY : HATRED ::
    (A) sweetness : bitterness
    (B) segregation : integration
    (C) fanaticism : intolerance
    (D) sugar : grain

3. ASSIST : SAVE ::
    (A) request : command
    (B) rely : descry
    (C) hurt : aid
    (D) declare : deny

4. 2 : 5 ::
    (A) 5 : 7
    (B) 6 : 17
    (C) 6 : 15
    (D) 5 : 14

5. DOUBLEHEADER : TRIDENT ::
    (A) twins : troika
    (B) ballgame : three bagger
    (C) chewing gum : toothpaste
    (D) freak : zoo

6. BOUQUET : FLOWER ::
    (A) key : door
    (B) air : balloon
    (C) skin : body
    (D) chain : link

7. LETTER : WORD ::
    (A) club : people
    (B) homework : school
    (C) page : book
    (D) product : factory

8. 36 : 4 ::
    (A) 3 : 27
    (B) 9 : 1
    (C) 12 : 4
    (D) 5 : 2

9. GERM : DISEASE ::
    (A) trichinosis : pork
    (B) men : woman
    (C) doctor : medicine
    (D) war : destruction

10. WAVE : CREST ::
    (A) pinnacle : nadir
    (B) mountain : peak
    (C) sea : ocean
    (D) breaker : swimming

VERBAL ANALOGY TEST FOUR

DIRECTIONS: In each question the two capitalized words have a certain relationship to each other. Select the letter of the pair of words which are related in the same way as the two capitalized words. Correct answers and explanations will be found at the end of the chapter.

1. CONTROL : ORDER ::
   (A) joke : clown
   (B) teacher : pupil
   (C) disorder : climax
   (D) anarchy : chaos

2. WOOD : CARVE ::
   (A) trees : sway
   (B) paper : burn
   (C) clay : mold
   (D) pipe : blow

3. STATE : BORDER ::
   (A) nation : state
   (B) property : fence
   (C) Idaho : Montana
   (D) planet : satellite

4. SOLDIER : REGIMENT ::
   (A) navy : army
   (B) lake : river
   (C) star : constellation
   (D) amphibian : frog

5. APOGEE : PERIGEE ::
   (A) dog : pedigree.
   (B) opposite : composite
   (C) inappropriate : apposite
   (D) effigy : statue

6. ASYLUM : REFUGEE ::
   (A) flight : escape.
   (B) destination : traveler
   (C) lunatic : insanity
   (D) accident : injury

7. WORRIED : HYSTERICAL ::
   (A) hot : cold
   (B) happy : ecstatic
   (C) lonely : crowded
   (D) happy : serious

8. WORD : CHARADE ::
   (A) phrase : act
   (B) idea : philosophy
   (C) fun : party
   (D) message : code

9. PLAYER : TEAM ::
   (A) fawn : doe
   (B) book : story
   (C) ball : bat
   (D) fish : school

10. BANANA : BUNCH ::
    (A) city : state
    (B) world : earth
    (C) president : nation
    (D) people : continent

VERBAL ANALOGY TEST FIVE

DIRECTIONS: In each question the two capitalized words have a certain relationship to each other. Select the letter of the pair of words which are related in the same way as the two capitalized words. Correct answers and explanations will be found at the end of the chapter.

1. MOTH : CLOTHING ::
   (A) egg : larva
   (B) suit : dress
   (C) hole : repair
   (D) stigma : reputation

2. LINCOLN : NEBRASKA ::
   (A) Washington : D. C.
   (B) Trenton : New Jersey
   (C) New York : U. S.
   (D) Chicago : New York

3. BUZZ : HUM ::
   (A) noise : explosion
   (B) reverberation : peal
   (C) tinkle : clang
   (D) echo : sound

4. BOXER : GLOVES ::
   (A) swimmer : water
   (B) bacteriologist : microscope
   (C) businessman : bills
   (D) fruit : pedlar

5. DECISION : CONSIDERATION ::
   (A) gift : party
   (B) plea : request
   (C) fulfillment : wish
   (D) conference : constitution

6. ILLUSION : MIRAGE ::
   (A) haunter : specter
   (B) imagination : concentration
   (C) dream : reality
   (D) mirror : glass

7. FRANCE : EUROPE ::
   (A) Australia : New Zealand
   (B) Paris : France
   (C) Israel : Egypt
   (D) Algeria : Africa

8. INSULT : INVULNERABLE ::
   (A) success : capable
   (B) poverty : miserable
   (C) purchase : refundable
   (D) assault : impregnable

9. POISON : DEATH ::
   (A) book : pages
   (B) music : violin
   (C) kindness : cooperation
   (D) life : famine

10. ROCK : SLATE ::
    (A) wave : sea
    (B) boat : kayak
    (C) swimmer : male
    (D) lifeguard : beach

VERBAL ANALOGY TEST SIX

DIRECTIONS: In each question the two capitalized words have a certain relationship to each other. Select the letter of the pair of words which are related in the same way as the two capitalized words. Correct answers and explanations will be found at the end of the chapter.

1. LAW : CITIZEN ::
   (A) democracy : communism
   (B) weapon : peace
   (C) reins : horse
   (D) gangster : policeman

2. JOY : ECSTASY ::
   (A) admiration : love
   (B) weather : humidity
   (C) happiness : sorrow
   (D) life : hope

3. LARCENY : GRAND ::
   (A) theft : daring
   (B) school : elementary
   (C) pepper : bitter
   (D) silence : peaceful

4. ANTISEPTIC : GERMS ::
   (A) bullet : death
   (B) mosquitoes : disease
   (C) lion : prey
   (D) doctor : medicine

5. HORSE : RIDE ::
   (A) sharpener : sharpen
   (B) instrument : play
   (C) use : reuse
   (D) break : crack

6. MYSTERY : CLUE ::
   (A) book : reader
   (B) fruit : bowl
   (C) door : key
   (D) detective : crime

7. PENCIL : SHARPEN ::
   (A) wood : saw
   (B) carpenter : build
   (C) blow : puff
   (D) well : fill

8. GARBAGE : SQUALOR ::
   (A) filth : cleanliness
   (B) fame : knowledge
   (C) diamonds : magnificence
   (D) color : brush

9. MYTH : STORY ::
   (A) fiction : reality
   (B) bonnet : hat
   (C) literature : poetry
   (D) flower : redness

10. DUNCE : CLEVER ::
    (A) idiot : stupid
    (B) courage : fearful
    (C) help : weak
    (D) worry : poor

VERBAL ANALOGY TEST SEVEN

DIRECTIONS: In each question the two capitalized words have a certain relationship to each other. Select the letter of the pair of words which are related in the same way as the two capitalized words. Correct answers and explanations will be found at the end of the chapter.

1. CROWN : ROYAL ::
   (A) gun : military
   (B) cola : sweet
   (C) crucifix : religious
   (D) wrap : ermine

2. ISLAND : OCEAN ::
   (A) hill : stream
   (B) forest : valley
   (C) oasis : desert
   (D) tree : field

3. MATHEMATICS : NUMEROLOGY ::
   (A) biology : botany
   (B) psychology : physiology
   (C) anatomy : medicine
   (D) astronomy : astrology

4. DISLIKABLE : ABHORRENT ::
   (A) trustworthy : helpful
   (B) difficult : arduous
   (C) silly : young
   (D) tender : hard

5. RETINUE : MONARCH ::
   (A) cortege : escort
   (B) princess : queen
   (C) moon : earth
   (D) second : first

6. WOOD : CORD ::
   (A) tree : pasture
   (B) nature : industry
   (C) milk : quart
   (D) leaf : cow

7. MINARET : MOSQUE ::
   (A) Christian : Moslem
   (B) steeple : church
   (C) dainty : grotesque
   (D) modern : classic

8. WHEAT : CHAFF ::
   (A) wine : dregs
   (B) bread : roll
   (C) laughter : raillery
   (D) oat : oatmeal

9. DRAMA : DIRECTOR ::
   (A) class : principal
   (B) magazine : editor
   (C) actor : playwright
   (D) tragedy : Sophocles

10. COMMONPLACE : CLICHÉ ::
    (A) serious : play
    (B) annoying : pun
    (C) appreciated : gift
    (D) terse : maxim

VERBAL ANALOGY TEST EIGHT

DIRECTIONS: In each question the two capitalized words have a certain relationship to each other. Select the letter of the pair of words which are related in the same way as the two capitalized words. Correct answers and explanations will be found at the end of the chapter.

1. AFFLUENT : LUCK ::
   (A) charitable : stinginess
   (B) greedy : cruelty
   (C) free-flowing : barrier
   (D) impoverished : laziness

2. PICCOLO : TUBA ::
   (A) orchestra : band
   (B) violin : bass
   (C) trumpet : trombone
   (D) sweet : sour

3. PLEASED : THRILLED ::
   (A) tipsy : drunken
   (B) sensible : lively
   (C) intelligent : dumb
   (D) liberal : tolerant

4. MORALITY : LEGALITY ::
   (A) home : court
   (B) man : law
   (C) sin : crime
   (D) priest : attorney

5. ELLIPSE : CURVE ::
   (A) stutter : speech
   (B) triangle : base
   (C) revolution : distance
   (D) square : polygon

6. SUGAR : SACCHARIN ::
   (A) candy : cake
   (B) butter : margarine
   (C) cane : stalk
   (D) spice : pepper

7. REQUEST : DEMAND ::
   (A) reply : respond
   (B) regard : reject
   (C) inquire : require
   (D) wish : crave

8. WATER : FAUCET ::
   (A) fuel : throttle
   (B) H_2O : O
   (C) kitchen : sink
   (D) steam : solid

9. FLASK : BOTTLE ::
   (A) whiskey : milk
   (B) metal : glass
   (C) brochure : tome
   (D) quart : pint

10. MONEY : GREED ::
    (A) finance : creed
    (B) property : desire
    (C) dollar sign : capitalism
    (D) food : voracity

VERBAL ANALOGY TEST NINE

DIRECTIONS: Each of the following items contains a pair of words in capital letters, followed by four pairs of words. Choose the pair that best expresses a relationship similar to the one expressed by the capitalized pair. Correct answers and explanations will be found at the end of the chapter.

1. HAIR : BALDNESS ::
   (A) wig : head
   (B) egg : eggshell
   (C) rain : drought
   (D) skin : scar

2. BOAT : SHIP ::
   (A) book : volume
   (B) canoe : paddle
   (C) oar : water
   (D) aft : stern

3. SCYTHE : DEATH ::
   (A) fall : winter
   (B) knife : murder
   (C) arrow : love
   (D) harvest : crops

4. CARNIVORE : ANIMALS ::
   (A) omnivore : omelets
   (B) vegetarian : vegetables
   (C) trace : minerals
   (D) herbivore : healthy

5. MAUVE : COLOR ::
   (A) basil : spice
   (B) colorless : colored
   (C) light : dark
   (D) tan : brown

6. MUFFLE : SILENCE ::
   (A) cover : bell
   (B) sound : hearing
   (C) cry : glove
   (D) stymie : defeat

7. DEARTH : PAUCITY ::
   (A) few : many
   (B) scarcity : shortage
   (C) shortage : plethora
   (D) empty : container

8. WATERMARK : BIRTHMARK ::
   (A) buoy : stamp
   (B) paper : person
   (C) tide : character
   (D) line : signal

9. BRIGHT : BRILLIANT ::
   (A) color : red
   (B) yellow : red
   (C) contented : overjoyed
   (D) light : fire

10. DISCIPLINE : ORDER ::
    (A) military : rank
    (B) authority : follower
    (C) parent : child
    (D) training : preparation

VERBAL ANALOGY TEST TEN

DIRECTIONS: Each of the following items contains a pair of words in capital letters, followed by four pairs of words. Choose the pair that best expresses a relationship similar to the one expressed by the capitalized pair. Correct answers and explanations will be found at the end of the chapter.

1. NEWS REPORT : DESCRIPTIVE ::
   (A) weather report : unpredictable
   (B) editorial : one-sided
   (C) feature story : newsworthy
   (D) commercial : prescriptive

2. AGREEMENT : CONSENSUS ::
   (A) discord : harmony
   (B) pleasure : hatred
   (C) pacific : tranquil
   (D) argument : solution

3. WATER : HYDRAULIC ::
   (A) energy : atomic
   (B) power : electric
   (C) air : pneumatic
   (D) pressure : compress

4. STABLE : HORSE ::
   (A) barn : cow
   (B) sty : hog
   (C) fold : ram
   (D) coop : hen

5. ROLE : ACTOR ::
   (A) aria : soprano
   (B) private : soldier
   (C) melody : singer
   (D) position : ballplayer

6. PROW : SHIP ::
   (A) snout : hog
   (B) nose : airplane
   (C) bird : beak
   (D) wheel : car

7. MAXIMUM : MINIMUM ::
   (A) pessimist : optimist
   (B) minimum : optimum
   (C) best : good
   (D) most : least

8. SENSATION : ANESTHETIC ::
   (A) breath : lung
   (B) drug : reaction
   (C) satisfaction : disappointment
   (D) poison : antidote

9. DISEMBARK : SHIP ::
   (A) board : train
   (B) dismount : horse
   (C) intern : jail
   (D) discharge : navy

10. PROTEIN : MEAT ::
    (A) calories : cream
    (B) energy : sugar
    (C) cyclamates : diet
    (D) starch : potatoes

VERBAL ANALOGY TEST ELEVEN

DIRECTIONS: *Each of the following items contains a pair of words in capital letters, followed by four pairs of words. Choose the pair that* best *expresses a relationship similar to the one expressed by the capitalized pair. Correct answers and explanations will be found at the end of the chapter.*

1. NECK : NAPE ::
   (A) foot : heel
   (B) head : forehead
   (C) arm : wrist
   (D) stomach : back

2. GRIPPING : PLIERS ::
   (A) chisel : gouging
   (B) breaking : hammer
   (C) elevating : jack
   (D) killing : knife

3. RADIUS : CIRCLE ::
   (A) rubber : tire
   (B) spoke : wheel
   (C) equator : earth
   (D) cord : circumference

4. MISDEMEANOR : FELONY ::
   (A) mild : seriously
   (B) thief : burglar
   (C) murder : manslaughter
   (D) cracked : broken

5. HYGROMETER : HUMIDITY ::
   (A) thermometer : temperature
   (B) gauge : pressure
   (C) odometer : speed
   (D) barometer : weather

6. ASTUTE : STUPID ::
   (A) scholar : idiotic
   (B) agile : clumsy
   (C) lonely : clown
   (D) dunce : ignorant

7. WHALE : FISH ::
   (A) collie : dog
   (B) fly : insect
   (C) bat : bird
   (D) clue : detective

8. GOLD : PROSPECTOR ::
   (A) medicine : doctor
   (B) prayer : preacher
   (C) wood : carpenter
   (D) clue : detective

9. COUPLET : POEM ::
   (A) page : letter
   (B) sentence : paragraph
   (C) number : address
   (D) epic : poetry

10. OIL : WELL ::
    (A) water : faucet
    (B) iron : ore
    (C) silver : mine
    (D) gas : pump

VERBAL ANALOGY TEST TWELVE

DIRECTIONS: *Each of the following items contains a pair of words in capital letters, followed by four pairs of words. Choose the pair that best expresses a relationship similar to the one expressed by the capitalized pair. Correct answers and explanations will be found at the end of the chapter.*

1. RUDDER : SHIP ::
   (A) wheel : car
   (B) motor : truck
   (C) row : boat
   (D) kite : string

2. STALLION : ROOSTER ::
   (A) buck : doe
   (B) mare : hen
   (C) horse : chicken
   (D) foal : calf

3. READ : BOOK ::
   (A) taste : salty
   (B) attend : movie
   (C) smell : odor
   (D) listen : record

4. PARROT : SPARROW ::
   (A) dog : poodle
   (B) elephant : ant
   (C) goldfish : guppy
   (D) lion : cat

5. BONES : LIGAMENT ::
   (A) break : stretch
   (B) muscle : tendon
   (C) fat : cell
   (D) knuckle : finger

6. SPICY : INSIPID ::
   (A) pepper : salt
   (B) hot : creamy
   (C) exciting : dull
   (D) pickle : pepper

7. BURL : TREE ::
   (A) pearl : oyster
   (B) bronze : copper
   (C) plank : wood
   (D) glass : sand

8. YEAST : LEAVEN ::
   (A) soda : bubble
   (B) iodine : antiseptic
   (C) aspirin : medicine
   (D) flour : dough

9. NUMEROUS : POLYGON ::
   (A) circumference : circle
   (B) hypotenuse : triangle
   (C) four : square
   (D) degree : angle

10. EXPURGATE : PASSAGES ::
    (A) defoliate : leaves
    (B) cancel : checks
    (C) incorporate : ideas
    (D) invade : privacy

SYNONYM TEST ANSWER KEY

TEST 1

#	Ans	#	Ans	#	Ans	#	Ans	#	Ans
1.	D	5.	C	9.	A	13.	B	17.	D
2.	C	6.	B	10.	B	14.	D	18.	A
3.	C	7.	C	11.	D	15.	C		
4.	D	8.	A	12.	B	16.	D		

TEST 2

#	Ans	#	Ans	#	Ans	#	Ans	#	Ans
1.	D	3.	B	5.	D	7.	B	9.	C
2.	A	4.	B	6.	C	8.	A	10.	B

TEST 3

#	Ans	#	Ans	#	Ans	#	Ans	#	Ans
1.	F	5.	F	9.	F	13.	F	17.	F
2.	T	6.	T	10.	F	14.	F	18.	T
3.	T	7.	T	11.	T	15.	T	19.	T
4.	F	8.	F	12.	F	16.	F	20.	T

TEST 4

#	Ans	#	Ans	#	Ans	#	Ans	#	Ans
1.	B	5.	C	9.	D	13.	B	17.	C
2.	A	6.	D	10.	A	14.	B	18.	B
3.	D	7.	C	11.	C	15.	B		
4.	C	8.	B	12.	C	16.	D		

TEST 5

#	Ans	#	Ans	#	Ans	#	Ans	#	Ans
1.	C	3.	D	5.	A	7.	C	9.	B
2.	B	4.	B	6.	B	8.	D	10.	D

TEST 6

#	Ans	#	Ans	#	Ans	#	Ans	#	Ans
1.	C	5.	C	9.	C	13.	A	17.	B
2.	C	6.	A	10.	D	14.	C	18.	A
3.	B	7.	A	11.	D	15.	C	19.	A
4.	C	8.	C	12.	C	16.	C	20.	C

TEST 7

#	Ans	#	Ans	#	Ans	#	Ans	#	Ans
1.	B	5.	D	9.	B	13.	B	17.	D
2.	A	6.	B	10.	C	14.	A	18.	B
3.	D	7.	B	11.	D	15.	C	19.	D
4.	A	8.	D	12.	D	16.	C	20.	A

SYNONYM TEST ANSWER KEY

TEST 8

1. B	5. B	9. B	13. B	17. B
2. A	6. A	10. B	14. C	18. D
3. C	7. D	11. B	15. C	19. A
4. A	8. D	12. B	16. C	20. D

TEST 9

1. C	5. C	9. D	13. B	17. A
2. A	6. B	10. B	14. A	18. C
3. A	7. A	11. A	15. D	19. A
4. B	8. B	12. B	16. C	20. B

TEST 10

1. D	5. C	9. A	13. B	17. B
2. A	6. C	10. A	14. A	18. C
3. C	7. D	11. C	15. C	19. A
4. B	8. A	12. D	16. B	20. C

TEST 11

1. B	5. C	9. D	13. A	17. A
2. D	6. A	10. D	14. D	18. C
3. D	7. B	11. B	15. D	19. C
4. A	8. D	12. A	16. D	

ANTONYM TEST ANSWER KEY

TEST 1

1. Ⓐ Ⓑ ● Ⓓ	3. Ⓐ Ⓑ ● Ⓓ	5. Ⓐ ● Ⓒ Ⓓ	7. Ⓐ Ⓑ Ⓒ ●	9. Ⓐ ● Ⓒ Ⓓ
2. Ⓐ Ⓑ ● Ⓓ	4. Ⓐ Ⓑ ● Ⓓ	6. Ⓐ ● Ⓒ Ⓓ	8. Ⓐ Ⓑ ● Ⓓ	10. Ⓐ Ⓑ Ⓒ ●

TEST 2

1. Ⓐ ● Ⓒ Ⓓ	3. ● Ⓑ Ⓒ Ⓓ	5. Ⓐ ● Ⓒ Ⓓ	7. Ⓐ Ⓑ ● Ⓓ	9. Ⓐ ● Ⓒ Ⓓ
2. Ⓐ Ⓑ ● Ⓓ	4. Ⓐ Ⓑ ● Ⓓ	6. ● Ⓑ Ⓒ Ⓓ	8. Ⓐ ● Ⓒ Ⓓ	10. Ⓐ Ⓑ Ⓒ ●

TEST 3

1. Ⓐ ● Ⓒ Ⓓ	3. Ⓐ Ⓑ Ⓒ ●	5. Ⓐ ● Ⓒ Ⓓ	7. Ⓐ ● Ⓒ Ⓓ	9. ● Ⓑ Ⓒ Ⓓ
2. Ⓐ ● Ⓒ Ⓓ	4. Ⓐ Ⓑ ● Ⓓ	6. Ⓐ Ⓑ Ⓒ ●	8. Ⓐ Ⓑ Ⓒ ●	10. Ⓐ Ⓑ ● Ⓓ

TEST 4

1. Ⓐ Ⓑ ● Ⓓ	3. ● Ⓑ Ⓒ Ⓓ	5. Ⓐ ● Ⓒ Ⓓ	7. Ⓐ Ⓑ ● Ⓓ	9. ● Ⓑ Ⓒ Ⓓ
2. Ⓐ Ⓑ ● Ⓓ	4. Ⓐ Ⓑ Ⓒ ●	6. Ⓐ ● Ⓒ Ⓓ	8. Ⓐ Ⓑ ● Ⓓ	10. Ⓐ ● Ⓒ Ⓓ

TEST 5

1. Ⓐ Ⓑ Ⓒ ●	3. Ⓐ ● Ⓒ Ⓓ	5. Ⓐ Ⓑ Ⓒ ●	7. Ⓐ ● Ⓒ Ⓓ	9. Ⓐ ● Ⓒ Ⓓ
2. Ⓐ Ⓑ ● Ⓓ	4. Ⓐ ● Ⓒ Ⓓ	6. Ⓐ ● Ⓒ Ⓓ	8. Ⓐ Ⓑ Ⓒ ●	10. Ⓐ Ⓑ ● Ⓓ

TEST 6

1. Ⓐ Ⓑ ● Ⓓ	3. Ⓐ Ⓑ Ⓒ ●	5. Ⓐ Ⓑ ● Ⓓ	7. Ⓐ Ⓑ Ⓒ ●	9. Ⓐ ● Ⓒ Ⓓ
2. Ⓐ ● Ⓒ Ⓓ	4. Ⓐ ● Ⓒ Ⓓ	6. ● Ⓑ Ⓒ Ⓓ	8. ● Ⓑ Ⓒ Ⓓ	10. Ⓐ Ⓑ Ⓒ ●

TEST 7

1. Ⓐ Ⓑ ● Ⓓ	3. Ⓐ Ⓑ ● Ⓓ	5. Ⓐ ● Ⓒ Ⓓ	7. Ⓐ Ⓑ ● Ⓓ	9. Ⓐ ● Ⓒ Ⓓ
2. ● Ⓑ Ⓒ Ⓓ	4. ● Ⓑ Ⓒ Ⓓ	6. Ⓐ Ⓑ ● Ⓓ	8. Ⓐ Ⓑ Ⓒ ●	10. Ⓐ ● Ⓒ Ⓓ

TEST 8

1. Ⓐ Ⓑ ● Ⓓ	3. Ⓐ ● Ⓒ Ⓓ	5. Ⓐ ● Ⓒ Ⓓ	7. Ⓐ Ⓑ ● Ⓓ	9. ● Ⓑ Ⓒ Ⓓ
2. Ⓐ ● Ⓒ Ⓓ	4. Ⓐ Ⓑ Ⓒ ●	6. Ⓐ Ⓑ Ⓒ ●	8. Ⓐ ● Ⓒ Ⓓ	10. Ⓐ Ⓑ Ⓒ ●

ANTONYM TEST ANSWER KEY

TEST 9

1. B	3. C	5. C	7. C	9. D
2. D	4. A	6. B	8. C	10. C

TEST 10

1. C	3. C	5. C	7. A	9. A
2. B	4. A	6. B	8. D	10. A

SENTENCE COMPLETION TEST
ANSWER KEY

TEST 1

1. Ⓐ Ⓑ ● Ⓓ	4. Ⓐ Ⓑ Ⓒ ●	7. Ⓐ Ⓑ ● Ⓓ	10. ● Ⓑ Ⓒ Ⓓ
2. Ⓐ Ⓑ Ⓒ ●	5. Ⓐ ● Ⓒ Ⓓ	8. Ⓐ Ⓑ ● Ⓓ	11. Ⓐ Ⓑ ● Ⓓ
3. Ⓐ Ⓑ ● Ⓓ	6. ● Ⓑ Ⓒ Ⓓ	9. Ⓐ Ⓑ ● Ⓓ	12. Ⓐ Ⓑ ● Ⓓ

TEST 2

1. Ⓐ ● Ⓒ Ⓓ	4. Ⓐ ● Ⓒ Ⓓ	7. Ⓐ Ⓑ ● Ⓓ	10. Ⓐ ● Ⓒ Ⓓ
2. Ⓐ Ⓑ Ⓒ ●	5. Ⓐ Ⓑ ● Ⓓ	8. Ⓐ Ⓑ Ⓒ ●	11. Ⓐ Ⓑ Ⓒ ●
3. Ⓐ Ⓑ ● Ⓓ	6. Ⓐ ● Ⓒ Ⓓ	9. Ⓐ ● Ⓒ Ⓓ	12. Ⓐ Ⓑ ● Ⓓ

TEST 3

1. ● Ⓑ Ⓒ Ⓓ	4. ● Ⓑ Ⓒ Ⓓ	7. Ⓐ Ⓑ ● Ⓓ	10. Ⓐ Ⓑ Ⓒ ●
2. Ⓐ ● Ⓒ Ⓓ	5. Ⓐ Ⓑ Ⓒ ●	8. Ⓐ Ⓑ ● Ⓓ	11. Ⓐ Ⓑ ● Ⓓ
3. Ⓐ Ⓑ ● Ⓓ	6. ● Ⓑ Ⓒ Ⓓ	9. Ⓐ ● Ⓒ Ⓓ	12. Ⓐ ● Ⓒ Ⓓ

TEST 4

1. Ⓐ Ⓑ Ⓒ ●	4. Ⓐ ● Ⓒ Ⓓ	7. ● Ⓑ Ⓒ Ⓓ	10. Ⓐ Ⓑ ● Ⓓ
2. Ⓐ Ⓑ Ⓒ ●	5. Ⓐ ● Ⓒ Ⓓ	8. Ⓐ Ⓑ ● Ⓓ	11. Ⓐ Ⓑ Ⓒ ●
3. Ⓐ Ⓑ ● Ⓓ	6. Ⓐ ● Ⓒ Ⓓ	9. Ⓐ Ⓑ Ⓒ ●	12. ● Ⓑ Ⓒ Ⓓ

TEST 5

1. Ⓐ ● Ⓒ Ⓓ	4. Ⓐ ● Ⓒ Ⓓ	7. Ⓐ ● Ⓒ Ⓓ	10. Ⓐ Ⓑ ● Ⓓ
2. Ⓐ Ⓑ ● Ⓓ	5. Ⓐ Ⓑ Ⓒ ●	8. Ⓐ Ⓑ Ⓒ ●	11. ● Ⓑ Ⓒ Ⓓ
3. Ⓐ Ⓑ ● Ⓓ	6. ● Ⓑ Ⓒ Ⓓ	9. Ⓐ ● Ⓒ Ⓓ	12. Ⓐ ● Ⓒ Ⓓ

TEST 6

1. Ⓐ Ⓑ ● Ⓓ	4. ● Ⓑ Ⓒ Ⓓ	7. ● Ⓑ Ⓒ Ⓓ	10. ● Ⓑ Ⓒ Ⓓ
2. Ⓐ Ⓑ ● Ⓓ	5. Ⓐ Ⓑ Ⓒ ●	8. Ⓐ Ⓑ Ⓒ ●	11. Ⓐ ● Ⓒ Ⓓ
3. ● Ⓑ Ⓒ Ⓓ	6. Ⓐ Ⓑ Ⓒ ●	9. Ⓐ Ⓑ ● Ⓓ	12. Ⓐ Ⓑ ● Ⓓ

TEST 7

1. Ⓐ Ⓑ Ⓒ ●	4. ● Ⓑ Ⓒ Ⓓ	7. Ⓐ Ⓑ ● Ⓓ	10. Ⓐ Ⓑ Ⓒ ●
2. ● Ⓑ Ⓒ Ⓓ	5. Ⓐ ● Ⓒ Ⓓ	8. Ⓐ Ⓑ Ⓒ ●	11. Ⓐ Ⓑ ● Ⓓ
3. Ⓐ ● Ⓒ Ⓓ	6. Ⓐ Ⓑ Ⓒ ●	9. Ⓐ ● Ⓒ Ⓓ	12. Ⓐ ● Ⓒ Ⓓ

SENTENCE COMPLETION TEST
ANSWER KEY

TEST 8

1.	●BCD	4.	ABC●	7.	AB●D	10.	ABC●
2.	A●CD	5.	AB●D	8.	AB●D	11.	A●CD
3.	●BCD	6.	ABC●	9.	ABC●	12.	●BCD

TEST 9

1.	AB●D	4.	ABC●	7.	ABC●	10.	●BCD
2.	●BCD	5.	A●CD	8.	ABC●	11.	AB●D
3.	A●CD	6.	A●CD	9.	ABC●	12.	●BCD

TEST 10

1.	ABC●	4.	A●CD	7.	A●CD	10.	AB●D
2.	●BCD	5.	AB●D	8.	AB●D	11.	●BCD
3.	●BCD	6.	●BCD	9.	ABC●	12.	AB●D

VERBAL ANALOGY ANSWER KEY

TEST 1

1. Ⓐ ● Ⓒ Ⓓ   3. Ⓐ Ⓑ ● Ⓓ   5. Ⓐ ● Ⓒ Ⓓ   7. ● Ⓑ Ⓒ Ⓓ   9. Ⓐ Ⓑ ● Ⓓ
2. Ⓐ ● Ⓒ Ⓓ   4. Ⓐ Ⓑ ● Ⓓ   6. Ⓐ Ⓑ ● Ⓓ   8. Ⓐ Ⓑ Ⓒ ●   10. Ⓐ ● Ⓒ Ⓓ

1. **(B)** To intimidate is to inspire fear; to astonish is to inspire wonder.

2. **(B)** A stove is often part of a kitchen; a sink is often part of a bathroom.

3. **(C)** You happily celebrate a marriage; you sorrowfully lament a bereavement.

4. **(C)** Margarine is a manufactured substitute for butter; nylon is a manufactured substitute for silk.

5. **(B)** A person may be negligent in meeting a requirement; he may similarly be remiss in performing his duty.

6. **(C)** A gazelle is known to be swift; a swan is known to be graceful.

7. **(A)** One falls into ignominy if he shows disloyalty; one gains fame if he shows heroism.

8. **(D)** *Saturnine* and *mercurial* are antonyms; so are *allegro* and *adagio*.

9. **(C)** Marmalade is made from oranges; ketchup is made from tomatoes.

10. **(B)** An apostate is banished (sent away); an ally is welcomed (brought in).

TEST 2

1. Ⓐ Ⓑ Ⓒ ●   3. Ⓐ Ⓑ Ⓒ ●   5. Ⓐ Ⓑ Ⓒ ●   7. ● Ⓑ Ⓒ Ⓓ   9. ● Ⓑ Ⓒ Ⓓ
2. Ⓐ Ⓑ ● Ⓓ   4. Ⓐ ● Ⓒ Ⓓ   6. Ⓐ Ⓑ ● Ⓓ   8. Ⓐ ● Ⓒ Ⓓ   10. Ⓐ ● Ⓒ Ⓓ

1. **(D)** All four are round: circle, sphere, wheel, and orange.

2. **(C)** Open is the opposite of secretive; forthright is the opposite of snide.

3. **(D)** When you affirm, you are direct; when you hint, you are indirect. When you charge, you are direct; when you insinuate, you are indirect.

4. **(B)** One throws a ball and one shoots a gun.

5. **(D)** A greyhound is proverbially speedy; on the other hand, a sloth is proverbially sluggish.

6. **(C)** A triangle is a three-sided plane figure; a pyramid is a three-sided solid figure. A square is a four-sided plane figure; a box is a four-sided solid figure.

7. **(A)** To impeach is to charge or challenge; if the impeachment proceedings are successful, the charged person is dismissed. To arraign is to call into court as a result of accusation; if the accusation is proved correct, the arraigned person is convicted.

8. **(B)** To emulate is to imitate another person's good points; to mimic is to imitate everything about another person. To praise is to speak well of another person's good points; to flatter is to praise everything about another person.

9. **(A)** For people the horny sheaths at the end of the hand are called nails; for animals the horny sheaths at the end of the paws are called claws.

10. **(B)** A diamond is a partially compressed square; an ellipse is a partially compressed circle.

VERBAL ANALOGY ANSWER KEY

TEST 3

1. Ⓐ ● Ⓒ Ⓓ   3. ● Ⓑ Ⓒ Ⓓ   5. ● Ⓑ Ⓒ Ⓓ   7. Ⓐ Ⓑ ● Ⓓ   9. Ⓐ Ⓑ Ⓒ ●
2. Ⓐ Ⓑ ● Ⓓ   4. Ⓐ Ⓑ ● Ⓓ   6. Ⓐ Ⓑ Ⓒ ●   8. Ⓐ ● Ⓒ Ⓓ   10. Ⓐ ● Ⓒ Ⓓ

1. **(B)** A woodsman cuts with an axe; a carpenter cuts with a saw.

2. **(C)** Bigotry breeds hatred; fanaticism breeds intolerance.

3. **(A)** When you assist, you help; when you save, you help a great deal. When you request, you ask; when you command, you are very strong in what you ask for.

4. **(C)** $2\frac{1}{2} \times 2 = 5$; $2\frac{1}{2} \times 6 = 15$.

5. **(A)** A doubleheader has two parts; a trident has three teeth. Twins are two of a kind; a troika is a vehicle drawn by three horses.

6. **(D)** A flower is part of a bouquet; a link is part of a chain.

7. **(C)** Letters make up a word; pages make up a book.

8. **(B)** $36 \div 9 = 4$; $9 \div 9 = 1$.

9. **(D)** A germ often causes disease; a war often causes destruction.

10. **(B)** The top of the wave is the crest; the top of the mountain is the peak.

TEST 4

1. Ⓐ Ⓑ Ⓒ ●   3. Ⓐ ● Ⓒ Ⓓ   5. Ⓐ Ⓑ ● Ⓓ   7. Ⓐ ● Ⓒ Ⓓ   9. Ⓐ Ⓑ Ⓒ ●
2. Ⓐ Ⓑ ● Ⓓ   4. Ⓐ Ⓑ ● Ⓓ   6. Ⓐ ● Ⓒ Ⓓ   8. Ⓐ Ⓑ Ⓒ ●   10. ● Ⓑ Ⓒ Ⓓ

1. **(D)** Control results in order; anarchy results in chaos.

2. **(C)** One creates something by carving wood; one creates something by molding clay.

3. **(B)** A border separates one state from another; a fence separates one property from another.

4. **(C)** A soldier is part of a regiment; a star is part of a constellation.

5. **(C)** *Apogee* and *perigee* are opposites; so are *inappropriate* and *apposite*.

6. **(B)** A refugee seeks asylum; a traveler seeks a destination.

7. **(B)** One who is greatly worried may become hysterical; one who is very happy may well be ecstatic.

8. **(D)** A word may be disguised by a charade; a message may be disguised by a code.

9. **(D)** A player is part of a team; a fish is part of a school.

10. **(A)** A banana is one of several bananas in a bunch; a city is one of several cities in a state.

VERBAL ANALOGY ANSWER KEY

TEST 5

1. Ⓐ Ⓑ Ⓒ ●   3. Ⓐ Ⓑ ● Ⓓ   5. Ⓐ Ⓑ ● Ⓓ   7. Ⓐ Ⓑ Ⓒ ●   9. Ⓐ Ⓑ ● Ⓓ
2. Ⓐ ● Ⓒ Ⓓ   4. Ⓐ ● Ⓒ Ⓓ   6. ● Ⓑ Ⓒ Ⓓ   8. Ⓐ Ⓑ Ⓒ ●   10. Ⓐ ● Ⓒ Ⓓ

1. **(D)** A moth will injure clothing; a stigma will injure a reputation.

2. **(B)** Lincoln is the capital of Nebraska; Trenton is the capital of New Jersey.

3. **(C)** The words *buzz* and *hum* are onomatopoetic; so are the words *tinkle* and *clang*.

4. **(B)** A boxer uses gloves in his profession; a bacteriologist uses a microscope in his profession.

5. **(C)** Consideration is a likely preliminary before making a decision; a wish is preliminary to the fulfillment of that wish.

6. **(A)** An illusion is a mirage; a haunter is a specter.

7. **(D)** France is a country in Europe; Algeria is a country in Africa.

8. **(D)** A person who is invulnerable cannot be hurt by an insult; a city which is impregnable cannot be hurt by an assault.

9. **(C)** Poison often results in death; kindness often results in cooperation.

10. **(B)** Slate is a type of rock; a kayak is a type of boat.

TEST 6

1. Ⓐ Ⓑ ● Ⓓ   3. Ⓐ ● Ⓒ Ⓓ   5. Ⓐ ● Ⓒ Ⓓ   7. ● Ⓑ Ⓒ Ⓓ   9. Ⓐ ● Ⓒ Ⓓ
2. ● Ⓑ Ⓒ Ⓓ   4. Ⓐ Ⓑ ● Ⓓ   6. Ⓐ Ⓑ ● Ⓓ   8. Ⓐ Ⓑ ● Ⓓ   10. Ⓐ ● Ⓒ Ⓓ

1. **(C)** Law controls the citizen; reins control the horse.

2. **(A)** Joy is a milder form of ecstasy; admiration is a milder form of love.

3. **(B)** A level of larceny is grand larceny; a level of school is elementary school.

4. **(C)** An antiseptic kills germs; a lion kills his prey.

5. **(B)** One rides a horse; one plays an instrument.

6. **(C)** One employs a clue to unlock a mystery; one uses a key to unlock a door.

7. **(A)** One sharpens a pencil and one saws wood.

8. **(C)** Garbage leads to a condition of squalor; diamonds lead to a condition of magnificence.

9. **(B)** A myth is a type of story; a bonnet is a type of hat.

10. **(B)** One who is a dunce is certainly not clever; one who has courage is certainly not fearful.

VERBAL ANALOGY ANSWER KEY

TEST 7

1. Ⓐ Ⓑ ● Ⓓ   3. Ⓐ Ⓑ Ⓒ ●   5. Ⓐ Ⓑ ● Ⓓ   7. Ⓐ ● Ⓒ Ⓓ   9. Ⓐ ● Ⓒ Ⓓ
2. Ⓐ Ⓑ ● Ⓓ   4. Ⓐ ● Ⓒ Ⓓ   6. Ⓐ Ⓑ ● Ⓓ   8. ● Ⓑ Ⓒ Ⓓ   10. Ⓐ Ⓑ Ⓒ ●

1. **(C)** A crown (when worn) indicates a royal state; a crucifix (when worn) indicates a religious attachment.

2. **(C)** An island is surrounded by the ocean; an oasis is surrounded by the desert.

3. **(D)** Mathematics is the science of numbers and numerology is the occult science of numbers; astronomy is the science of celestial bodies and astrology is the occult science of celestial bodies.

4. **(B)** To be abhorrent is to be extremely dislikable; to be arduous is to be extremely difficult.

5. **(C)** A retinue attends a person of rank such as a monarch; the moon is a satellite (smaller body attending upon a larger one)

attending upon and revolving round the earth.

6. **(C)** A cord is a wood unit of measurement; a quart is a milk unit of measurement.

7. **(B)** A minaret is a high tower attached to a mosque; a steeple is a high structure rising above a church.

8. **(A)** Chaff is that worthless part of the wheat left over after threshing; dregs are the worthless residue in the process of making wine.

9. **(B)** A director is responsible for the production of the drama; an editor is responsible for the publication of the magazine.

10. **(D)** A cliché is always commonplace; a maxim is always terse.

TEST 8

1. Ⓐ Ⓑ Ⓒ ●   3. ● Ⓑ Ⓒ Ⓓ   5. Ⓐ Ⓑ Ⓒ ●   7. Ⓐ Ⓑ Ⓒ ●   9. Ⓐ Ⓑ ● Ⓓ
2. Ⓐ ● Ⓒ Ⓓ   4. Ⓐ Ⓑ ● Ⓓ   6. Ⓐ ● Ⓒ Ⓓ   8. ● Ⓑ Ⓒ Ⓓ   10. Ⓐ Ⓑ Ⓒ ●

1. **(D)** A person may become affluent because of luck; a person may become impoverished because of laziness.

2. **(B)** A piccolo is a wind instrument pitched an octave higher than an ordinary flute, whereas a tuba is a much larger and lower-pitched wind instrument; a violin, in comparison with a bass, is smaller and higher-pitched.

3. **(A)** To be thrilled is to be extremely pleased; to be drunken is to be extremely tipsy.

4. **(C)** A sin is immoral; a crime is illegal.

5. **(D)** An ellipse is a kind of curve; a square is a kind of polygon.

6. **(B)** Saccharin is a chemical compound used as a substitute for sugar; margarine, made from vegetable oils and milk, is a substitute for butter.

7. **(D)** To demand is to request in a strong manner; to crave is to wish in a strong manner.

8. **(A)** A faucet controls the flow of water; a throttle controls the flow of fuel.

9. **(C)** A flask is a smaller version of a bottle; a brochure is a smaller version of a tome.

10. **(D)** Some people have an insatiable desire (greed) for money; some have an insatiable desire (voracity) for food.

VERBAL ANALOGY ANSWER KEY

TEST 9

1. (A) (B) ● (D) 3. (A) (B) ● (D) 5. ● (B) (C) (D) 7. (A) ● (C) (D) 9. (A) (B) ● (D)
2. ● (B) (C) (D) 4. (A) ● (C) (D) 6. (A) (B) (C) ● 8. (A) ● (C) (D) 10. (A) (B) (C) ●

1. **(C)** To be bald is to lack hair. In a drought there is a lack of rain.

2. **(A)** A ship is a synonym for boat, and a volume for book.

3. **(C)** A scythe symbolizes death, as an arrow symbolizes love.

4. **(B)** A carnivore eats animals; a vegetarian eats vegetables.

5. **(A)** Mauve is a color, and basil is a spice.

6. **(D)** To muffle something is almost to silence it. To stymie something is almost to defeat it.

7. **(B)** *Paucity* is a synonym for *dearth,* and *shortage* for *scarcity.*

8. **(B)** Paper is sometimes identified by a watermark, and a person by a birthmark.

9. **(C)** A person who is extremely bright is brilliant. A person who is extremely contented is overjoyed.

10. **(D)** Discipline brings about order rather than disorder. Training brings about preparation rather than lack of preparation.

TEST 10

1. (A) (B) (C) ● 3. (A) (B) ● (D) 5. (A) (B) (C) ● 7. (A) (B) (C) ● 9. (A) ● (C) (D)
2. (A) (B) ● (D) 4. (A) ● (C) (D) 6. (A) ● (C) (D) 8. (A) (B) (C) ● 10. (A) (B) (C) ●

1. **(D)** A news report is descriptive of an event, but a commercial is prescriptive, recommending rather than describing.

2. **(C)** A consensus is a general agreement. *Tranquil* and *pacific* both mean peaceful.

3. **(C)** *Hydraulic* describes something that is operated by means of water; *pneumatic* describes something that is operated by means of air.

4. **(B)** A horse is usually kept and fed in a stable; a hog is usually kept and fed in a sty. The parallel to horse and hog would be chicken, not hen.

5. **(D)** The actor plays a role, as a ballplayer plays a position.

6. **(B)** The prow is the forward part of the ship, as the nose is the forward part of the airplane.

7. **(D)** *Maximum* and *minimum* mark extremes in quantity, as do *most* and *least.*

8. **(D)** One can counteract a sensation with an anesthetic and a poison with an antidote.

9. **(B)** One leaves a ship by disembarking and a horse by dismounting.

10. **(D)** Meat is a food that supplies us with protein; potatoes are a food that supplies us with starch.

VERBAL ANALOGY ANSWER KEY

TEST 11

1. ●ⒷⒸⒹ   3. Ⓐ●ⒸⒹ   5. ●ⒷⒸⒹ   7. ⒶⒷ●Ⓓ   9. Ⓐ●ⒸⒹ
2. ⒶⒷ●Ⓓ   4. ⒶⒷⒸ●   6. Ⓐ●ⒸⒹ   8. ⒶⒷⒸ●   10. ⒶⒷ●Ⓓ

1. **(A)** The nape is the back of the neck, and the heel is the back of the foot.

2. **(C)** Pliers are designed for gripping, and a jack for elevating.

3. **(B)** The radius moves from the center of the circle to the edge, as the spoke moves from the center of the wheel to the edge.

4. **(D)** A misdemeanor, though serious, is not as serious as a felony. Though something that is cracked is damaged, it is not as seriously damaged as a broken object.

5. **(A)** A hygrometer is used to measure humidity, and a thermometer, temperature.

6. **(B)** As *astute* is in emphatic opposition to *stupid,* so *agile* is in opposition to *clumsy.*

7. **(C)** A whale is a mammal that is mistakenly thought to be a fish, and a bat is a mammal that is mistakenly thought to be a bird.

8. **(D)** A prospector seeks gold, and a detective seeks a clue.

9. **(B)** A couplet makes up part of a poem, and a sentence makes up part of a paragraph.

10. **(C)** Oil is extracted from the earth by means of a well, and silver by means of a mine.

TEST 12

1. ●ⒷⒸⒹ   3. ⒶⒷⒸ●   5. Ⓐ●ⒸⒹ   7. ●ⒷⒸⒹ   9. ⒶⒷ●Ⓓ
2. Ⓐ●ⒸⒹ   4. ⒶⒷ●Ⓓ   6. ⒶⒷ●Ⓓ   8. Ⓐ●ⒸⒹ   10. ●ⒷⒸⒹ

1. **(A)** A rudder is used in directing a ship. A wheel is used in directing a car.

2. **(B)** A stallion and a rooster are two different animals of the same sex, as are a mare and a hen.

3. **(D)** We assimilate a book through reading, and a record through listening.

4. **(C)** A parrot and a sparrow are two very different sorts of birds. A goldfish and a guppy are two very different sorts of fish.

5. **(B)** Muscles are connected to bone by tendons just as bones are connected to bones by ligaments.

6. **(C)** Food that is insipid is dull and uninteresting, whereas spicy food can be said to be exciting.

7. **(A)** A burl is an outgrowth of a tree, and a pearl is an outgrowth of an oyster.

8. **(B)** Yeast is used as a leaven, and iodine as an antiseptic. These functions are more specific than aspirin's function as a medicine.

9. **(C)** A polygon has numerous sides. A square has four sides.

10. **(A)** Passages can be eliminated by expurgation, and leaves by defoliation.

PART IV
BUILDING AND TESTING YOUR SPELLING SKILLS

IMPROVING YOUR SPELLING SKILLS

Spelling questions require careful attention to detail. You can raise your spelling score by working to improve your ability in each of these areas:

- **VISUAL MEMORY** helps you to remember the spelling of words you may have seen only once or twice.

- **SPELLING RULES** are generalizations about certain spelling situations. These can help you to spell special groups of words.

- **RESPONSE STRATEGIES** will explain the most efficient way to answer spelling questions.

PLANNING A STRATEGY

- Read the directions thoroughly. Carefully note which word you are asked to find—the incorrectly spelled word? the misspelled word? the correctly spelled word?

- Read through each item carefully. Examine each word before choosing a response.

- Answer the easiest questions first. Tackle the more difficult items next.

- Eliminate obviously wrong answers immediately. Try to eliminate as many choices as possible before you take a guess.

- If the test directions discourage guessing, don't respond to any question unless you can first eliminate at least one, and preferably two, choices.

HOW TO ANSWER THE QUESTIONS

Spelling questions usually use several formats. Regardless of format, you are usually given four or five answer choices.

The most common type of spelling question provides a list of words and asks you to find the one that is *incorrectly* spelled.

EXAMPLE: (A) enclosure (B) reinforcement   The incorrectly spelled word
(C) analycis (D) antidote   in this group is (C). The
correct spelling is *analysis*.

EXAMPLE: (A) liability (B) cappacity   The incorrectly spelled word
                (C) guidance (D) illegible   in this group is (B). The
                                                correct spelling is *capacity*.

A spelling question may be written so that all but one word are misspelled. You are asked to find the one correctly spelled word.

EXAMPLE: (A) attitude (B) soloes   The correctly spelled word is (A).
                (C) occured (D) policys

EXAMPLE: (A) purchace (B) oponent   The correctly spelled word is (C).
                (C) criticism (D) origional

A third type of test question measures your ability to detect misspelled words in a text. A series of sentences are given; all except one contain misspelled words. You are asked to find the completely correct sentence in the group.

EXAMPLE: (A) Learning another langue will undoubedly enable you to apreciate your vacaton more.
                (B) The easiest way to learn is by studying with casette recordings of the languge.
                (C) A booklet accompanies the recordings, explaining the grammar of the language.
                (D) This combination alows you to learn quickly and easly.

The correctly spelled sentence is (C).

A fourth type of spelling test is a list of words, both correctly and incorrectly spelled. You are asked to identify those spelled incorrectly and to spell them correctly.

EXAMPLE: 1. keepsake   4. evaporate
                2. eufemism   5. carnival
                3. kilogram   6. carreer

The answers are (2) and (6). The correct spellings are *euphemism* and *career*.

EIGHT EASY SPELLING RULES

SPELLING RULE 1

- **If a one-syllable word ends with a short vowel and one consonant, DOUBLE THE FINAL CONSONANT before adding a suffix that begins with a vowel.**

-er	-er, -est	-y	-en	-ing	-ed
blotter	biggest	baggy	bidden	budding	rubbed
chopper	dimmer	blurry	bitten	quitting	scarred
clipper	fattest	funny	fatten	clipping	skipped
fitter	flatter	furry	flatten	dropping	stabbed
hopper	gladdest	muddy	gladden	fanning	stepped
plotter	grimmer	sloppy	hidden	fretting	stopped
quitter	hottest	starry	madden	grinning	tanned
shipper	madder	stubby	sadden	gripping	nodded
shopper	reddest	sunny	trodden	hopping	plotted

- **DO NOT DOUBLE THE FINAL CONSONANT if the word ends in two consonants, if the final consonant is preceded by a double vowel, or if the suffix begins with a consonant.**

-ing, -ed, -er	-ly	-ness	-ful	-y
acting	badly	baseness	boastful	dirty
burned	dimly	bigness	baleful	dusky
cooker	gladly	coldness	doleful	fishy
climber	madly	dimness	fitful	frosty
coasting	manly	fatness	fretful	leafy
farmer	nearly	grimness	sinful	misty
feared	sadly	sadness		rainy
feasting	thinly	redness		soapy
quoted	trimly	wetness		weedy

SPELLING RULE 2

- If a word of more than one syllable ends with a short vowel and one consonant, DOUBLE THE FINAL CONSONANT before adding a suffix that begins with a vowel, if the accent is on the last syllable.

-ing, ed	-ence, -ent	-ance	-at
befitting	abhorrence	acquittance	acquittal
befogged	concurrent	admittance	transmittal
committing	excellence	remittance	noncommittal
compelled	intermittent		
controlling	occurrence		
disbarred	recurrent		
impelling			
incurred			
omitting			

	-er	-en	-able
permitted			
propelling	beginner	forbidden	controllable
regretted	propeller	forgotten	forgettable
submitting	transmitter		regrettable

- DO NOT DOUBLE THE FINAL CONSONANT if the word ends in two consonants, if the final consonant is preceded by a double vowel, if the accent is not on the last syllable, or if the suffix begins with a consonant.

ENDING IN 2 CONSONANTS	2 VOWELS BEFORE THE FINAL CONSONANT	ACCENT NOT ON THE FINAL SYLLABLE	SUFFIX BEGINS WITH A CONSONANT
-ing, -ed	-ing, -ed	-ing, ed	-ment
consenting	concealing	benefiting	allotment
converted	contained	blossomed	annulment
demanding	detaining	differed	commitment
diverted	disdained	gathered	deferment
requesting	refraining	limiting	equipment
subsisted	remounted	profited	interment
supplanting	restraining	quarreling	preferment
supported	retained	soliciting	
transcending	revealing	summoned	

SPELLING RULE 3

If a word ends with a silent *e* . . .

- **DROP THE *E* before adding a suffix that begins with a vowel.**

-ing, -ed	-able	-ation	-ive
achieving	believable	admiration	abusive
balanced	debatable	continuation	appreciative
believing	desirable	declaration	creative
capsized	endurable	derivation	decorative
relieved	excitable	duplication	expensive
revolving	imaginable	exhalation	exclusive
telephoned	measurable	inclination	illustrative
trembling	observable	inhalation	intensive
trembled	pleasurable	quotation	repulsive

- **DO NOT DROP THE *E* before a suffix that begins with a consonant.**

-ful	-ment	-ly	-ness
careful	achievement	accurately	completeness
disgraceful	amusement	affectionately	cuteness
distasteful	announcement	bravely	fineness
fateful	engagement	extremely	genuineness
hopeful	enlargement	genuinely	lameness
prideful	enslavement	immediately	lateness
tasteful	entanglement	intensely	likeness
vengeful	management	intimately	ripeness
wasteful	replacement	sincerely	whiteness

EXCEPTIONS			
acknowledgment	changeable	judgment	peaceable
acreage	chargeable	manageable	pronounceable
advantageous	duly	noticeable	replaceable
argument	dyeing	outrageous	serviceable
awful	exchanging		

SPELLING RULE 4

To make a word plural . . .

• ADD -*ES* to words ending in *s, x, l, ch,* or *sh*.	
annexes	fizzes
birches	hoaxes
brushes	marshes
caresses	witnesses
coaches	

• ADD -*S* to all other words.	
advantages	croutons
angles	distances
beacons	effects
briquets	rings
candles	

SPELLING RULE 5

If a word ends with a *y* that has a vowel sound . . .

• CHANGE THE *Y* TO *I* before adding any suffix except one that begins with *i*.			
-er, -est, -ly, -ness	-ous	-ance, -ant	-able, -ful
craftier	ceremonious	alliance	beautiful
daintiest	harmonious	appliance	fanciful
healthier	industrious	compliant	justifiable
heavily	injurious	defiant	merciful
moldiness	luxurious	pliant	pitiable
moodiest	melodious	reliance	pliable
murkiness	mysterious		
steadily	studious		
sleepiness	victorious		

• DO NOT CHANGE THE *Y* if it is preceded by another vowel, or if the suffix begins with *i*.
-ing
allaying
applying
complying
relaying
multiplying
sprayer
grayer
player

EXCEPTIONS	
-ly, -ness	-ous
dryly	beauteous
dryness	bounteous
shyly	miscellaneous
shyness	piteous
slyly	plenteous
slyness	
spryly	
wryly	

SPELLING RULE 6

Put *i* before *e*, except after *c*, or when sounded like *a*, as in *neighbor* or *weigh*.

I BEFORE *E* EXCEPT AFTER *C* OR SOUNDS LIKE *A*			EXCEPTIONS
achieve	conceit	deign	ancient
believe	conceive	eight	conscience
fiend	ceiling	freight	deficient
fierce	deceit	inveigh	efficient
grief	deceive	neighbor	either
relieve	perceive	reign	foreign
reprieve	receipt	skein	glacier
retrieve	receive	vein	heifer
sieve		weigh	leisure
			neither
			proficient
			weird

SPELLING RULE 7

The suffix *-ful* never has two *l*'s. When *-ful* is added to a word, the spelling of the base word does not change.

EXAMPLES		
careful	disdainful	distasteful
forceful	grateful	hopeful
masterful	powerful	sorrowful

SPELLING RULE 8

When the suffix *-ly* is added to a word, the spelling of the base word does not change.

EXAMPLES	EXCEPTIONS		
frankly	When the base word ends with *-ble*, the *-ble* is changed to *-bly*.		
quickly			
coyly	forcibly	despicably	illegibly
forcefully	indelibly	probably	suitably
swiftly			
	When the base word ends with a *y* following a consonant, the *y* is changed to *i* before *-ly*.		
	busily	daintily	heavily
	luckily	merrily	sleepily

400 FREQUENTLY MISSPELLED WORDS

A poor speller can, in almost every case, become an excellent speller with perseverance and practice. The first step in spelling improvement is to find out which words are troublesome for you. The list that follows contains some of the most frequently misspelled words. Ask a friend to dictate this list to you. Write each word as it is read to you, then compare what you have written with the printed list. Place an X next to each word that you spelled incorrectly (and next to each word that you spelled correctly but were not sure of). For every word you misspelled:

1. LOOK at the word carefully.
2. PRONOUNCE each syllable clearly.
3. PICTURE the word in your mind.
4. WRITE the word correctly at least three times.

Test yourself again—and again—until you have mastered this entire list.

A

aberration
abscess
absence
abundance
accessible
accidental
accommodate
accumulation
accurately
achievement
acknowledgment
acquaint
address
adjunct
affectionate
aggravate
aisle
alleged
all right
amateur
amendment
American
ancestor
ancient
anecdote
annoyance
antarctic
anticipate
apparatus
apparently

arctic
argue
arraignment
arrange
ascertain
asparagus
assessment
assistance
attaché
audience
August
author
available
awkward

B

bankruptcy
barbarian
barren
basically
beautiful
because
beggar
begun
beleaguered
besiege
bewilder
bicycle
breathe
bulletin

bureau
burial

C

cabinet
cafeteria
caffeine
calendar
campaign
capital
capitol
career
ceiling
cemetery
changeable
character
charlatan
chauffeur
chief
chimney
choose
college
column
committal
committee
community
competitor
confectionery
conscience
conscious
consequence

conquer
consul
continuous
correlation
counsel
courageous
criticism
crucial
crystallized
culpable
currency
curtain
customer

D

dairy
deceit
December
decide
deferred
demur
derogatory
desecrated
desert
descendant
desperate
dessert
diary
dictatorship
difficulty
dilapidated
diphtheria
disappearance
disappoint
disastrous
disease
dismal
dissatisfied
distinguished
doubt
dying

E

ecstasy
eczema
eight
either
embarrass
eminent
emphasis
emphatically
ephemeral

equipment
essential
exaggerate
exceed
except
exercise
exhaust
exhibition
exhortation
existence
explain
extension
extraordinary

F

familiar
fascinated
February
feudal
fiend
fierce
financier
freight
Friday
friend
forehead
foreign
foreword
forfeit
forward
furniture
further

G

gaseous
gelatin
geography
ghost
gingham
glacier
glandular
gnash
gonorrhea
government
grammar
grain
grandeur
grievous
guarantee
guard
guess
guidance

H

hallelujah
harassed
hearth
heathen
heavily
height
heinous
heretic
heritage
heroes
hieroglyphic
hindrance
hippopotamus
horrify
humorous
hundredth
hygienic
hymn
hypocrisy

I

imaginary
immediate
imminent
impartiality
incongruous
incumbent
independent
indict
inimitable
instantaneous
integrity
intercede
interference
interruption
introduce
irreparably

J

January
jealous
jeopardy
jewelry
journal
judgment
judicial
justice
justification

K

kernel
kindergarten

kiln
kilometer
kilowatt
kitchen
knee
knot
knowledge

L

laboratory
labyrinth
lacquer
leisure
legible
length
lieutenant
lightning
liquidate
literature
loneliness
loose
lovable

M

maintenance
maneuver
marriage
masquerade
materialize
mathematics
matinee
mechanical
medallion
medicine
medieval
memoir
mischievous
misspell
muscle

N

naturally
necessary
negligible
neither
nickel
niece
ninth
noticeable
nucleus

O

oasis
obligatory
obsolescence
occasion
occurrence
official
omitted
ordinance
outrageous

P

pamphlet
panicky
parallel
paraphernalia
parliamentary
patient
peculiar
persuade
physician
picnicking
pneumonia
possession
precious
preferred
prejudice
presumptuous
privilege
propaganda
publicity
punctilious
pursuit

Q

quarrel
queue
quiescent
quiet
quite
quotient

R

receipt
recognize
reference
regrettable
rehearsal
relevant
religious
renascence
repetitious

requirement
reservoir
resilience
resources
restaurant
resurrection
rhetorical
rhythm
ridiculous
routine

S

sacrilegious
scenery
schedule
scissors
secretary
separate
siege
seizure
sophomore
source
sovereign
specialized
specifically
statute
staunch
subversive
succeed
sufficient
surgeon
surgical
surely
stationary
stationery
symmetrical
sympathetic

T

temperamental
temperature
tendency
thorough
through
tomorrow
tragedy
transferred
transient
truculent
Tuesday
typical

U–Z

umbrella
unctious
undoubtedly
unique
unusual
usage
usual
vacillate
vacuum

valuable
variety
vegetable
veil
vengeance
villain
Wednesday
weight
weird
whether

wholesome
wholly
wield
wouldn't
written
Xerox
xylophone
yacht
yield
zombie

SPELLING TEST ANSWER SHEET

TEST 1

1. Ⓐ Ⓑ Ⓒ Ⓓ	7. Ⓐ Ⓑ Ⓒ Ⓓ	13. Ⓐ Ⓑ Ⓒ Ⓓ	19. Ⓐ Ⓑ Ⓒ Ⓓ	25. Ⓐ Ⓑ Ⓒ Ⓓ
2. Ⓐ Ⓑ Ⓒ Ⓓ	8. Ⓐ Ⓑ Ⓒ Ⓓ	14. Ⓐ Ⓑ Ⓒ Ⓓ	20. Ⓐ Ⓑ Ⓒ Ⓓ	26. Ⓐ Ⓑ Ⓒ Ⓓ
3. Ⓐ Ⓑ Ⓒ Ⓓ	9. Ⓐ Ⓑ Ⓒ Ⓓ	15. Ⓐ Ⓑ Ⓒ Ⓓ	21. Ⓐ Ⓑ Ⓒ Ⓓ	27. Ⓐ Ⓑ Ⓒ Ⓓ
4. Ⓐ Ⓑ Ⓒ Ⓓ	10. Ⓐ Ⓑ Ⓒ Ⓓ	16. Ⓐ Ⓑ Ⓒ Ⓓ	22. Ⓐ Ⓑ Ⓒ Ⓓ	28. Ⓐ Ⓑ Ⓒ Ⓓ
5. Ⓐ Ⓑ Ⓒ Ⓓ	11. Ⓐ Ⓑ Ⓒ Ⓓ	17. Ⓐ Ⓑ Ⓒ Ⓓ	23. Ⓐ Ⓑ Ⓒ Ⓓ	29. Ⓐ Ⓑ Ⓒ Ⓓ
6. Ⓐ Ⓑ Ⓒ Ⓓ	12. Ⓐ Ⓑ Ⓒ Ⓓ	18. Ⓐ Ⓑ Ⓒ Ⓓ	24. Ⓐ Ⓑ Ⓒ Ⓓ	30. Ⓐ Ⓑ Ⓒ Ⓓ

TEST 2

1. Ⓐ Ⓑ Ⓒ Ⓓ	7. Ⓐ Ⓑ Ⓒ Ⓓ	13. Ⓐ Ⓑ Ⓒ Ⓓ	19. Ⓐ Ⓑ Ⓒ Ⓓ	25. Ⓐ Ⓑ Ⓒ Ⓓ
2. Ⓐ Ⓑ Ⓒ Ⓓ	8. Ⓐ Ⓑ Ⓒ Ⓓ	14. Ⓐ Ⓑ Ⓒ Ⓓ	20. Ⓐ Ⓑ Ⓒ Ⓓ	26. Ⓐ Ⓑ Ⓒ Ⓓ
3. Ⓐ Ⓑ Ⓒ Ⓓ	9. Ⓐ Ⓑ Ⓒ Ⓓ	15. Ⓐ Ⓑ Ⓒ Ⓓ	21. Ⓐ Ⓑ Ⓒ Ⓓ	27. Ⓐ Ⓑ Ⓒ Ⓓ
4. Ⓐ Ⓑ Ⓒ Ⓓ	10. Ⓐ Ⓑ Ⓒ Ⓓ	16. Ⓐ Ⓑ Ⓒ Ⓓ	22. Ⓐ Ⓑ Ⓒ Ⓓ	28. Ⓐ Ⓑ Ⓒ Ⓓ
5. Ⓐ Ⓑ Ⓒ Ⓓ	11. Ⓐ Ⓑ Ⓒ Ⓓ	17. Ⓐ Ⓑ Ⓒ Ⓓ	23. Ⓐ Ⓑ Ⓒ Ⓓ	29. Ⓐ Ⓑ Ⓒ Ⓓ
6. Ⓐ Ⓑ Ⓒ Ⓓ	12. Ⓐ Ⓑ Ⓒ Ⓓ	18. Ⓐ Ⓑ Ⓒ Ⓓ	24. Ⓐ Ⓑ Ⓒ Ⓓ	30. Ⓐ Ⓑ Ⓒ Ⓓ

TEST 3

1. Ⓐ Ⓑ Ⓒ Ⓓ	7. Ⓐ Ⓑ Ⓒ Ⓓ	13. Ⓐ Ⓑ Ⓒ Ⓓ	19. Ⓐ Ⓑ Ⓒ Ⓓ	25. Ⓐ Ⓑ Ⓒ Ⓓ
2. Ⓐ Ⓑ Ⓒ Ⓓ	8. Ⓐ Ⓑ Ⓒ Ⓓ	14. Ⓐ Ⓑ Ⓒ Ⓓ	20. Ⓐ Ⓑ Ⓒ Ⓓ	26. Ⓐ Ⓑ Ⓒ Ⓓ
3. Ⓐ Ⓑ Ⓒ Ⓓ	9. Ⓐ Ⓑ Ⓒ Ⓓ	15. Ⓐ Ⓑ Ⓒ Ⓓ	21. Ⓐ Ⓑ Ⓒ Ⓓ	27. Ⓐ Ⓑ Ⓒ Ⓓ
4. Ⓐ Ⓑ Ⓒ Ⓓ	10. Ⓐ Ⓑ Ⓒ Ⓓ	16. Ⓐ Ⓑ Ⓒ Ⓓ	22. Ⓐ Ⓑ Ⓒ Ⓓ	28. Ⓐ Ⓑ Ⓒ Ⓓ
5. Ⓐ Ⓑ Ⓒ Ⓓ	11. Ⓐ Ⓑ Ⓒ Ⓓ	17. Ⓐ Ⓑ Ⓒ Ⓓ	23. Ⓐ Ⓑ Ⓒ Ⓓ	29. Ⓐ Ⓑ Ⓒ Ⓓ
6. Ⓐ Ⓑ Ⓒ Ⓓ	12. Ⓐ Ⓑ Ⓒ Ⓓ	18. Ⓐ Ⓑ Ⓒ Ⓓ	24. Ⓐ Ⓑ Ⓒ Ⓓ	30. Ⓐ Ⓑ Ⓒ Ⓓ

TEST 4

1. Ⓐ Ⓑ Ⓒ Ⓓ	7. Ⓐ Ⓑ Ⓒ Ⓓ	13. Ⓐ Ⓑ Ⓒ Ⓓ	19. Ⓐ Ⓑ Ⓒ Ⓓ	25. Ⓐ Ⓑ Ⓒ Ⓓ
2. Ⓐ Ⓑ Ⓒ Ⓓ	8. Ⓐ Ⓑ Ⓒ Ⓓ	14. Ⓐ Ⓑ Ⓒ Ⓓ	20. Ⓐ Ⓑ Ⓒ Ⓓ	26. Ⓐ Ⓑ Ⓒ Ⓓ
3. Ⓐ Ⓑ Ⓒ Ⓓ	9. Ⓐ Ⓑ Ⓒ Ⓓ	15. Ⓐ Ⓑ Ⓒ Ⓓ	21. Ⓐ Ⓑ Ⓒ Ⓓ	27. Ⓐ Ⓑ Ⓒ Ⓓ
4. Ⓐ Ⓑ Ⓒ Ⓓ	10. Ⓐ Ⓑ Ⓒ Ⓓ	16. Ⓐ Ⓑ Ⓒ Ⓓ	22. Ⓐ Ⓑ Ⓒ Ⓓ	28. Ⓐ Ⓑ Ⓒ Ⓓ
5. Ⓐ Ⓑ Ⓒ Ⓓ	11. Ⓐ Ⓑ Ⓒ Ⓓ	17. Ⓐ Ⓑ Ⓒ Ⓓ	23. Ⓐ Ⓑ Ⓒ Ⓓ	29. Ⓐ Ⓑ Ⓒ Ⓓ
6. Ⓐ Ⓑ Ⓒ Ⓓ	12. Ⓐ Ⓑ Ⓒ Ⓓ	18. Ⓐ Ⓑ Ⓒ Ⓓ	24. Ⓐ Ⓑ Ⓒ Ⓓ	30. Ⓐ Ⓑ Ⓒ Ⓓ

TEST 5

1. Ⓐ Ⓑ Ⓒ Ⓓ	7. Ⓐ Ⓑ Ⓒ Ⓓ	13. Ⓐ Ⓑ Ⓒ Ⓓ	19. Ⓐ Ⓑ Ⓒ Ⓓ	25. Ⓐ Ⓑ Ⓒ Ⓓ
2. Ⓐ Ⓑ Ⓒ Ⓓ	8. Ⓐ Ⓑ Ⓒ Ⓓ	14. Ⓐ Ⓑ Ⓒ Ⓓ	20. Ⓐ Ⓑ Ⓒ Ⓓ	26. Ⓐ Ⓑ Ⓒ Ⓓ
3. Ⓐ Ⓑ Ⓒ Ⓓ	9. Ⓐ Ⓑ Ⓒ Ⓓ	15. Ⓐ Ⓑ Ⓒ Ⓓ	21. Ⓐ Ⓑ Ⓒ Ⓓ	27. Ⓐ Ⓑ Ⓒ Ⓓ
4. Ⓐ Ⓑ Ⓒ Ⓓ	10. Ⓐ Ⓑ Ⓒ Ⓓ	16. Ⓐ Ⓑ Ⓒ Ⓓ	22. Ⓐ Ⓑ Ⓒ Ⓓ	28. Ⓐ Ⓑ Ⓒ Ⓓ
5. Ⓐ Ⓑ Ⓒ Ⓓ	11. Ⓐ Ⓑ Ⓒ Ⓓ	17. Ⓐ Ⓑ Ⓒ Ⓓ	23. Ⓐ Ⓑ Ⓒ Ⓓ	29. Ⓐ Ⓑ Ⓒ Ⓓ
6. Ⓐ Ⓑ Ⓒ Ⓓ	12. Ⓐ Ⓑ Ⓒ Ⓓ	18. Ⓐ Ⓑ Ⓒ Ⓓ	24. Ⓐ Ⓑ Ⓒ Ⓓ	

SPELLING TEST ANSWER SHEET

TEST 6

1. Ⓐ Ⓑ Ⓒ Ⓓ	4. Ⓐ Ⓑ Ⓒ Ⓓ	7. Ⓐ Ⓑ Ⓒ Ⓓ	10. Ⓐ Ⓑ Ⓒ Ⓓ	13. Ⓐ Ⓑ Ⓒ Ⓓ
2. Ⓐ Ⓑ Ⓒ Ⓓ	5. Ⓐ Ⓑ Ⓒ Ⓓ	8. Ⓐ Ⓑ Ⓒ Ⓓ	11. Ⓐ Ⓑ Ⓒ Ⓓ	14. Ⓐ Ⓑ Ⓒ Ⓓ
3. Ⓐ Ⓑ Ⓒ Ⓓ	6. Ⓐ Ⓑ Ⓒ Ⓓ	9. Ⓐ Ⓑ Ⓒ Ⓓ	12. Ⓐ Ⓑ Ⓒ Ⓓ	15. Ⓐ Ⓑ Ⓒ Ⓓ

TEST 7

1. Ⓒ Ⓘ	21. Ⓒ Ⓘ	41. Ⓒ Ⓘ	61. Ⓒ Ⓘ	81. Ⓒ Ⓘ
2. Ⓒ Ⓘ	22. Ⓒ Ⓘ	42. Ⓒ Ⓘ	62. Ⓒ Ⓘ	82. Ⓒ Ⓘ
3. Ⓒ Ⓘ	23. Ⓒ Ⓘ	43. Ⓒ Ⓘ	63. Ⓒ Ⓘ	83. Ⓒ Ⓘ
4. Ⓒ Ⓘ	24. Ⓒ Ⓘ	44. Ⓒ Ⓘ	64. Ⓒ Ⓘ	84. Ⓒ Ⓘ
5. Ⓒ Ⓘ	25. Ⓒ Ⓘ	45. Ⓒ Ⓘ	65. Ⓒ Ⓘ	85. Ⓒ Ⓘ
6. Ⓒ Ⓘ	26. Ⓒ Ⓘ	46. Ⓒ Ⓘ	66. Ⓒ Ⓘ	86. Ⓒ Ⓘ
7. Ⓒ Ⓘ	27. Ⓒ Ⓘ	47. Ⓒ Ⓘ	67. Ⓒ Ⓘ	87. Ⓒ Ⓘ
8. Ⓒ Ⓘ	28. Ⓒ Ⓘ	48. Ⓒ Ⓘ	68. Ⓒ Ⓘ	88. Ⓒ Ⓘ
9. Ⓒ Ⓘ	29. Ⓒ Ⓘ	49. Ⓒ Ⓘ	69. Ⓒ Ⓘ	89. Ⓒ Ⓘ
10. Ⓒ Ⓘ	30. Ⓒ Ⓘ	50. Ⓒ Ⓘ	70. Ⓒ Ⓘ	90. Ⓒ Ⓘ
11. Ⓒ Ⓘ	31. Ⓒ Ⓘ	51. Ⓒ Ⓘ	71. Ⓒ Ⓘ	91. Ⓒ Ⓘ
12. Ⓒ Ⓘ	32. Ⓒ Ⓘ	52. Ⓒ Ⓘ	72. Ⓒ Ⓘ	92. Ⓒ Ⓘ
13. Ⓒ Ⓘ	33. Ⓒ Ⓘ	53. Ⓒ Ⓘ	73. Ⓒ Ⓘ	93. Ⓒ Ⓘ
14. Ⓒ Ⓘ	34. Ⓒ Ⓘ	54. Ⓒ Ⓘ	74. Ⓒ Ⓘ	94. Ⓒ Ⓘ
15. Ⓒ Ⓘ	35. Ⓒ Ⓘ	55. Ⓒ Ⓘ	75. Ⓒ Ⓘ	95. Ⓒ Ⓘ
16. Ⓒ Ⓘ	36. Ⓒ Ⓘ	56. Ⓒ Ⓘ	76. Ⓒ Ⓘ	96. Ⓒ Ⓘ
17. Ⓒ Ⓘ	37. Ⓒ Ⓘ	57. Ⓒ Ⓘ	77. Ⓒ Ⓘ	97. Ⓒ Ⓘ
18. Ⓒ Ⓘ	38. Ⓒ Ⓘ	58. Ⓒ Ⓘ	78. Ⓒ Ⓘ	98. Ⓒ Ⓘ
19. Ⓒ Ⓘ	39. Ⓒ Ⓘ	59. Ⓒ Ⓘ	79. Ⓒ Ⓘ	99. Ⓒ Ⓘ
20. Ⓒ Ⓘ	40. Ⓒ Ⓘ	60. Ⓒ Ⓘ	80. Ⓒ Ⓘ	100. Ⓒ Ⓘ

SPELLING TEST ANSWER SHEET

TEST 8

1. Ⓐ Ⓑ Ⓒ Ⓓ	7. Ⓐ Ⓑ Ⓒ Ⓓ	13. Ⓐ Ⓑ Ⓒ Ⓓ	19. Ⓐ Ⓑ Ⓒ Ⓓ	25. Ⓐ Ⓑ Ⓒ Ⓓ
2. Ⓐ Ⓑ Ⓒ Ⓓ	8. Ⓐ Ⓑ Ⓒ Ⓓ	14. Ⓐ Ⓑ Ⓒ Ⓓ	20. Ⓐ Ⓑ Ⓒ Ⓓ	26. Ⓐ Ⓑ Ⓒ Ⓓ
3. Ⓐ Ⓑ Ⓒ Ⓓ	9. Ⓐ Ⓑ Ⓒ Ⓓ	15. Ⓐ Ⓑ Ⓒ Ⓓ	21. Ⓐ Ⓑ Ⓒ Ⓓ	27. Ⓐ Ⓑ Ⓒ Ⓓ
4. Ⓐ Ⓑ Ⓒ Ⓓ	10. Ⓐ Ⓑ Ⓒ Ⓓ	16. Ⓐ Ⓑ Ⓒ Ⓓ	22. Ⓐ Ⓑ Ⓒ Ⓓ	28. Ⓐ Ⓑ Ⓒ Ⓓ
5. Ⓐ Ⓑ Ⓒ Ⓓ	11. Ⓐ Ⓑ Ⓒ Ⓓ	17. Ⓐ Ⓑ Ⓒ Ⓓ	23. Ⓐ Ⓑ Ⓒ Ⓓ	29. Ⓐ Ⓑ Ⓒ Ⓓ
6. Ⓐ Ⓑ Ⓒ Ⓓ	12. Ⓐ Ⓑ Ⓒ Ⓓ	18. Ⓐ Ⓑ Ⓒ Ⓓ	24. Ⓐ Ⓑ Ⓒ Ⓓ	30. Ⓐ Ⓑ Ⓒ Ⓓ

TEST 9

1. Ⓐ Ⓑ Ⓒ Ⓓ	7. Ⓐ Ⓑ Ⓒ Ⓓ	13. Ⓐ Ⓑ Ⓒ Ⓓ	19. Ⓐ Ⓑ Ⓒ Ⓓ	25. Ⓐ Ⓑ Ⓒ Ⓓ
2. Ⓐ Ⓑ Ⓒ Ⓓ	8. Ⓐ Ⓑ Ⓒ Ⓓ	14. Ⓐ Ⓑ Ⓒ Ⓓ	20. Ⓐ Ⓑ Ⓒ Ⓓ	26. Ⓐ Ⓑ Ⓒ Ⓓ
3. Ⓐ Ⓑ Ⓒ Ⓓ	9. Ⓐ Ⓑ Ⓒ Ⓓ	15. Ⓐ Ⓑ Ⓒ Ⓓ	21. Ⓐ Ⓑ Ⓒ Ⓓ	27. Ⓐ Ⓑ Ⓒ Ⓓ
4. Ⓐ Ⓑ Ⓒ Ⓓ	10. Ⓐ Ⓑ Ⓒ Ⓓ	16. Ⓐ Ⓑ Ⓒ Ⓓ	22. Ⓐ Ⓑ Ⓒ Ⓓ	28. Ⓐ Ⓑ Ⓒ Ⓓ
5. Ⓐ Ⓑ Ⓒ Ⓓ	11. Ⓐ Ⓑ Ⓒ Ⓓ	17. Ⓐ Ⓑ Ⓒ Ⓓ	23. Ⓐ Ⓑ Ⓒ Ⓓ	29. Ⓐ Ⓑ Ⓒ Ⓓ
6. Ⓐ Ⓑ Ⓒ Ⓓ	12. Ⓐ Ⓑ Ⓒ Ⓓ	18. Ⓐ Ⓑ Ⓒ Ⓓ	24. Ⓐ Ⓑ Ⓒ Ⓓ	30. Ⓐ Ⓑ Ⓒ Ⓓ

TEST 10

1. Ⓒ Ⓘ ___	4. Ⓒ Ⓘ ___	7. Ⓒ Ⓘ ___	10. Ⓒ Ⓘ ___	13. Ⓒ Ⓘ ___
2. Ⓒ Ⓘ ___	5. Ⓒ Ⓘ ___	8. Ⓒ Ⓘ ___	11. Ⓒ Ⓘ ___	14. Ⓒ Ⓘ ___
3. Ⓒ Ⓘ ___	6. Ⓒ Ⓘ ___	9. Ⓒ Ⓘ ___	12. Ⓒ Ⓘ ___	15. Ⓒ Ⓘ ___

Total Number of Questions 339
Total Incorrect −
_____
Total Correct = _____ × .29 = _____%
Score

SPELLING TEST ONE

DIRECTIONS: *This test gives four suggested spellings for each word listed. Choose the spelling you know to be* correct *and mark your answer accordingly. Correct answers to this test will be found at the end of the chapter.*

1. (A) transeint (B) transient (C) trancient (D) transent
2. (A) heratage (B) heritage (C) heiritage (D) heretage
3. (A) exibition (B) exhibition (C) exabition (D) exhebition
4. (A) intiative (B) enitiative (C) initative (D) initiative
5. (A) similiar (B) simmilar (C) similar (D) simuler
6. (A) sufficiantly (B) sufisiently (C) sufficiently (D) suficeintly
7. (A) anticipate (B) antisipate (C) anticapate (D) antisapate
8. (A) intelligence (B) inteligence (C) intellegence (D) intelegence
9. (A) referance (B) referrence (C) referense (D) reference
10. (A) conscious (B) consious (C) conscius (D) consceous
11. (A) paralell (B) parellel (C) parellell (D) parallel
12. (A) abundence (B) abundance (C) abundants (D) abundents
13. (A) spesifically (B) specificaly (C) specifically (D) specefically
14. (A) elemanate (B) elimenate (C) elliminate (D) eliminate
15. (A) resonance (B) resonnance (C) resonence (D) reasonance

16. (A) benaficial (B) beneficial (C) benefitial (D) bennaficial
17. (A) retrievable (B) retreivable (C) retrievible (D) retreavable
18. (A) collosal (B) colossal (C) colosal (D) collossal
19. (A) inflameable (B) inflamable (C) enflamabel (D) inflammable
20. (A) auxillary (B) auxilliary (C) auxilary (D) auxiliary
21. (A) corregated (B) corrigated (C) corrugated (D) coregated
22. (A) accumalation (B) accumulation (C) acumulation (D) accumullation
23. (A) consumation (B) consummation (C) consumeation (D) consomation
24. (A) retorical (B) rhetorical (C) rhetorrical (D) retorrical
25. (A) inimitable (B) iminitable (C) innimitable (D) inimitible
26. (A) proletarian (B) prolletarian (C) prolatarian (D) proleterian
27. (A) appelate (B) apellate (C) appellate (D) apelate
28. (A) esential (B) essencial (C) essential (D) essantial
29. (A) assessment (B) assesment (C) asessment (D) assesmant
30. (A) ordinence (B) ordinnance (C) ordinanse (D) ordinance

SPELLING TEST TWO

DIRECTIONS: *This test gives four suggested spellings for each word listed. Choose the spelling you know to be* correct *and mark your answer accordingly. Correct answers to this test will be found at the end of the chapter.*

1. (A) disapearance (B) disappearance
    (C) disappearense (D) disappearence

2. (A) attendence (B) attendanse
    (C) attendance (D) atendance

3. (A) acertain (B) assertain
    (C) ascertain (D) asertain

4. (A) specimen (B) speciman
    (C) spesimen (D) speceman

5. (A) relevant (B) relevent
    (C) rellevent (D) relavant

6. (A) anesthetic (B) aenesthetic
    (C) anestitic (D) annesthetic

7. (A) foriegn (B) foreign
    (C) forriegn (D) forreign

8. (A) interuption (B) interruption
    (C) interrupsion (D) interrupcion

9. (A) acquiesence (B) acquiescence
    (C) aquiescense (D) acquiesance

10. (A) exceed (B) exsede
    (C) exseed (D) excede

11. (A) maneuver (B) manuver
    (C) maneuvere (D) manneuver

12. (A) correlation (B) corrolation
    (C) corellation (D) corralation

13. (A) hinderence (B) hindranse
    (C) hindrance (D) hindrence

14. (A) existence (B) existance
    (C) existense (D) existince

15. (A) bankrupcy (B) bankruptcy
    (C) bankruptsy (D) bankrupsy

16. (A) receipts (B) receits
    (C) reciepts (D) recieps

17. (A) impromtu (B) inpromtu
    (C) impromptu (D) impromptue

18. (A) pronounciation (B) pronunciatun
    (C) pronunciation (D) pronounciatun

19. (A) entirly (B) entirely
    (C) entirley (D) entireley

20. (A) complecation (B) complicasion
    (C) complication (D) complacation

21. (A) condem (B) condemn
    (C) condemm (D) condenm

22. (A) ocassion (B) occassion
    (C) ocasion (D) occasion

23. (A) contagious (B) contageous
    (C) contagous (D) contagiose

24. (A) perminent (B) permenant
    (C) permanent (D) permanant

25. (A) proceed (B) procede
    (C) prosede (D) proseed

26. (A) embarassment (B) embarrasment
    (C) embarasment (D) embarrassment

27. (A) cematary (B) cemetary
    (C) cemitery (D) cemetery

28. (A) believable (B) believeable
    (C) believeble (D) believible

29. (A) council (B) counsil
    (C) counsle (D) councel

30. (A) achievement (B) acheivment
    (C) achievment (D) acheivement

SPELLING TEST THREE

DIRECTIONS: *This test gives four suggested spellings for each word listed. Choose the spelling you know to be* correct *and mark your answer accordingly. Correct answers to this test will be found at the end of the chapter.*

1. (A) Wendesday   (B) Wensday
   (C) Wednesday   (D) Wendnesday

2. (A) classify   (B) classafy
   (C) classefy   (D) classifey

3. (A) concensus   (B) concencus
   (C) consencus   (D) consensus

4. (A) suffiscent   (B) sufficient
   (C) sufficiant   (D) suffiscient

5. (A) responsable   (B) responseable
   (C) responsibil   (D) responsible

6. (A) remittence   (B) remmittence
   (C) remmittance   (D) remittance

7. (A) probible   (B) probable
   (C) probbable   (D) probabil

8. (A) weigt   (B) wieght
   (C) weight   (D) waight

9. (A) argument   (B) argumint
   (C) argumant   (D) arguement

10. (A) priceing   (B) prising
    (C) priseing   (D) pricing

11. (A) ballanced   (B) balanced
    (C) balansed   (D) balanct

12. (A) operateing   (B) oparating
    (C) oparrating   (D) operating

13. (A) privelege   (B) privilege
    (C) privelige   (D) privilige

14. (A) expenses   (B) expences
    (C) expensses   (D) expensces

15. (A) mispell   (B) misspell
    (C) misspel   (D) mispel

16. (A) occurrance   (B) occurence
    (C) occurrence   (D) ocurrence

17. (A) changable   (B) changeable
    (C) changible   (D) changeabel

18. (A) conscience   (B) conscence
    (C) consciense   (D) conscense

19. (A) deterent   (B) deterrant
    (C) deterant   (D) deterrent

20. (A) exagerate   (B) exagerrate
    (C) exaggerate   (D) exaggerrate

21. (A) noticable   (B) noticible
    (C) noticeable   (D) noticeble

22. (A) passable   (B) passible
    (C) passeble   (D) passeable

23. (A) dissplaid   (B) displayed
    (C) dissplayed   (D) displaid

24. (A) tryeing   (B) trieing
    (C) trying   (D) triing

25. (A) imaterial   (B) immaterial
    (C) imaterrial   (D) imatterial

26. (A) balancing   (B) balanceing
    (C) balansing   (D) balanseing

27. (A) conceed   (B) consede
    (C) concede   (D) conseed

28. (A) innumerible   (B) innumerable
    (C) inumerable   (D) inumerible

29. (A) maintainance   (B) maintenance
    (C) maintenance   (D) maintanance

30. (A) guarantee   (B) guarantie
    (C) garantee   (B) guarrantee

SPELLING TEST FOUR

DIRECTIONS: Each of the following four word groups contains one word that is spelled correctly. Choose the correctly spelled word. Correct answers to this test will be found at the end of the chapter.

1. (A) authority (B) similiar
    (C) refering (D) preferebly

2. (A) suficient (B) wheather
    (C) acuteally (D) minimum

3. (A) volentary (B) syllabus
    (C) embodyeing (D) pertanent

4. (A) simplified (B) comunity
    (C) emfasis (D) advant

5. (A) approppriate (B) expedient
    (C) adopshun (D) satisfactarily

6. (A) unconsiously (B) pamflet
    (C) asess (D) adjacent

7. (A) mortgages (B) infalible
    (C) eradecated (D) sourse

8. (A) predescessor (B) obsolete
    (C) unimpared (D) sporadicaly

9. (A) impenitrable (B) recognisable
    (C) paresite (D) vigilance

10. (A) emfatically (B) manefold
    (C) anxieties (D) expence

11. (A) emfatically (B) inculcate
    (C) skilfel (D) indigense

12. (A) indespensable (B) incumbrance
    (C) intolerible (D) desicration

13. (A) exibit (B) critisism
    (C) recieved (D) conspicuous

14. (A) biennial (B) monatary
    (C) beninant (D) complacensy

15. (A) propriaty (B) legalety
    (C) acquiesce (D) conversant

16. (A) ajusted (B) porportionate
    (C) inaugurated (D) dubeous

17. (A) responsability (B) soceity
    (C) individuel (D) increments

18. (A) subordonate (B) transaction
    (C) buisness (D) effitiency

19. (A) condemnation (B) exsees
    (C) ordinerily (D) capasity

20. (A) discuscion (B) statistics
    (C) producktion (D) disguissed

21. (A) constrictive (B) proposel
    (C) partisipated (D) desision

22. (A) comtroller (B) inadequasy
    (C) resolusion (D) promotion

23. (A) progresive (B) reciepts
    (C) dependent (D) secsion

24. (A) seperate (B) speciallized
    (C) funshions (D) publicity

25. (A) instrament (B) vicinity
    (C) offical (D) journale

26. (A) unecessary
    (B) responsebility
    (C) suprintendent
    (D) recommendation

27. (A) resonable (B) curency
    (C) occur (D) critisise

28. (A) apetite (B) preliminary
    (C) concilatory (D) cruseal

29. (A) afilliation (B) amendement
    (C) ansient (D) patient

30. (A) recipeint (B) pretious
    (C) uncertainty (D) maritial

SPELLING TEST FIVE

DIRECTIONS: *In this test all words but one of each group are spelled correctly.*
Indicate the misspelled *word in each group. Correct answers to this test will be*
found at the end of this chapter.

1. (A) extraordinary   (B) statesmen
    (C) array   (D) financeer

2. (A) materialism   (B) indefatigible
    (C) moribund   (D) rebellious

3. (A) queue   (B) equillibrium
    (C) contemporary   (D) structure

4. (A) acquatic
    (B) fascinated
    (C) bogged
    (D) accommodations

5. (A) embarrassment   (B) sosialization
    (C) imposition   (D) incredulous

6. (A) politisians   (B) psychology
    (C) susceptible   (D) antipathy

7. (A) convincing   (B) vicissetudes
    (C) negligible   (D) foreign

8. (A) characters   (B) veracity
    (C) testimony   (D) apolagetic

9. (A) shriek   (B) carelogue
    (C) impeccable   (D) ruthless

10. (A) ocassions
    (B) accomplishment
    (C) assumed
    (D) distinguished

11. (A) servicable   (B) preparation
    (C) exceptional   (D) initiative

12. (A) primarely   (B) available
    (C) paragraph   (D) routine

13. (A) ligament   (B) preseding
    (C) mechanical   (D) anecdote

14. (A) judgment   (B) conclusion
    (C) circumlocution   (D) breifly

15. (A) censor   (B) personel
    (C) counterfeit   (D) advantageous

16. (A) liquifyed   (B) adage
    (C) ancient   (D) imitation

17. (A) lapse   (B) questionnaire
    (C) concieve   (D) staunch

18. (A) calendar   (B) typographical
    (C) inexcusable   (D) sallient

19. (A) carreer   (B) eminently
    (C) nevertheless   (D) fourth

20. (A) corperal   (B) sergeant
    (C) lieutenant   (D) commandant

21. (A) partial   (B) business
    (C) through   (D) comission

22. (A) accounts   (B) financial
    (C) reciept   (D) answer

23. (A) except   (B) conection
    (C) altogether   (D) credentials

24. (A) whose   (B) written
    (C) strenth   (D) therefore

25. (A) catalogue   (B) familiar
    (C) formerly   (D) secretery

26. (A) debtor   (B) shipment
    (C) fileing   (D) correspond

27. (A) courtesy   (B) dictionery
    (C) extremely   (D) exactly

28. (A) probaly   (B) directory
    (C) acquired   (D) hurriedly

29. (A) hauled   (B) freight
    (C) hankerchief   (D) millionaire

SPELLING TEST SIX

DIRECTIONS: This test measures your ability to detect misspelled words in a text. In each of the following groups of four sentences, there is only one which does not contain a misspelled word. Choose the completely correct *sentence in each group. Correct answers to this test will be found at the end of the chapter.*

1. (A) In accordance with their usual custom, the employees presented a gift to the retiring president.
   (B) It is difficult not to critisize them under the circumstances.
   (C) The company has not paid a divedend to the owners of the preferred stock since the beginning of the depression.
   (D) At the time it was thought that any improvement on the invention was impossible.

2. (A) Whether the percentage of profit was as immence as has been charged is doubtful.
   (B) In the early years of the depression, transient and local homeless were sheltered together because of their common lack of funds to pay for domicile.
   (C) It is easier and wiser to suspend judgement until the facts are known.
   (D) The responsability for the situation was put squarely on those to whom it belonged.

3. (A) The recommendations of the committee were adopted by the convention.
   (B) It is usually considered unecessary to analyse the statistics under the present circumstances.
   (C) Hearafter, the company will refuse to sell hinges on credit.
   (D) The lieutenent to whom you referred in your last letter has been transferred to another post.

4. (A) It has been found impossible to adjust the requirements.
   (B) Advancement is slow because oportunities for promotion are infrequent.
   (C) A carrear in the civil service is the ambition of the majority of young entrants.
   (D) Because he has been closly connected with the management of the enterprise for so long, he is well informed on the matter.

5. (A) The indictment supersedes the original document.
   (B) The responsibility of soceity to the individual is a matter of serious moment.
   (C) After the middle of the month, all salary incraments will be adjusted according to the new scheme of proportionate distribution.
   (D) He was given explisit directions to limit expenses as far as possible.

6. (A) They were somewhat dubious as to the propriety and quality of the procedure as contemplated.
   (B) It was certain that he would acquiese, once conversant with the full details.
   (C) Although only a bienniel publication, its influence was far-reaching and its circulation extensive.
   (D) It was difficult to arouse him to any appreciation of the monatary aspects of the situation.

7. (A) His attitude throughout was one of benign complacency, in spite of the derision of the multitude.
   (B) The exhibit deserved a more conspicious location and more favorable criticism than it received.
   (C) It should have been considered an incumbrance rather than an advantage, since it was not indespensable and added greatly to the total load.
   (D) The situation has become intolerable and further desicration of the premises should be discouraged emphatically.

8. (A) To inculcate steadfast principals of economy and skillful administration is the task that confronts us.
   (B) The degree of indigence is relative, fluctuating with the rise and fall of the country's general prosperity.

(C) The duties of the position are mane-fold, the anxieties great, and the emoluments scarcely in keeping with the expense of energy demanded.

(D) Though at first the gloom seemed impenitrable, shadows and, finally, objects became visible and later distinctly recognizable.

9. (A) Investigation into the nature of the parisites, which continually affect the vegetation, demands constant vigilance and unremitting care.

(B) The example set by his predescessor enabled him to embark on his mission secure in the confidence of the majority of the citizens.

(C) Customs which are obsolete in most communities are found sporadically in all their primitive vigor, unimpaired by the passage of time.

(D) Formerly, guaranteed morgages were considered to be infallible investments, even by the most conservative.

10. (A) The signature of every recipiant must be secured before the list of donations is turned over to the organization.

(B) The tendency to deviate from the proper scientific point of view in these matters should be eradecated at its source.

(C) The authorship of the pamphlet was recently acknowledged, and an explanation of its appearance offered.

(D) Income tax payers provided 46 per cent of all internal revenue reciepts during the last fiscal year.

11. (A) International peace is attainable, dependant only on the acceptance and application of certain principles.

(B) What is expected to become a struggle between the radical and conservative sections was precipitated today.

(C) He said that his action to stop further payments accorded with the request of the comptroler.

(D) He regarded state legislation alone as inadiquate to deal with the issue.

12. (A) The sponsors of the resolution, in a joint statement, defended their propo-

sel as a constructive step toward the promotion of world peace.

(B) A large number of persons participated in the conference.

(C) The most dramatic, and doubtless the most important, ruling was the desision of the court reversing its own previous opinion on the question of state minimum wage laws.

(D) Included in the report to be presented to the delegates as a basis for discuscion are statistics covering production in the various countries.

13. (A) He held fast to his original opinion that much of present research was disguissed promotion material.

(B) The tranquillity in which the session of the House of Representatives was ending was shattered by the bombshell of disagreement.

(C) His decision to assess adjacent property was widely condemmed.

(D) The majority of the approppriation acts and resolutions were special in nature.

14. (A) Is it expedient to amend the constitution by the adoption of the subjoined?

(B) It was the general opinion that this system had not functioned satisfactorily and that it needed to be simplefied.

(C) In the early days, protection against fire was provided by volentary fire departments.

(D) If you would oppose home rule for Illinois cities, draft a provision embodyeing your ideas as to the constitutional relationship which should exist between a state and a municipality.

15. (A) An attempt has been made to give the pertinent facts in sufficient detail so that the student may determine whether the decision actually made was sound.

(B) Should they also have been given authorety to review local bond issues under a plan similar to that adopted in Indiana?

(C) A corperal ranks below either a sergeant or a lieutenant.

(D) A carreer system is eminently desirable for the proper administration of civil service.

SPELLING TEST SEVEN

DIRECTIONS: *In the following list, some words are spelled correctly, some misspelled. On your answer sheet, blacken* C *for those words correctly spelled. Blacken* I *for each incorrectly spelled word and spell out the word correctly on the blank provided. Correct answers to this test will be found at the end of the chapter.*

1. unparalleled
2. gastliness
3. mediocrity
4. exibition
5. posessing
6. lucritive
7. coresspondence
8. accellerated
9. labirynth
10. duplisity
11. repitious
12. jepardy
13. impartiallity
14. sobriquet
15. accesable
16. incredible
17. connoisseurs
18. fallibility
19. litagation
20. piquansy
21. fuedal
22. predetory
23. desparado
24. incongruity
25. delibarate
26. competetive
27. beleaguered
28. leiutenant
29. equinoxial
30. derogatory
31. denuncietory
32. panickey
33. calendar
34. belligerence

35. abolition
36. predjudice
37. propoganda
38. adolesents
39. irresistible
40. exortation
41. renascence
42. counsil
43. bullitin
44. aberation
45. integraty
46. cristallized
47. irrepairably
48. punctillious
49. catagory
50. parlament
51. medalion
52. bountious
53. aggrevate
54. midgit
55. wierd
56. elliminate
57. murmering
58. hystrionic
59. goverment
60. clamerous
61. garantee
62. presumptious
63. comemmerate
64. indispensible
65. bookeeping
66. disatisfied
67. tremendious
68. interseed

69. inaugerate
70. rehersel
71. nucleous
72. benefiting
73. wholy
74. discription
75. alright
76. representitive
77. mischievious
78. ingenuous
79. accidently
80. exilerate
81. pronounciation
82. fourty
83. mackeral
84. rescind
85. kleptomania
86. summerize
87. resillience
88. regretable
89. questionaire
90. privelege
91. judgment
92. plagiarism
93. vengence
94. subpoena
95. rythm
96. derth
97. impromtue
98. incumbant
99. forfiet
100. maintainance

SPELLING TEST EIGHT

DIRECTIONS: In this test all words but one of each group are spelled correctly. Indicate the misspelled word in each group. Correct answers to this test will be found at the end of the chapter.

1. (A) proscenium   (B) resilient
    (C) biennial   (D) connoisseur

2. (A) queue   (B) equable
    (C) ecstacy   (D) obsequious

3. (A) quizes   (B) frolicking
    (C) maelstrom   (D) homonym

4. (A) pseudonym   (B) annihilate
    (C) questionaire   (D) irascible

5. (A) diptheria   (B) annular
    (C) acolyte   (D) descendant

6. (A) truculant   (B) rescind
    (C) dilettante   (D) innuendo

7. (A) prevalence   (B) discrete
    (C) efrontery   (D) admissible

8. (A) igneous   (B) annullment
    (C) dissipate   (D) abattoir

9. (A) quiescent   (B) apologue
    (C) myrrh   (D) inocuous

10. (A) propoganda   (B) gaseous
    (C) iridescent   (D) similar

11. (A) supercede   (B) tyranny
    (C) beauteous   (D) victuals

12. (A) geneology   (B) tragedy
    (C) soliloquy   (D) prejudice

13. (A) remittance   (B) shoeing
    (C) category   (D) gutteral

14. (A) catarrh   (B) parlamentary
    (C) villain   (D) omitted

15. (A) vengeance   (B) parallel
    (C) nineth   (D) mayoralty

16. (A) changeable   (B) therefor
    (C) incidently   (D) dissatisfy

17. (A) orifice   (B) deferrment
    (C) harass   (D) accommodate

18. (A) picnicking   (B) proceedure
    (C) hypocrisy   (D) seize

19. (A) vilify   (B) efflorescence
    (C) sarcophagus   (D) sacreligious

20. (A) paraphenalia   (B) apothecaries
    (C) occurrence   (D) plagiarize

21. (A) irreparably   (B) comparitively
    (C) lovable   (D) audible

22. (A) nullify   (B) siderial
    (C) salability   (D) irrelevant

23. (A) asinine   (B) dissonent
    (C) opossum   (D) indispensable

24. (A) discomfit   (B) sapient
    (C) exascerbate   (D) sarsaparilla

25. (A) valleys   (B) maintainance
    (C) abridgment   (D) reticence

26. (A) tolerance   (B) circumferance
    (C) insurance   (D) dominance

27. (A) diameter   (B) tangent
    (C) paralell   (D) perimeter

28. (A) providential   (B) personal
    (C) accidental   (D) diagonel

29. (A) development   (B) retarded
    (C) homogenious   (D) intelligence

30. (A) noticeable   (B) forceible
    (C) practical   (D) erasable

SPELLING TEST NINE

DIRECTIONS: In the following test, one word in each group is incorrectly spelled. On your answer sheet, blacken the letter preceding the word which is incorrectly spelled. Correct answers to this test will be found at the end of the chapter.

1. (A) census   (B) fundimental
    (C) analysis   (D) grateful

2. (A) retrieve   (B) installment
    (C) concede   (D) dissappear

3. (A) accidentaly   (B) dismissal
    (C) indelible   (D) conscientious

4. (A) perceive   (B) carreer
    (C) anticipate   (D) acquire

5. (A) assortment   (B) guidance
    (C) facillity   (D) reimburse

6. (A) advantageous   (B) pamphlet
    (C) plentiful   (D) similar

7. (A) across   (B) omission
    (C) guarrantee   (D) repel

8. (A) liable   (B) anouncement
    (C) maintenance   (D) always

9. (A) grievance   (B) altogether
    (C) pospone   (D) excessive

10. (A) commit   (B) condemn
    (C) exaggerate   (D) sieze

11. (A) absence
    (B) acknowledgment
    (C) accummulate
    (D) audible

12. (A) benificiary   (B) disbursement
    (C) incidentally   (D) exorbitant

13. (A) acquire   (B) liaison
    (C) noticable   (D) inoculate

14. (A) permissible   (B) persuade
    (C) peddler   (D) pertenant

15. (A) responsable   (B) substantial
    (C) reconciliation   (D) sizable

16. (A) innumerable   (B) revenge
    (C) applicant   (D) dictionery

17. (A) heroes   (B) folios
    (C) sopranos   (D) usuel

18. (A) typical   (B) descend
    (C) summarize   (D) continuel

19. (A) courageous   (B) recomend
    (C) omission   (D) eliminate

20. (A) compliment   (B) illuminate
    (C) auxilary   (D) installation

21. (A) preliminary   (B) aquainted
    (C) syllable   (D) analysis

22. (A) accustomed   (B) negligible
    (C) interupted   (D) bulletin

23. (A) summoned   (B) managment
    (C) mechanism   (D) sequence

24. (A) comittee   (B) surprise
    (C) noticeable   (D) emphasize

25. (A) occurrance   (B) likely
    (C) accumulate   (D) grievance

26. (A) obstacle   (B) particuliar
    (C) baggage   (D) fascinating

27. (A) written   (B) permenent
    (C) similar   (D) convenient

28. (A) cooperation   (B) duplicate
    (C) negotiable   (D) Febuary

29. (A) experience   (B) interupt
    (C) cylinder   (D) campaign

30. (A) cordialy   (B) completely
    (C) sandwich   (D) respectfully

SPELLING TEST TEN

DIRECTIONS: One word has been misspelled in some of the sentences below. Where you find a word incorrectly spelled, blacken I *and write the word out correctly on your answer sheet. If all words in the sentence are spelled* correctly, *blacken the* C *on your sheet. Correct answers to this test will be found at the end of the chapter.*

1. Amusement and pastime are nearly equivelent.

2. Hostility is enmity in action.

3. He who baffles does so by skill, forthought, address.

4. An attack is foild which is made to miss its mark.

5. The extent of one's knowledge bears a distinct relation to one's efficiency.

6. A perdicament is a situation that may be disagreeable or comical.

7. Agent's at all times should show forebearance and courtesy to passengers.

8. A successful agent is one who tends strictly to his duties.

9. Inflammable materials, such as naptha, must not be carried on subway cars.

10. A jolly, picnicing party of children was very obedient to the agent's admonition to be quiet on the train.

11. The students were eager and confident.

12. Tastefull refers to that in which the element of taste is more prominent.

13. Under all conditions a teacher must have pateince.

14. Use and useage denote the manner of using something.

15. An agent who does not report all cases of insubordination is generally surplanted by another.

SPELLING TEST ANSWER KEY

TEST 1

1. B	7. A	13. C	19. D	25. A
2. B	8. A	14. D	20. D	26. A
3. B	9. D	15. A	21. C	27. C
4. D	10. A	16. B	22. B	28. C
5. C	11. D	17. A	23. B	29. A
6. C	12. B	18. B	24. B	30. D

TEST 2

1. B	7. B	13. C	19. B	25. A
2. C	8. B	14. A	20. C	26. D
3. C	9. B	15. B	21. B	27. D
4. A	10. A	16. A	22. D	28. A
5. A	11. A	17. C	23. A	29. A
6. A	12. A	18. C	24. C	30. A

TEST 3

1. C	7. B	13. B	19. D	25. B
2. A	8. C	14. A	20. C	26. A
3. D	9. A	15. B	21. C	27. C
4. B	10. D	16. C	22. A	28. B
5. C	11. B	17. B	23. B	29. B
6. D	12. D	18. A	24. C	30. A

TEST 4

1. A	7. A	13. D	19. A	25. B
2. D	8. B	14. A	20. B	26. D
3. B	9. D	15. C	21. C	27. C
4. A	10. C	16. C	22. D	28. D
5. B	11. B	17. D	23. C	29. D
6. D	12. B	18. B	24. D	30. C

TEST 5

1. D	7. B	13. B	19. A	25. D
2. B	8. D	14. D	20. A	26. C
3. B	9. B	15. B	21. D	27. B
4. A	10. A	16. A	22. C	28. A
5. B	11. A	17. C	23. B	29. C
6. A	12. A	18. D	24. C	

SPELLING TEST ANSWER KEY

TEST 6

#	Answer	#	Answer	#	Answer	#	Answer	#	Answer
1.	A	4.	A	7.	A	10.	C	13.	B
2.	B	5.	A	8.	B	11.	B	14.	A
3.	A	6.	A	9.	C	12.	B	15.	A

TEST 7

1. correct
2. ghastliness
3. correct
4. exhibition
5. possessing
6. lucrative
7. correspondence
8. accelerated
9. labyrinth
10. duplicity
11. repetitious
12. jeopardy
13. impartiality
14. correct
15. accessible
16. correct
17. correct
18. correct
19. litigation
20. piquancy
21. feudal
22. predatory
23. desperado
24. correct
25. deliberate
26. competitive
27. correct
28. lieutenant
29. equinoctial
30. correct
31. denunciatory
32. panicky
33. correct
34. correct
35. correct
36. prejudice
37. propaganda
38. adolescents
39. correct
40. exhortation
41. correct
42. counsel, council
43. bulletin
44. aberration
45. integrity
46. crystallized
47. irreparably
48. punctilious
49. category
50. parliament
51. medallion
52. bounteous
53. aggravate
54. midget
55. weird
56. eliminate
57. murmuring
58. histrionic
59. government
60. clamorous
61. guarantee
62. presumptuous
63. commemorate
64. indispensable
65. bookkeeping
66. dissatisfied
67. tremendous
68. intercede
69. inaugurate
70. rehearsal
71. nucleus
72. correct
73. wholly
74. description
75. all right
76. representative
77. mischievous
78. correct
79. accidentally
80. exhilarate
81. pronunciation
82. forty
83. mackerel
84. correct
85. correct
86. summarize
87. resilience
88. regrettable
89. questionnaire
90. privilege
91. correct
92. correct
93. vengeance
94. correct
95. rhythm
96. dearth
97. impromptu
98. incumbent
99. forfeit
100. maintenance

TEST 8

#	Answer	#	Answer	#	Answer	#	Answer	#	Answer
1.	B	7.	C	13.	D	19.	D	25.	B
2.	C	8.	B	14.	B	20.	A	26.	B
3.	A	9.	D	15.	C	21.	B	27.	C
4.	C	10.	A	16.	C	22.	B	28.	D
5.	A	11.	A	17.	B	23.	B	29.	C
6.	A	12.	A	18.	B	24.	C	30.	B

SPELLING TEST ANSWER KEY

TEST 9

1.	Ⓐ ● Ⓒ Ⓓ	7.	Ⓐ Ⓑ ● Ⓓ	13.	Ⓐ Ⓑ ● Ⓓ	19.	Ⓐ ● Ⓒ Ⓓ	25.	● Ⓑ Ⓒ Ⓓ
2.	Ⓐ Ⓑ Ⓒ ●	8.	Ⓐ ● Ⓒ Ⓓ	14.	Ⓐ Ⓑ Ⓒ ●	20.	Ⓐ Ⓑ ● Ⓓ	26.	Ⓐ ● Ⓒ Ⓓ
3.	● Ⓑ Ⓒ Ⓓ	9.	Ⓐ Ⓑ ● Ⓓ	15.	● Ⓑ Ⓒ Ⓓ	21.	Ⓐ ● Ⓒ Ⓓ	27.	Ⓐ ● Ⓒ Ⓓ
4.	Ⓐ ● Ⓒ Ⓓ	10.	Ⓐ Ⓑ Ⓒ ●	16.	Ⓐ Ⓑ Ⓒ ●	22.	Ⓐ Ⓑ ● Ⓓ	28.	Ⓐ Ⓑ Ⓒ ●
5.	Ⓐ Ⓑ ● Ⓓ	11.	Ⓐ Ⓑ ● Ⓓ	17.	Ⓐ Ⓑ Ⓒ ●	23.	Ⓐ ● Ⓒ Ⓓ	29.	Ⓐ ● Ⓒ Ⓓ
6.	● Ⓑ Ⓒ Ⓓ	12.	● Ⓑ Ⓒ Ⓓ	18.	Ⓐ Ⓑ Ⓒ ●	24.	● Ⓑ Ⓒ Ⓓ	30.	● Ⓑ Ⓒ Ⓓ

TEST 10

1. equivalent
2. correct
3. forethought
4. foiled
5. correct
6. predicament
7. Agents
8. correct
9. naphtha
10. picnicking
11. correct
12. tasteful
13. patience
14. usage
15. supplanted

PART V
BUILDING AND TESTING YOUR GRAMMAR SKILLS

HOW THE ENGLISH LANGUAGE WORKS

It really isn't necessary to be familiar with all the labels that describe the fine points of English mechanics. If your goal is to speak and write with confidence—and to score high on tests—it's more important that you understand how and why the language works. So, briefly, before we get into the *how,* let's look at the *why.*

English is actually a hybrid of many languages, primarily Germanic and Latinate, with a healthy dose of words borrowed from just about every tongue ever spoken. This explains why English has more words and a larger proportion of **synonyms** and **antonyms** than any other language (see **Etymology,** p. 11). It also explains why we can so casually switch from calling a pair of slacks *jeans* (Italian) to *denims* (French) to *dungarees* (Hindi).

Along with this colorful blend of words comes a borrowed **grammar,** the body of rules for speaking and writing. The traditional grammar most of us learned as children is actually a description of how Latin works. English, being only partly a Latinate language, doesn't quite fit into that pattern and tends to poke out in all directions with exceptions, contradictions, and unconvincing explanations.

WORD ORDER: THE PATTERN

If you want to understand the uniqueness of the English language and *how* it works, the easiest place to start with is **word order.** Unlike many languages, English doesn't rely heavily on changes within a word itself to signal its meaning and function within a sentence. Very often our only clue is where the word occurs within the sequence of words in a sentence. Take, for example, the word *rose.* A rose is a rose, you say. True. But notice what happens in the following examples:

The *rose* stands in the vase.

She threw the *rose* over the balcony to him.

He *rose* from the chair.

She wore *rose* lipstick.

In the first example, *rose* means a particular flower and, as a noun, functions as the subject of the verb *stands.* In the second example, *rose* is still a noun, yet now it functions as the object of the verb *threw. Rose* changes meaning and function completely in the last two examples: first, as a past tense of an action having nothing to do with flowers, and second, as an adjective denoting a quality—the color of a lipstick.

Many words in English do, of course, undergo internal changes when their meanings or functions change: verbs (*rise/rose*), pronouns (*he/him*), and the plural *s* give clear signals of these changes. But, because of the subtlety of English word order, you need to pay particular attention to where a word occurs in a sentence and to its relationship to other words if you are to be sure of its meaning and function.

PARTS OF SPEECH: THE PIECES

The **parts of speech,** as we have always called them, are convenient categories for a language's words. Imagine that an entire vocabulary of a language is a pie, and that each slice is a particular "part of speech." There are words that describe physical objects and mental "objects"—**nouns,** and their substitutes, **pronouns.** There are words that signal physical activity and mental "activity"—**verbs.** There are those that denote distinguishing characteristics or qualities—**adjectives** and **adverbs.** There are linkers that point to spatial or temporal relationships—**prepositions**—or to logical relationships—**conjunctions.** And then there are the emotion words—**interjections.** When they're all wedged back together into a pie, they collectively describe the world we know and experience—objects, time, motion, feelings, and so forth.

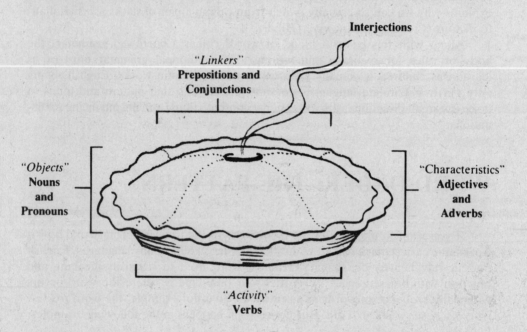

Interjections

"Linkers"
**Prepositions and
Conjunctions**

"Objects"
**Nouns
and
Pronouns**

"Characteristics"
**Adjectives
and
Adverbs**

"Activity"
Verbs

By looking at each category more closely and examining the subtle messages embedded in each word, we discover that every sentence we utter is a complex intertwining of matched parts.

Verb	*Run.*
+Noun	*Boys* run.
= Pronoun	*They* run.
+Adverbs	Boys run *very quickly.*
+Adjective	*Young* boys run very quickly.
+Preposition	Young boys run very quickly *into* the pool.
+Conjunction	Young boys *and* girls run very quickly into the pool.
+Interjection	*Wow!* Young boys and girls run very quickly into the pool!

VERBS

Verbs are the basis for all communication. Someone can come up to you and yell "Run!" and you get the message clearly. But if the same person had come up to you and yelled "Cat!" or "Vanilla-flavored!" or "Although!", you'd be left scratching your head. Strictly speaking, "Run!" includes information about **mood** (imperative), **voice** (active), **person** (2nd singular, "you" understood), and **tense** (present)—quite a bit for just three letters.

Mood is, literally, the speaker's frame of mind—factual thinking (**indicative**), wishful thinking (**subjunctive**), or forceful thinking (**imperative**). **Voice** signals the verb's relationship to its subject: a straightforward, dynamic relationship (**active**— I hit him) or a round-about, static relationship (**passive**—He was hit by me). **Person,** too, refers to a particular relationship between a subject and a verb. When we see *walks* in a sentence, we know that *he/she/it* (3rd person singular) must be before it if the pieces of the sentence are to match.

Attributes of a Verb

Mood	*I laugh.* (indicative)
	If I were laughing . . . (subjunctive)
	Laugh! (imperative)
Voice	*I moved the chair.* (active)
	The chair was moved by me. (passive)
Agreement of Persons and Number	*We don't know.* (1st person plural subject and verb)
	He doesn't know. (3rd person singular subject and verb)
Tense	*I laugh.* (present)
	We had laughed. (past perfect)
	She will be laughing. (future progressive)

Types of Verbs

Transitive	completed by a noun or pronoun
	We invited our friends.
Intransitive	completed in itself or by an adverb
	She fell. She fell down.
Copulative	a form of *is* or a sensory/seeming verb
	She is pretty. We felt bad. He appeared depressed.

Tense is a verb's time signal. There are languages with more than a dozen separate divisions of time, but in English we do quite nicely with six, the three simple tenses (**past, present, future**) and each of their **perfects.** These, too, can be subdivided into even finer points with even more subtle distinctions. The **simple** present (*I eat*) is the "always" present. The **progressive** present (*I am eating*) is the "specific" present. The **emphatic** present (*I do eat*) adds an extra measure of forcefulness to a statement.

Once we move beyond the present tense, verbs undergo complex changes. The word itself can be transformed with added-on signals (*walked*), or it can change shape internally (*eat/ate*), or it can be coupled with a form of *be* or *have* (*was walking/have eaten*). The logic behind how each verb changes is pretty much dictated by its history, and only by being thoroughly familiar with the principal parts of each verb can you be sure about the correct form of each tense.

Principal Parts of a Verb

	Present	Past	Present Perfect
Regular	walk	walked	have walked
	bathe	bathed	have bathed
Irregular	ring	rang	have rung
	eat	ate	have eaten

English Verb Time Lines

Simple Tenses	Past	Present	Future
Simple	I walked	I walk	I will walk
Progressive	I was walking	I am walking	I will be walking
Emphatic	I did walk	I do walk	———

Perfect Tenses	Past Perfect	Present Perfect	Future Perfect
	I had walked	I have walked	I will have walked
	I had walked three miles by the time you caught up with me.	I have walked three miles to get here.	I will have walked three miles by the time you catch up with me.
	activity begun and completed in the past before some other past action	activity begun in the past, completed in the present	activity begun at any time and completed in the future

Verbals are verb forms that serve as other parts of speech. Again, word order is the primary clue to the word's function, particularly since a verbal looks exactly like the verb form from which it's derived. All you have to remember is that if it stands in for another part of speech, it is bound by the same links and relationships as that part of speech would be.

Uses of Verbals

Type	Form	as adjective	as noun	as adverb
Infinitive	to ———	a book *to read*	*To swim* is fun.	He went *to play* ball.
Gerund	———ing	———	*Swimming* is fun.	———
Participle (present)	———ing + noun	a *closing* door	———	———
Participle (past)	———ed + noun	a *closed* door	———	———

NOUNS AND PRONOUNS

Nouns are those words that denote physical objects and mental concepts. Nouns, too, have extra meaning and information embedded in them, such as **number, case,** and **gender,** beyond the simple meaning of the word itself.

Number pertains to whether there's more than one of the noun (cat/cats), and is almost always signaled by the added *s*. There are a few irregularly formed plural nouns (child/children, index/indices), but they are easily memorized. There are also collective nouns that, although they refer to a group of people or objects, are treated as singular nouns (crowd is . . . , flock has . . .). It is important to remember that in a complete sentence, the verb will always agree with the number of the noun used as its subject.

Case signals a noun's particular relationship to a verb (**nominative/objective**), to a preposition (**objective**), or to another noun (**possessive**). A noun's case is determined by where it appears in the sentence's word order. Generally, if the noun is used as the verb's subject, it will come *before* the verb and will be in the **nominative case.** True, a sentence can be switched around in such a way that the subject comes *after* the verb (There *is* a *cat* on the chair). But the most economical structure for the essential meaning is the subject-verb word order (A *cat is* on the chair).

A noun in the **objective case** will look exactly like a noun in the nominative case, but it will complete the meaning of a transitive verb or a preposition by coming *after* it (Gerry opened the *door*. The box was behind the *door*). In the first example, the sentence word order can't be toyed with without making radical changes in the nature of the verb. For example: *The door was opened by Gerry* does make *door* the subject of the sentence, but the verb is now in the passive voice. In the second example, the only real alternative is *Behind the door was the box*. A bit more dramatic, perhaps, but *door* is still the object of the preposition *behind*.

Possessive case (the *man's* hat) is easily distinguished from the nominative and objective forms of the noun. The *'s* is a clear signal, and it will usually appear before the other noun, the noun "possessed." The only tip to remember is that if the noun itself ends in an *s* the apostrophe is usually sufficient to signal possessive case: *Charles' car, the DiSantos' dog, soldiers' weapons.*

Gender is usually easy enough to detect in a noun. Unlike many languages which assign masculine and feminine classifications to all nouns (signaled by such articles as *il, el, la, le*), English uses the all-purpose *the* and lets the individual noun point out its own gender when necessary. For example, we have pairs of words with clear gender distinctions, such as *ram/ewe, baron/baroness,* but the overwhelming majority of English nouns are neuter.

Pronouns are economical devices which substitute for or refer back to a noun. After we've mentioned *Mr. Smith* once in a long passage, we use *he* or *him* thereafter. In a compound or complex sentence, we do the same thing (When *the boys* saw the ice cream truck, *they* ran home for money). It's important to remember that when a pronoun is used, it must have the same number, case, and gender as the noun it stands for. Pronouns are also used for emphasis immediately after a noun (The children *themselves* wanted to rest).

Personal pronouns undergo many variations, much like verbs, as they are used in so many different ways. Because they are used to substitute for a noun in a sentence, pronouns follow the same rules of case—nominative, objective, possessive.

John owns the book. *He* owns the book.

The book belongs to *John*. The book belongs to *him*.

The *book* belongs to John. *It* belongs to John.

The book is *John's*. The book is *his*.

Functions of Pronouns

Type	Examples	Function
Demonstrative	this, that, these, those	points to
Interrogative	who, which, what	asks
Reflexive	myself, herself, themselves	reflects back
Relative	who, which, that, what	refers back to
Personal		

Number	Person	Nominative	Objective	Possessive
Singular	1st	I	me	mine
	2nd	you	you	yours
	3rd	he, she, it	him, her, it	his, hers, its
Plural	1st	we	us	ours
	2nd	you	you	yours
	3rd	they	them	theirs

ADJECTIVES AND ADVERBS

Adjectives and **adverbs** are similar in that they both supply added information about another part of speech. Adjectives are always linked to nouns and pronouns, and adverbs are always linked to verbs and adjectives. If someone asked you to rummage through a pile of laundry to find a specific sweater, it would be easier to find a *soft, blue* sweater than just a sweater. By the same token, if you were standing on a busy street corner, it would be easier for you to find the man who is walking *rapidly*—or the *rapidly* walking man—than just a man walking.

Adjectives and adverbs often look exactly the same. (The *fast* movement frightened the horse. Julio ran *fast*.) Here again, word order is the only sure clue to the word's function. Linked to *movement*, a noun, *fast* serves as an adjective. Linked to *ran*, a verb, *fast* serves as an adverb. Usually, though, an **adverb** will look like an adjective with **-ly** added to it. (The *cold* water made him shiver. Mrs. Howard eyed him *coldly*.) A quick test to distinguish between an adjective form and an adverb form of the same word would be to ask *how? when? where?* after the verb. Adverbs are natural answers to these questions.

Adjectives—any word or phrase used to illuminate a noun—are actually transformations of other parts of speech. They echo verbs (the *crying* child), nouns (a *chocolate* cake), pronouns (*their* house). And, as their primary function is to distinguish something from something else, adjectives can change their shape to show even finer distinctions: *the pretty woman* (one), *the prettier woman* (one of two), *the prettiest woman* (one of at least three). Adjectives can even signal whether we're talking about a specific item (*the* lamp) or that kind of item in general (*a* lamp).

Forms of Adjectives

Borrowed from Verb Forms

Past Participle:	a closed door	(_____-ed + noun)
Present Participle:	a closing door	(_____-ing + noun)

Borrowed from Pronoun Forms

Possessive: my, your, his, her, its, our, your, their
Demonstrative: this, that, these, those
Interrogative: whose, which, what
Indefinite: any, some, all

} + noun

PREPOSITIONS AND CONJUNCTIONS

A **preposition** performs an extremely subtle function in that it explains the relationship between the word before it (a noun or a verb) and the word after it (a noun or a pronoun). Spatial relationships (the man *in* the moon; He walked *through* the house), temporal relationships (working *since* this morning; home *by* five o'clock), possession (home *of* the brave; land *of* the free)— all are denoted by prepositions. Very often a particular preposition is so closely associated with a particular word that the two words become forged into an idiomatic expression (infer from; prior to; coincide with).

Conjunctions are another part of speech that link. Their job is to signal the logical relationship between two thoughts. Equality (I like ice cream *and* I like burritos), contradiction (He considers himself an honest man, *yet* he cheats on his taxes), concession (I don't want to go, *but* I will for your sake)—any number of logical relationships can be signaled by a conjunction.

INTERJECTIONS

Interjections, those expressive little bulges in an otherwise orderly sentence, are usually detached from the normal sequence in some way to show that they are not part of the essential meaning:

> *Ouch!* That hurts!
>
> It was—*wow!*—the weirdest thing I'd ever seen!
>
> They've sent me (*sheesh!*) another bill!

SENTENCE STRUCTURE AND PUNCTUATION: THE PATTERN REFINED

Now that we've surveyed the verbal components of a sentence, it's time to move on to the overall structure of a sentence and to those nonverbal sentence components, **punctuation marks.**

Simply put, there are only three "formulas" for forming a sentence, and each one is a variation of the basic rule: A sentence is a complete thought. We established that a complete thought can be as economical as *Run!* By the same token, as more and more links and relationships are grafted onto that economical device, a sentence can also grow to be mind-bogglingly long.

The first sentence formula is the **simple sentence:** a subject (stated or implied) and verb (Run!/He runs), or a subject, verb, and object (Peter loves Carla).

The second formula is the **compound sentence,** which is nothing more than two simple sentences (now called **clauses**) linked by a conjunction: *I work hard and I deserve a raise.*

The third formula is the **complex sentence,** where a complete thought (the main/independent clause) is linked with an incomplete thought (the subordinate/ dependent clause): *Because I was late, I wasn't able to meet you at the station.* The first part of the sentence (Because I was late) would make no sense if uttered alone, and would be called a **fragment** if written alone. Variations on these three formulas are endless, but they are the basis for communicating all complete thoughts.

Punctuation often mimics in writing what our tone of voice does in speaking. When we utter a complete thought, our voice can drop (He is a fool.), or it can rise (He is a fool?), or it can boom (He is a fool!). Thus, the **period,** the **question mark,** and the **exclamation point** are **sentence enders.**

With other punctuation marks, we can imitate hesitation (We were . . . not impressed), excitement (Robert Redford—I can't believe it!—is on the phone!), or sober formality (We request the following items: desks, chairs, lamps, rugs).

The **comma** is the most versatile (and misused) punctuation mark. Roughly speaking, it mimics a pause or dip in voice, but there are also certain agreed-upon conventions that everyone should remember about comma use. Many sample illustrations you've read in this chapter illustrate common uses of the comma. For example, when a sentence contains a series of parallel items (corn, beets, and spinach; walking, talking, and waving), the pattern is A, B, and/or C.

> Case signals a noun's particular relationship
> to a verb, to a preposition, or to another noun.
> A   ,   B   ,   and/or   C

The trend is toward leaving out the comma before the conjunction (A, B and/or C), but this pattern often results in confusion.

In a long **compound sentence,** a comma is used to separate the two clauses; if the two clauses are brief, the comma is usually not necessary.

> The house we had hoped to buy was sold before we got to the realtor's office, so we decided to call ahead next time to save ourselves the annoyance of a useless trip.

> I like ice cream and I like burritos.

In a **complex** sentence, a comma separates the incomplete thought from the complete thought when the incomplete thought comes first.

> Although she was sad, she continued to smile.

When a person is addressed directly, the name is separated from the rest of the sentence with a comma or commas.

> Jane, please come here.

> I think, Bill, that we should go now.

Commas are also used to block off any part of a sentence not absolutely essential to the basic meaning of the sentence.

She was not, however, willing to take the chance.

The customer, who had dawdled until closing, finally made his purchase.

If a sentence contains a **direct quotation,** two simple formulas can help you use the commas correctly. When the quotation begins the entire sentence, the formula is open quote, comma, closed quote (" ,").

"We might consider it," Stan said.

If the quotation ends the sentence, the formula is comma, open quote, sentence ender, closed quote (, "(./?/!)").

Mary then shouted, "I've had enough!"

Both formulas are used if a quotation is split in half within a sentence (" ," , "(./?/!)").

"I never realized," he groaned, "how heavy this is!"

Commas are also used in minor ways to indicate a pause: after salutations in a personal letter (Dear Dr. Gomez, Sincerely yours,), when writing out dates and locations (He was born on January 16, 1918, in Hoboken, New Jersey), and in certain sentence constructions where confusion would result if the reader weren't forced to pause (After planting, the farmer had his dinner).

A **colon** is a formal mark used in only two instances: to distinguish a formal business salutation (Dear Sirs:) from a personal salutation (Dear Mom,), or to indicate that the beginning statement will be amplified by either a listing (as in this sentence) or an explanation. This second usage of the colon has a curious mirror image in one of the uses of the **dash:**

These are the subjects I have taken: biology, history, drama, calculus.

Biology, history, drama, calculus—these are the subjects I have taken.

With the colon, the particulars come after; with the dash, they come before.

A **semicolon** is a rather troublesome hybrid used well infrequently and misued frequently. It can often be used in the same spot where a period might appear, but it's usually best to avoid it if you're not absolutely sure. It can be used to link short sentences of contrasting implication (War is destructive; peace is constructive), and also following a colon to separate items in a listing which contains a potentially confusing assortment of commas and periods:

The requests came in as follows: Mrs. Vitali asked for $4.50; John, Marie, and Paul asked for $12.47; Rachel and Mike asked for $27.02.

The **apostrophe,** a silent device, has three functions: to denote possession (Henry's; the children's); to signal a dropped letter (it's=it is, don't=do not, Hallowe'en=Hallow[ed ev]en[ing]); and to form the plural of letters and numerals (three R's; several 6's).

The final punctuation mark, the **hyphen,** is another silent device used to divide compound nouns (sister-in-law) and compound adjectives (third-grade students), and to signal the syllabic break of a word in a line of printing. It is not the same thing as a **dash,** which is a longer mark denoting a statement made on the side or parenthetically (see examples under INTERJECTIONS). Dashes are often used in this way to substitute for parentheses. It is useful to remember that, on a typewriter, a hyphen is (-) and a dash is (--).

CAPITALIZATION RULES

Always capitalize:

1. **The first word of a sentence.**

With cooperation, a depression can be avoided.

2. **All proper names.**

America, Santa Fe Chief, General Motors, Abraham Lincoln

3. **Days of the week and months.**

The check was mailed on *Thursday*.
Note: The seasons are not capitalized. In Florida, *winter* is mild.

4. **The word *dear* when it is the first word in the salutation of a letter.**

Dear Mr. Jones: (but: *My* dear Mr. Jones:)

5. **The first word of the complimentary close of a letter.**

Truly yours,   (but: *Very* truly yours,)

6. **The first, and the important words in a title.**

The *Art* of *Salesmanship*

7. **A word used as part of a proper name.**

William *Street* (but: That *street* is narrow.) Morningside *Terrace* (but: We have a *terrace* apartment.)

8. **Titles, when they refer to a particular official or family member.**

The report was read by *Secretary* Marshall. (but: Miss Shaw, our *secretary*, is ill.)
Let's visit *Uncle* Harry. (but: I have three *uncles*.)

9. **Points of a compass, when they refer to particular regions of a country.**

We're going *South* next week. (but: New York is *south* of Albany.)
Note: the Far West, the Pacific Coast, the Middle East, etc.

10. **The first word of a direct quotation.**

It was Alexander Pope who wrote, "*A* little learning is a dangerous thing."
Note: When a direct quotation sentence is broken, the *first* word of the *second half* of the sentence is not capitalized.

"Don't phone," Lily told me, "*because* they're not in yet."

CORRECT USAGE TEST
ANSWER SHEET

TEST 1

1. Ⓐ Ⓑ Ⓒ Ⓓ   3. Ⓐ Ⓑ Ⓒ Ⓓ   5. Ⓐ Ⓑ Ⓒ Ⓓ   7. Ⓐ Ⓑ Ⓒ Ⓓ
2. Ⓐ Ⓑ Ⓒ Ⓓ   4. Ⓐ Ⓑ Ⓒ Ⓓ   6. Ⓐ Ⓑ Ⓒ Ⓓ   8. Ⓐ Ⓑ Ⓒ Ⓓ

TEST 2

1. Ⓐ Ⓑ Ⓒ Ⓓ   3. Ⓐ Ⓑ Ⓒ Ⓓ   5. Ⓐ Ⓑ Ⓒ Ⓓ   7. Ⓐ Ⓑ Ⓒ Ⓓ   9. Ⓐ Ⓑ Ⓒ Ⓓ
2. Ⓐ Ⓑ Ⓒ Ⓓ   4. Ⓐ Ⓑ Ⓒ Ⓓ   6. Ⓐ Ⓑ Ⓒ Ⓓ   8. Ⓐ Ⓑ Ⓒ Ⓓ

TEST 3

1. Ⓐ Ⓑ Ⓒ Ⓓ   3. Ⓐ Ⓑ Ⓒ Ⓓ   5. Ⓐ Ⓑ Ⓒ Ⓓ   7. Ⓐ Ⓑ Ⓒ Ⓓ   9. Ⓐ Ⓑ Ⓒ Ⓓ
2. Ⓐ Ⓑ Ⓒ Ⓓ   4. Ⓐ Ⓑ Ⓒ Ⓓ   6. Ⓐ Ⓑ Ⓒ Ⓓ   8. Ⓐ Ⓑ Ⓒ Ⓓ

TEST 4

1. Ⓐ Ⓑ Ⓒ Ⓓ   3. Ⓐ Ⓑ Ⓒ Ⓓ   5. Ⓐ Ⓑ Ⓒ Ⓓ   7. Ⓐ Ⓑ Ⓒ Ⓓ   9. Ⓐ Ⓑ Ⓒ Ⓓ
2. Ⓐ Ⓑ Ⓒ Ⓓ   4. Ⓐ Ⓑ Ⓒ Ⓓ   6. Ⓐ Ⓑ Ⓒ Ⓓ   8. Ⓐ Ⓑ Ⓒ Ⓓ   10. Ⓐ Ⓑ Ⓒ Ⓓ

TEST 5

1. Ⓐ Ⓑ Ⓒ Ⓓ   3. Ⓐ Ⓑ Ⓒ Ⓓ   5. Ⓐ Ⓑ Ⓒ Ⓓ   7. Ⓐ Ⓑ Ⓒ Ⓓ
2. Ⓐ Ⓑ Ⓒ Ⓓ   4. Ⓐ Ⓑ Ⓒ Ⓓ   6. Ⓐ Ⓑ Ⓒ Ⓓ   8. Ⓐ Ⓑ Ⓒ Ⓓ

TEST 6

1. Ⓐ Ⓑ Ⓒ Ⓓ   3. Ⓐ Ⓑ Ⓒ Ⓓ   5. Ⓐ Ⓑ Ⓒ Ⓓ   7. Ⓐ Ⓑ Ⓒ Ⓓ   9. Ⓐ Ⓑ Ⓒ Ⓓ
2. Ⓐ Ⓑ Ⓒ Ⓓ   4. Ⓐ Ⓑ Ⓒ Ⓓ   6. Ⓐ Ⓑ Ⓒ Ⓓ   8. Ⓐ Ⓑ Ⓒ Ⓓ   10. Ⓐ Ⓑ Ⓒ Ⓓ

TEST 7

1. Ⓐ Ⓑ Ⓒ Ⓓ   3. Ⓐ Ⓑ Ⓒ Ⓓ   5. Ⓐ Ⓑ Ⓒ Ⓓ   7. Ⓐ Ⓑ Ⓒ Ⓓ
2. Ⓐ Ⓑ Ⓒ Ⓓ   4. Ⓐ Ⓑ Ⓒ Ⓓ   6. Ⓐ Ⓑ Ⓒ Ⓓ   8. Ⓐ Ⓑ Ⓒ Ⓓ

TEST 8

1. Ⓐ Ⓑ Ⓒ Ⓓ   3. Ⓐ Ⓑ Ⓒ Ⓓ   5. Ⓐ Ⓑ Ⓒ Ⓓ   7. Ⓐ Ⓑ Ⓒ Ⓓ   9. Ⓐ Ⓑ Ⓒ Ⓓ
2. Ⓐ Ⓑ Ⓒ Ⓓ   4. Ⓐ Ⓑ Ⓒ Ⓓ   6. Ⓐ Ⓑ Ⓒ Ⓓ   8. Ⓐ Ⓑ Ⓒ Ⓓ   10. Ⓐ Ⓑ Ⓒ Ⓓ

CORRECT USAGE TEST
ANSWER SHEET

TEST 9

1. Ⓐ Ⓑ Ⓒ Ⓓ   3. Ⓐ Ⓑ Ⓒ Ⓓ   5. Ⓐ Ⓑ Ⓒ Ⓓ   7. Ⓐ Ⓑ Ⓒ Ⓓ   9. Ⓐ Ⓑ Ⓒ Ⓓ
2. Ⓐ Ⓑ Ⓒ Ⓓ   4. Ⓐ Ⓑ Ⓒ Ⓓ   6. Ⓐ Ⓑ Ⓒ Ⓓ   8. Ⓐ Ⓑ Ⓒ Ⓓ   10. Ⓐ Ⓑ Ⓒ Ⓓ

TEST 10

1. Ⓐ Ⓑ Ⓒ Ⓓ   5. Ⓐ Ⓑ Ⓒ Ⓓ   8. Ⓐ Ⓑ Ⓒ Ⓓ   11. Ⓐ Ⓑ Ⓒ Ⓓ   14. Ⓐ Ⓑ Ⓒ Ⓓ
2. Ⓐ Ⓑ Ⓒ Ⓓ   6. Ⓐ Ⓑ Ⓒ Ⓓ   9. Ⓐ Ⓑ Ⓒ Ⓓ   12. Ⓐ Ⓑ Ⓒ Ⓓ   15. Ⓐ Ⓑ Ⓒ Ⓓ
3. Ⓐ Ⓑ Ⓒ Ⓓ   7. Ⓐ Ⓑ Ⓒ Ⓓ   10. Ⓐ Ⓑ Ⓒ Ⓓ   13. Ⓐ Ⓑ Ⓒ Ⓓ   16. Ⓐ Ⓑ Ⓒ Ⓓ
4. Ⓐ Ⓑ Ⓒ Ⓓ

TEST 11

1. Ⓐ Ⓑ   5. Ⓐ Ⓑ   8. Ⓐ Ⓑ   11. Ⓐ Ⓑ   14. Ⓐ Ⓑ
2. Ⓐ Ⓑ   6. Ⓐ Ⓑ   9. Ⓐ Ⓑ   12. Ⓐ Ⓑ   15. Ⓐ Ⓑ
3. Ⓐ Ⓑ   7. Ⓐ Ⓑ   10. Ⓐ Ⓑ   13. Ⓐ Ⓑ   16. Ⓐ Ⓑ
4. Ⓐ Ⓑ

TEST 12

1. Ⓐ Ⓑ   5. Ⓐ Ⓑ   8. Ⓐ Ⓑ   11. Ⓐ Ⓑ   14. Ⓐ Ⓑ
2. Ⓐ Ⓑ   6. Ⓐ Ⓑ   9. Ⓐ Ⓑ   12. Ⓐ Ⓑ   15. Ⓐ Ⓑ
3. Ⓐ Ⓑ   7. Ⓐ Ⓑ   10. Ⓐ Ⓑ   13. Ⓐ Ⓑ   16. Ⓐ Ⓑ
4. Ⓐ Ⓑ

Total Number of Questions 130
Total Incorrect—
Total Correct   × .76 = _____%
Score

CORRECT USAGE TEST ONE

DIRECTIONS: In each of the following groups of sentences, select the one sentence that is grammatically incorrect. Mark the answer sheet with the letter of that incorrect sentence. Correct answers to this test will be found at the end of the chapter.

1. (A) Everyone at camp must have his medical certificate on file before participating in competitive sports.
   (B) A crate of oranges were sent from Florida for all the children in cabin six.
   (C) John and Danny's room looks as if they were prepared for inspection.
   (D) Three miles is too far for a young child to walk.

2. (A) The game over, the spectators rushed out on the field and tore down the goalposts.
   (B) The situation was aggravated by disputes over the captaincy of the team.
   (C) Yesterday they lay their uniforms aside with the usual end-of-the-season regret.
   (D) It is sometimes thought that politics is not for the high-minded.

3. (A) Sandburg's autobiography, as well as his poems, are familiar to many readers.
   (B) A series of authentic records of the American Indian tribes is being published.
   (C) The Smokies is the home of the descendants of this brave tribe.
   (D) Five dollars is really not too much to pay for a book of this type.

4. (A) Being tired, I stretched out on a grassy knoll.
   (B) While we were rowing on the lake, a sudden squall almost capsized the boat.
   (C) Entering the room, a strange mark on the floor attracted my attention.
   (D) Mounting the curb, the empty car crossed the sidewalk and came to rest against a building.

5. (A) The text makes the process of developing and sustaining a successful home

zoo appear to be a pleasant and profitable one.
   (B) The warmth and humor, the clear characterization of the Walmsey family, which includes three children, two dogs and two cats, is such fun to read that this reviewer found herself reading it all over again.
   (C) You will be glad, I am sure, to give the book to whoever among your young friends has displayed an interest in animals.
   (D) The consensus among critics of children's literature is that the book is well worth the purchase price.

6. (A) Not one in a thousand readers take the matter seriously.
   (B) He was able partially to accomplish his purpose.
   (C) You are not as tall as he.
   (D) The people began to realize how much she had done.

7. (A) In the case of members who are absent, a special letter will be sent.
   (B) The visitors were all ready to see it.
   (C) I like Burns's poem, "To a Mountain Daisy."
   (D) John told William that he was sure he seen it.

8. (A) B. Nelson & Co. has a sale of sport shirts today.
   (B) Venetian blinds—called that although they probably did not originate in Venice—are no longer used as extensively as they were at one time.
   (C) He determined to be guided by the opinion of whoever spoke first.
   (D) There was often disagreement as to whom was the better Shakespearean actor, Evans or Gielgud.

CORRECT USAGE TEST TWO

DIRECTIONS: *In each of the following groups of sentences, select the one sentence that is grammatically incorrect. Mark the answer sheet with the letter of that incorrect sentence. Correct answers to this test will be found at the end of the chapter.*

1. (A) Everyone can have a wonderful time in New York if they will just not try to see the entire city in one week.
   (B) Being a stranger in town myself, I know how you feel.
   (C) New York is a city of man-made wonders, as awe-inspiring as those found in nature.
   (D) He felt deep despair (as who has not?) at the evidence of man's inhumanity to man.

2. (A) A clerk should be careful as well as punctual, even though he or she are otherwise efficient.
   (B) Regardless of whether it may be true, some students are not very studious.
   (C) Not every writer can say that his opinion is always the best.
   (D) We often think of people who assume airs as being affected.

3. (A) This is the woman whom I saw.
   (B) She could solve even this problem.
   (C) She divided the money among the three of us.
   (D) Either she or I are guilty.

4. (A) Consider that the person which is always idle can never be happy.
   (B) Because a man understands a woman does not mean they are necessarily compatible.
   (C) He said that accuracy and speed are both essential.
   (D) Can it be said that the better of the two books is less expensive?

5. (A) Neither the critics nor the author were right about the reaction of the public.
   (B) The senator depended upon whoever was willing to assist him.

   (C) I don't recall any time when Edgar has broken his word.
   (D) Every one of the campers but John and me is going on the hike.

6. (A) Everyone entered promptly but her.
   (B) Each of the messengers were busily occupied.
   (C) At which exit did you leave him?
   (D) The work was not done well.

7. (A) Never before have I seen anyone who has the skill John has when he repairs engines.
   (B) If anyone can be wholly just in his decisions, it is he.
   (C) Because of his friendliness, the new neighbor was immediately accepted by the community.
   (D) Imagine our embarrassment when us girls saw Miss Maltinge sitting with her beau in the front row.

8. (A) I wondered why it was that the Mayor objected to the Governor's reference to the new tax law.
   (B) I have never read *Les Miserables*, but I plan to do so this summer.
   (C) After much talk and haranguing, the workers received an increase in wages.
   (D) The author and myself were the only cheerful ones at the macabre gathering.

9. (A) The doctor had carelessly left all the instruments on the operating table.
   (B) Was it them whom the professor regarded with such contempt?
   (C) Despite all the power he has, I should still hate to be in his shoes.
   (D) I feel bad because I gave such a poor performance in the play tonight.

CORRECT USAGE TEST THREE

DIRECTIONS: In each of the following groups of sentences, select the one sentence that is grammatically incorrect. Mark the answer sheet with the letter of that incorrect sentence. Correct answers to this test will be found at the end of the chapter.

1. (A) The general regarded whomever the colonel honored with disdain.
   (B) Everyone who reads this book will think themselves knights errant on missions of heroism.
   (C) The reason why the new leader was so unsuccessful was that he had fewer responsibilities.
   (D) All the new mechanical devices we have today have made our daily living a great deal simpler, it is said.

2. (A) The town consists of three distinct sections, of which the western one is by far the larger.
   (B) Of London and Paris, the former is the wealthier.
   (C) Chicago is larger than any other city in Illinois.
   (D) America is the greatest nation, and of all other nations England is the greatest.

3. (A) I can but do my best.
   (B) I cannot help comparing him with his predecessor.
   (C) I wish that I was in Florida now.
   (D) I like this kind of grapes better than any other.

4. (A) Neither Tom nor John was present for the rehearsal.
   (B) The happiness or misery of men's lives depends on their early training.
   (C) Honor as well as profit are to be gained by these studies.
   (D) The egg business is only incidental to the regular business of the general store.

5. (A) It was superior in every way to the book previously used.
   (B) His testimony today is different from that of yesterday.
   (C) If you would have studied the problem carefully, you would have found the solution more quickly.
   (D) The flowers smelled so sweet that the whole house was perfumed.

6. (A) When either or both habits become fixed, the student improves.
   (B) Neither his words nor his action was justifiable.
   (C) A calm almost always comes before a storm.
   (D) The gallery with all its pictures were destroyed.

7. (A) Who did they say won?
   (B) The man whom I thought was my friend deceived me.
   (C) Send whoever will do the work.
   (D) The question of who should be leader arose.

8. (A) A box of choice figs was sent him for Christmas.
   (B) Neither Charles nor his brother finished his assignment.
   (C) There goes the last piece of cake and the last spoonful of ice cream.
   (D) Diamonds are more desired than any other precious stones.

9. (A) As long as you are ready, you may as well start promptly.
   (B) My younger brother insists that he is as tall as me.
   (C) We walked as long as there was any light to guide us.
   (D) Realizing I had forgotten my gloves, I returned to the theater.

CORRECT USAGE TEST FOUR

DIRECTIONS: In each of the following groups of sentences, select the one sentence that is grammatically incorrect. Mark the answer sheet with the letter of that incorrect sentence. Correct answers to this test will be found at the end of the chapter.

1. (A) His knowledge of methods and procedures enable him to assist the director in many ways.
   (B) A new set of rules and regulations has been made.
   (C) Reports that the strike has been settled were circulated yesterday.
   (D) The cracks in the teapot my aunts gave for Christmas make it useless.

2. (A) The Credit Bureau rates you as high as him.
   (B) He is no better than you or me.
   (C) You will be notified as soon as I.
   (D) We were ready sooner than they.

3. (A) Neither the stenographer nor the typist has returned from lunch.
   (B) Either the operators or the machines are at fault.
   (C) One or the other of those clerks are responsible for these errors.
   (D) Either the clerk or the receptionist is available by this time of day.

4. (A) The Board of Directors has prepared a manual for their own use.
   (B) The company has announced its new policy of advertising.
   (C) The jury were out about thirty minutes when they returned a verdict.
   (D) The flock of geese creates a health hazard for visitors with allergies.

5. (A) Who does he think he is?
   (B) Whom does he consider in making a decision?
   (C) Whom did they say is to be appointed?
   (D) Whom do they contact in such emergencies?

6. (A) Who shall I say called?
   (B) The water has frozen the pipes.
   (C) Everyone has left except them.
   (D) Every one of the salesmen must supply their own car.

7. (A) Two-thirds of the building is finished.
   (B) Where are Mr. Keene and Mr. Herbert?
   (C) Neither the salesladies nor the floorwalker want to work overtime.
   (D) The committee was agreed.

8. (A) Amends have been made for the damage to one of our cars.
   (B) Neither the customer nor the clerk were aware of the fire in the store.
   (C) A box of spare pencils is on the desk.
   (D) There is the total number of missing pens.

9. (A) The company insist on everyone's being prompt.
   (B) Each one of our salesmen takes an aptitude test.
   (C) It is the location that appeals to me.
   (D) Most of the men have left the building.

10. (A) The students in the dormitories were forbidden, unless they had special passes, from staying out after 11:30 p.m.
    (B) The Student Court rendered a decision satisfactory to both the defendant and the accuser.
    (C) Margarine is being substituted for butter to a considerable extent.
    (D) In this school there are at least fifteen minor accidents a year which are due to this traffic violation.

CORRECT USAGE TEST FIVE

DIRECTIONS: In each of the following groups of sentences, select the one sentence that is grammatically incorrect. Mark the answer sheet with the letter of that incorrect sentence. Correct answers to this test will be found at the end of the chapter.

1. (A) Sailing along New England's craggy coastline, you will relive a bygone era of far-roving whalers and graceful clipper ships.
   (B) The march of history is reenacted in folk festivals, outdoor pageants, and fiestas—local in theme, but national in import.
   (C) Visiting the scenes of the past, our interest in American history is renewed and enlivened.
   (D) What remained was a few unrecognizable fragments.

2. (A) I knew it to be him by the style of his clothes.
   (B) No one saw him doing it.
   (C) Her going away is a loss to the community.
   (D) Illness prevented him graduating in June.

3. (A) No one but her could have recognized him.
   (B) She knew the stranger to be him whom she had given up as lost.
   (C) He looked like he had been in some strange land where age advanced at a double pace.
   (D) It is impossible to include that item; the agenda has already been mimeographed.

4. (A) You have probably heard of the new innovation in the regular morning broadcast.
   (B) During the broadcast you are expected to stand, to salute, and to sing the fourth stanza of "America."
   (C) None of the rocks which form the solid crust of our planet is more than two billion years old.
   (D) "I have finished my assignment," said the pupil. "May I go home now?"

5. (A) The coming of peace effected a change in her way of life.
   (B) Spain is as weak, if not weaker than, she was in 1900.
   (C) In regard to that, I am not certain what my attitude will be.
   (D) That unfortunate family faces the problem of adjusting itself to a new way of life.

6. (A) Participation in active sports produces both release from tension as well as physical well-being.
   (B) The problem of taxes is still with them.
   (C) Every boy and every girl in the auditorium was thrilled when the curtain went up.
   (D) At length our club decided to send two representatives to the meeting, you and me.

7. (A) Remains of an ancient civilization were found near Mexico City.
   (B) It is interesting to compare the interior of one of the pyramids in Mexico with the interior of one of the pyramids in Egypt.
   (C) In two days' journey you will be reminded of political upheavals comparable to the volcanic eruptions still visible and audible in parts of Mexico.
   (D) There is little danger of the laws being broken, so drastic is the penalty.

8. (A) Instead of looking disdainfully at London grime, think of it as a mantle of tradition.
   (B) Nobody but the pilot and the co-pilot was permitted to handle the mysterious package.
   (C) Not only is industry anxious to hire all available engineers, but they are being offered commissions by the armed forces.
   (D) For immediate service go directly to the store manager.

CORRECT USAGE TEXT SIX

DIRECTIONS: *In each of the following groups of sentences, select the one sentence that is grammatically incorrect. Mark the answer sheet with the letter of that incorrect sentence. Correct answers to this test will be found at the end of the chapter.*

1. (A) The zinnia has the more vivid color, but the violet is the sweeter-smelling.
   (B) About three-fourths of the review I read was merely a summary of the story; the rest, criticism.
   (C) I shall insist that he not be accepted as a member, since he is very bad-tempered.
   (D) No sooner had he begun to speak when his auditors started to boo and hiss.

2. (A) The children's determination to find their dog almost resulted in tragedy.
   (B) They spent the first night in a house that was unlocked and with no one at home.
   (C) "What he asked me," said the boy, "was, 'Where can I find your father?' "
   (D) It was the whimpering of the younger child and the comforting words of her brother that a member of the search party heard about ten feet off the road.

3. (A) The quarrel is between the administration and me.
   (B) These questions are less difficult than those.
   (C) The former is considerably different with the latter.
   (D) We are not unaware of the consequences.

4. (A) This person also wished to state his case.
   (B) He came almost immediately.
   (C) Returning to the room, the book was missing.
   (D) They are very nearly alike in this respect.

5. (A) What kind of a job have you?
   (B) He did exactly as he was told.

(C) The red house is differently shaped than the blue.
   (D) We hoped to see you there.

6. (A) He found neither the money or the papers.
   (B) There are now two men in the room.
   (C) Who would file the summons was the question.
   (D) It is possible he may be here now.

7. (A) The choice finally remained between them and us.
   (B) Is this the gardener of whom you spoke?
   (C) The thieves divided the money among themselves.
   (D) Do you know who this package is to be addressed to?

8. (A) I shouldn't have done it.
   (B) After a wearying day, he lay down to rest.
   (C) These problems are difficult as the others.
   (D) She saw neither of us.

9. (A) The incident occurred when he took the book off the desk.
   (B) Helen thinks as clearly as John.
   (C) I cannot believe but what he is guilty.
   (D) He indicated that the two boys were to go.

10. (A) Our child will be successful without any assistance from either you or me.
    (B) Whom do you think we ought to consider for the chairmanship?
    (C) Deep in the forest, warmed by the dying embers of our campfire, sat the scoutmaster and I.
    (D) The part of the story I enjoyed most was where the heroine decided to leave her husband.

CORRECT USAGE TEST SEVEN

DIRECTIONS: In each of the following groups of sentences, select the one sentence that is grammatically incorrect. Mark the answer sheet with the letter of that incorrect sentence. Correct answers to this test will be found at the end of the chapter.

1. (A) "Which is the way to Paris?" asked the American tourist.
    (B) The physicist muttered in despair, "Will I always be surrounded by fools?".
    (C) I never feel badly if after trying hard I fail to win a prize; the effort gives me satisfaction.
    (D) Everywhere I go, I find grime and dirt in the air.

2. (A) Parents are the ones who we believe ought to insist upon their children's obeying orders.
    (B) The carpenters were lying on the ground and resting when I came in.
    (C) I do not understand why mother should object to me playing the piano at the party.
    (D) Lie in bed awhile until your aches and pains subside.

3. (A) She avoided my look of surprise, staring at the ceiling steadily.
    (B) When I told her I was sorry, I partly meant it.
    (C) My father enjoys fresh air, sunshine, and to take long walks.
    (D) The greatest pleasure I get is to see my favorite team win a ball game.

4. (A) Students who plan to become physicians are advised to study biology, chemistry, and German.
    (B) The critic asked the author which of his plays he considered the best.
    (C) I, who am your best friend, should have at least a fair chance of winning the prize.
    (D) If you go past the library tomorrow, please bring this book to the librarian who sits at the desk in the children's room.

5. (A) Writers no longer take for granted the mores of the society in which they live.
    (B) He is in this country now for five years, but he makes no attempt to speak our language.
    (C) The reason the child rebelled was that the order made no sense to him.
    (D) His written work has been done in so careless a manner that I refuse to read it.

6. (A) Being that I was obviously at fault, I was deprived of my chairmanship.
    (B) Neither the United States nor, for that matter, any other country has seriously regretted having joined the United Nations.
    (C) The members of the committee insisted upon presenting a preliminary report before adjournment today.
    (D) The truck with its huge load of crates was beginning to roll down the hill.

7. (A) "To eat sparingly is advisable," said the doctor.
    (B) When March winds blow, women's hats occupy a precarious perch.
    (C) While traveling through the Blue Ridge Mountains, the breathtaking scenes awed the travelers.
    (D) The doctor advised the patient to take two teaspoonfuls of the medicine daily.

8. (A) My experience in South Africa taught me that the climate there is quite different from ours.
    (B) The class had been in session two weeks, yet it seemed like we had been listening to lectures for years.
    (C) He turned out to be a much better student than I had expected.
    (D) Any writer who can write the way he does is either a fool or a cynic.

CORRECT USAGE TEST EIGHT

DIRECTIONS: *In each of the following groups of sentences, select the one sentence that is grammatically incorrect. Mark the answer sheet with the letter of that incorrect sentence. Correct answers to this test will be found at the end of the chapter.*

1. (A) The spectators agreed that the winner was a remarkable fine swimmer.
   (B) Oranges grown in California are packed while still green and shipped to the New York market.
   (C) My father, who was taken ill suddenly, is improving satisfactorily.
   (D) Any dissatisfied subscriber may have his or her money refunded promptly.

2. (A) What kind of a teacher would you like to be?
   (B) The temperature has dropped so much that it is likely to snow.
   (C) The improvements in the plan enable the teacher to save much time.
   (D) Offering people advice is often wasting one's breath.

3. (A) There are very good grounds for such a decision.
   (B) Due to bad weather, the game was postponed.
   (C) The door opens, and in walk John and Mary.
   (D) Where but in America is there greater prosperity?

4. (A) The remainder of the time was spent in prayer.
   (B) Immigration is when people come into a foreign country to live.
   (C) He coughed continually last winter.
   (D) The method is different from the one that was formerly used.

5. (A) Choose an author as you choose a friend.
   (B) Home is home, be it ever so humble.
   (C) You always look good in that sort of clothes.
   (D) We had no sooner entered the room when the bell rang.

6. (A) Never before, to the best of my recollection, have there been such promising students.
   (B) It is only because your manners are so objectionable that you are not invited to the party.
   (C) I fully expected that the children would be at their desks and to find them ready to begin work.
   (D) A complete system of railroads covers the entire country.

7. (A) Our vacation is over. I am sorry to say.
   (B) It is so dark that I can't hardly see.
   (C) Either you or I am right; we cannot both be right.
   (D) After it had lain in the rain all night, it was not fit for use again.

8. (A) I will not go unless I receive a special invitation.
   (B) The pilot shouted orders to his assistant as the plane burst into flames.
   (C) She acts as though her feelings were hurt.
   (D) Please come here and try and help me finish this piece of work.

9. (A) The convicted spy was hung at dawn.
   (B) His speech is so precise as to seem affected.
   (C) Besides the captain, there were six people on the boat.
   (D) We read each other's letters.

10. (A) The lines on the map are finely drawn.
    (B) He spoke very slowly.
    (C) The lady looked well in her new suit.
    (D) The cream tasted sour.

CORRECT USAGE TEST NINE

DIRECTIONS: In each of the following groups of sentences, select the one sentence that is grammatically incorrect. Mark the answer sheet with the letter of that incorrect sentence. Correct answers to this test will be found at the end of the chapter.

1. (A) The day is warm.
   (B) It should be called to his attention.
   (C) The girl was an unusually beautiful child.
   (D) He performed the job easy and quick.

2. (A) The company published its new catalogue last week.
   (B) The man who he introduced was Mr. Carey.
   (C) The Rolls-Royce is the fastest car in England.
   (D) He finished the job satisfactorily.

3. (A) She saw the letter laying here this morning.
   (B) They gave the poor man some food when he knocked on the door.
   (C) The plans were drawn before the fight started.
   (D) He was here when the messenger brought the news.

4. (A) I regret the loss caused by the error.
   (B) The students will have a new teacher.
   (C) We shall go irregardless.
   (D) They swore to bring out all the facts.

5. (A) If my trip is a success, I should be back on Thursday.
   (B) We will send a copy of the article to you if you wish it.
   (C) They will have gone before the notice is sent to their office.
   (D) Can I borrow your bicycle tomorrow?

6. (A) He likes these kind of pencils better than those kind.
   (B) That Jackson will be elected is evident.
   (C) He does not approve of my dictating the letter.
   (D) Jack should make some progress in his work each day.

7. (A) The company has moved into its new building.
   (B) They will approve him going to the concert.
   (C) That business is good appears to be true.
   (D) It was he who won the prize.

8. (A) It must be here somewhere.
   (B) The reason is that there is no gasoline.
   (C) I will try and attend one meeting.
   (D) He walked up the hill.

9. (A) A kite must have a tail in order to fly.
   (B) He placed the books upon the desk.
   (C) He was a little ways ahead of me.
   (D) He had an amused look on his face.

10. (A) I am sure that I have met you before.
    (B) He came a while ago.
    (C) I have already seen the play.
    (D) I'd as leave go as not.

CORRECT USAGE TEST TEN

DIRECTIONS: *For each of the following sentences, you are offered a choice of four words, one of which will complete the sentence correctly. Mark the answer sheet with the letter of that word. Correct answers to this test will be found at the end of the chapter.*

1. _____ of the clerks was instructed to do his own work.
   (A) All   (B) Some
   (C) Several   (D) Each

2. The woman arrived before the director had discussed the plan with him and _____.
   (A) I   (B) myself
   (C) she   (D) me

3. This book was written by an author _____ characters seem very real.
   (A) whose   (B) which
   (C) who's   (D) what

4. When the plan is presented, I shall favor _____ adoption.
   (A) our   (B) its
   (C) it's   (D) its'

5. We expect everyone to carry out _____ duty.
   (A) his or her   (B) our
   (C) there   (D) their

6. It looks _____ it might rain.
   (A) like   (B) as
   (C) as if   (D) that

7. They were the only men who received votes _____ me.
   (A) but   (B) besides
   (C) unless   (D) accept

8. Neither of the men _____ satisfactory work.
   (A) done   (B) haven't done
   (C) have done   (D) has done

9. The clerk _____ telephoned his superior in order to delay the conference.
   (A) could of   (B) ought to of
   (C) should of   (D) could have

10. The employee to _____ the salary increment was given resolved to maintain his high level of efficiency.
    (A) who   (B) whom
    (C) whoever   (D) whomever

11. A clerk, a stenographer, and _____ were chosen to represent the group.
    (A) me   (B) I
    (C) myself   (D) etc.

12. The sponsoring of social legislation seems to be divided _____ three or four civic agencies.
    (A) with   (B) from
    (C) among   (D) to

13. An agent _____ make mistakes.
    (A) don't   (B) does not
    (C) don't make no   (D) do not

14. The present outlook on social work has become different _____ that of the past.
    (A) by   (B) to
    (C) with   (D) from

15. The _____ important one of these five items warrants particular emphasis.
    (A) most   (B) greatest
    (C) more   (D) greater

16. One point is that, if the assignment is worked out _____, the worker will gain a power that would not be possible otherwise.
    (A) thoroughly   (B) good
    (C) thorough   (D) hardest

CORRECT USAGE TEST ELEVEN

DIRECTIONS: In each of the sentences below, only one of the two choices is correct. Blacken the letter of the correct choice on the answer sheet. Correct answers to this test will be found at the end of the chapter.

1. The thief _____ his wallet.
(A) robbed
(B) stole

2. We are very fond of _____ kind of apples.
(A) this
(B) these

3. Try _____ come.
(A) and
(B) to

4. Let us ask _____ person to settle this argument.
(A) an uninterested
(B) a disinterested

5. Don't put the cream _____ the radiator.
(A) beside
(B) besides

6. Will you be good enough to _____ me a dime?
(A) borrow
(B) lend

7. Don't _____ the customer alone at the counter.
(A) let
(B) leave

8. The deliverymen have _____ the cartons on the sidewalk.
(A) lain
(B) laid

9. The dog was _____ helpless in the street.
(A) lying
(B) laying

10. Your appearance is much different _____ what it used to be.
(A) than
(B) from

11. The school is arranging to have _____ boys form a cooking class.
(A) us
(B) we

12. When we reached the harbor, we found that the ship had _____.
(A) sunk
(B) sank

13. They let it _____ on the table.
(A) lay
(B) lie

14. The ice has _____.
(A) frozen
(B) froze

15. Overnight the river has _____ another foot.
(A) raised
(B) risen

16. Many a person lives to regret _____ hasty remarks.
(A) his
(B) their

CORRECT USAGE TEST TWELVE

DIRECTIONS: *For each of the following sentences, you are offered a choice of two words, one of which will complete the sentence correctly. Mark the answer sheet with the letter of that word. Correct answers to this test will be found at the end of the chapter.*

1. He told the boss that he would _____ the job.
   (A) accept
   (B) except

2. _____ Jim, Harry also went.
   (A) Beside
   (B) Besides

3. Please _____ this letter to the principal's office.
   (A) take
   (B) bring

4. It rained _____ for seven days without a moment of dry weather.
   (A) continuously
   (B) intermittently

5. Ask your brother whether I _____ borrow his book.
   (A) can
   (B) may

6. This school is different _____ my old one.
   (A) from
   (B) than

7. _____ her illness, we can't go.
   (A) Due to
   (B) Because of

8. You and I ought to cooperate with _____.
   (A) one another
   (B) each other

9. How does the new law _____ you?
   (A) affect
   (B) effect

10. He has _____ than I have.
    (A) fewer
    (B) less

11. I wonder _____ my friend will call me.
    (A) if
    (B) whether

12. I _____ from what he says that he likes me.
    (A) infer
    (B) imply

13. How many _____ have you sent out for the party?
    (A) invitations
    (B) invites

14. The child has _____ down to rest.
    (A) laid
    (B) lain

15. _____ us face it—it's too late to go.
    (A) Leave
    (B) Let

16. May I have a _____ of a dollar?
    (A) loan
    (B) lend

ARRANGING PARAGRAPHS IN LOGICAL ORDER

DIRECTIONS: In these questions, four given sentences may or may not be arranged in the order in which they would logically appear in a paragraph. Following the four given sentences are four suggested sequences, lettered A, B, C, and D from which you are to select the sequence that indicates the best arrangement of the sentences. For example: If, in the first question, you find that the fourth sentence should come first, the first sentence should be second, the second sentence should be third, and the third sentence should be fourth, you would look among the four choices for the answer 4-1-2-3 and circle the letter which precedes that sequence as your answer. Correct answers to this test will be found at the end of the chapter.

1. 1. There is also good reason for careful attention to internal communication.

    2. Effective communication with those inside the organization makes for fewer misunderstandings, and fewer disgruntled employees.

    3. Harmony within the business carries over into public relations with outsiders.

    4. In the area of office communication, primary attention is usually centered upon relations with outsiders—customers, suppliers, and others.
       (A) 2-3-1-4   (B) 4-1-2-3
       (C) 3-2-1-4   (D) 1-3-2-4

2. 1. A systematic plan for handling the mail will speed up the performance of office work.

    2. Regardless of the volume of mail, competent supervision and control are necessary.

    3. The provision of facilities for handling mail will depend largely upon the volume to be handled.

    4. The number of persons forming the mailroom staff, in turn, varies with the volume of correspondence to be handled and the degree to which mechanical equipment is used.
       (A) 1-3-4-2   (B) 2-1-3-4
       (C) 3-1-4-2   (D) 4-3-2-1

3. 1. A budget is a plan of financial requirements during a given time period.

    2. It necessarily is based upon analysis of the situation which faces the enterprise.

    3. It develops a course of action to be followed.

    4. The general uses of any budget are to plan financial needs in advance and provide a basis for controlling current expenditures.
       (A) 3-2-4-1   (B) 4-2-3-1
       (C) 2-4-3-1   (D) 1-2-3-4

4. 1. The employee has little control over any of them.

    2. The cost of the training period and its effectiveness will depend upon the degree to which these conditions are properly controlled by the employer.

    3. The conditions under which the employee must learn will materially affect the length of the training period.

    4. These conditions can be controlled by the employer.
       (A) 1-2-4-3   (B) 4-2-1-3
       (C) 3-4-2-1   (D) 2-4-3-1

5. 1. But once that effort is made, reappraisal and modification should be made in light of the skill and experience of the work force and the cost of perfectionism.

2. The second caution is that the development effort should be aimed at creating a simple, workable procedure as distinct from a perfect procedure.

3. As one speaker put it, "Hire a few workers to mop the floor so that you don't have to develop a perfect system that will keep 400 people from dropping things on the floor."

4. To be sure, the initial effort should be directed toward developing the ideal.
   (A) 4-1-3-2   (B) 3-1-4-2
   (C) 2-1-3-4   (D) 2-4-1-3

6. 1. They include computation and rate tables, codes, charts, price lists, wiring diagrams, account titles and definitions, and the like.

   2. The use and usefulness of these devices should be fully explored during the survey of work methods.

   3. In general, the analyst's objective should be to find out if all special data required to perform any part of the routine are readily available, conveniently arranged, and kept up to date.

   4. Work aids are the nonmechanical devices of many kinds used to facilitate repetitive clerical operations.
      (A) 1-2-3-4   (B) 4-1-2-3
      (C) 3-1-4-2   (D) 2-1-4-3

7. 1. This is just another way of stating the important principle that duplication is not always avoidable or wasteful.

   2. On this whole matter of combining forms, one point of caution needs to be stressed: The analyst must be careful not to go beyond the point of diminishing returns.

   3. In some situations it may be the simplest way of meeting the requirements.

   4. He must not fall into the error of seeking combination for its own sake.
      (A) 2-4-1-3   (B) 3-4-1-2
      (C) 4-1-2-3   (D) 1-3-4-2

8. 1. The big risk, of course, in funneling all proposed procedure instructions through a single point is that the adoption of worthwhile changes will be unnecessarily delayed.

   2. The approvals required must be clearly specified and held to a minimum, and the procedures staff must be geared to process recommended changes quickly.

   3. Unless this is done, operating personnel will soon become discouraged from submitting recommendations through the prescribed channels and will revert to making their own changes as the need arises.

   4. To avoid this danger, the path of revision must be short, easy to follow, and well understood by everyone.
      (A) 4-1-3-2   (B) 3-1-2-4
      (C) 1-4-2-3   (D) 2-4-1-3

9. 1. For one man, everything he does falls under the heading of administration.

   2. To a large extent, what the administrative functions of your job are depend on what you say they are.

   3. You can talk to a dozen executives without getting two to agree.

   4. Another executive will tell you only planning and decision making belong there.
      (A) 1-2-4-3   (B) 3-1-4-2
      (C) 3-2-4-1   (D) 4-1-2-3

10. 1. The importance of communications is axiomatic.

    2. When the phrase "two-way" precedes the word "communications," there is the feeling in some quarters that we have said everything there is to say on the subject.

    3. But communications may proceed in two directions and still not be inclusive enough to make it possible for you to do a thorough communications job.

    4. The fact is, the communications load of many executives tends to be decidedly uneven.
       (A) 4-3-1-2   (B) 2-3-4-1
       (C) 3-4-1-2   (D) 1-2-3-4

11. 1. In actuality, this isn't the case at all.

   2. The trouble with many approaches to problem solving is the mistaken idea that problems come to you spelled out in clear and simple terms.

   3. For example, a problem may grow so imperceptibly that it may actually have been around for years before it begins to take on the aspects of a problem.

   4. Or the facts of a case may be indistinguishable from the fancies.
      (A) 3-4-1-2   (B) 2-1-3-4
      (C) 1-3-2-4   (D) 4-2-1-3

12. 1. Regardless of the reason, the effects of the vacuum range from the disheartening to the deadly.

   2. People in management, more often than you might think, find themselves "in solitary."

   3. It's seldom calculated, but the fact remains, they have no one to talk to.

   4. Lack of direct channels to colleagues may reflect anything from poor personal relationships to faulty organizational setup.
      (A) 4-1-3-2   (B) 2-4-1-3
      (C) 2-3-4-1   (D) 3-1-4-2

13. 1. They must operate to accomplish any one of the primary tasks.

   2. These processes are planning, doing, and controlling.

   3. They cause the organization to function.

   4. Three processes are at work in an organization.
      (A) 4-3-2-1   (B) 1-2-3-4
      (C) 3-1-4-2   (D) 2-4-1-3

14. 1. Difficulty in the application of the principle of unity of command arises principally from its blind application to a static organization structure to meet a need that fluctuates with conditions and situations.

   2. The relationships shown on an organization chart seem as inflexible and static as the structure of the organization itself.

   3. If the organization is to serve its purpose, however, it cannot be entirely static because it is dealing with moving and changing situations.

   4. The relationships between the component units of the organization enable it to become a flexible, living organism.
      (A) 2-4-3-1   (B) 1-2-3-4
      (C) 3-4-1-2   (D) 2-1-3-4

15. 1. These may help, but good communications are possible only when there is mutual understanding—and trust—over a two-way circuit.

   2. Poor communication is basically the result of a lack of mutual confidence between management and labor.

   3. It can and does exist almost regardless of the number of memoranda, house organs, bulletin boards, and conferences.

   4. This occurs on all levels, between sections, departments, divisions, foremen, managers, executives.
      (A) 4-1-3-2   (B) 2-4-3-1
      (C) 3-1-2-4   (D) 1-4-3-2

16. 1. It cannot be answered by listing "qualities an executive should have" and then trying to assess executives accordingly.

   2. Quite simply, it is the lack of any precise means of judging executive ability.

   3. Of all the weaknesses in these development methods, however, only one is fundamental.

   4. Appraising performance is not difficult, but appraising qualities and potentialities involves the basic problem of the nature of leadership.
      (A) 4-3-2-1   (B) 2-1-3-4
      (C) 1-3-2-4   (D) 4-3-1-2

EFFECTIVE EXPRESSION TEST
ANSWER SHEET

1. Ⓐ Ⓑ Ⓒ Ⓓ	21. Ⓐ Ⓑ Ⓒ Ⓓ	41. Ⓐ Ⓑ Ⓒ Ⓓ	61. Ⓐ Ⓑ Ⓒ Ⓓ	81. Ⓐ Ⓑ Ⓒ Ⓓ
2. Ⓐ Ⓑ Ⓒ Ⓓ	22. Ⓐ Ⓑ Ⓒ Ⓓ	42. Ⓐ Ⓑ Ⓒ Ⓓ	62. Ⓐ Ⓑ Ⓒ Ⓓ	82. Ⓐ Ⓑ Ⓒ Ⓓ
3. Ⓐ Ⓑ Ⓒ Ⓓ	23. Ⓐ Ⓑ Ⓒ Ⓓ	43. Ⓐ Ⓑ Ⓒ Ⓓ	63. Ⓐ Ⓑ Ⓒ Ⓓ	83. Ⓐ Ⓑ Ⓒ Ⓓ
4. Ⓐ Ⓑ Ⓒ Ⓓ	24. Ⓐ Ⓑ Ⓒ Ⓓ	44. Ⓐ Ⓑ Ⓒ Ⓓ	64. Ⓐ Ⓑ Ⓒ Ⓓ	84. Ⓐ Ⓑ Ⓒ Ⓓ
5. Ⓐ Ⓑ Ⓒ Ⓓ	25. Ⓐ Ⓑ Ⓒ Ⓓ	45. Ⓐ Ⓑ Ⓒ Ⓓ	65. Ⓐ Ⓑ Ⓒ Ⓓ	85. Ⓐ Ⓑ Ⓒ Ⓓ
6. Ⓐ Ⓑ Ⓒ Ⓓ	26. Ⓐ Ⓑ Ⓒ Ⓓ	46. Ⓐ Ⓑ Ⓒ Ⓓ	66. Ⓐ Ⓑ Ⓒ Ⓓ	86. Ⓐ Ⓑ Ⓒ Ⓓ
7. Ⓐ Ⓑ Ⓒ Ⓓ	27. Ⓐ Ⓑ Ⓒ Ⓓ	47. Ⓐ Ⓑ Ⓒ Ⓓ	67. Ⓐ Ⓑ Ⓒ Ⓓ	87. Ⓐ Ⓑ Ⓒ Ⓓ
8. Ⓐ Ⓑ Ⓒ Ⓓ	28. Ⓐ Ⓑ Ⓒ Ⓓ	48. Ⓐ Ⓑ Ⓒ Ⓓ	68. Ⓐ Ⓑ Ⓒ Ⓓ	88. Ⓐ Ⓑ Ⓒ Ⓓ
9. Ⓐ Ⓑ Ⓒ Ⓓ	29. Ⓐ Ⓑ Ⓒ Ⓓ	49. Ⓐ Ⓑ Ⓒ Ⓓ	69. Ⓐ Ⓑ Ⓒ Ⓓ	89. Ⓐ Ⓑ Ⓒ Ⓓ
10. Ⓐ Ⓑ Ⓒ Ⓓ	30. Ⓐ Ⓑ Ⓒ Ⓓ	50. Ⓐ Ⓑ Ⓒ Ⓓ	70. Ⓐ Ⓑ Ⓒ Ⓓ	90. Ⓐ Ⓑ Ⓒ Ⓓ
11. Ⓐ Ⓑ Ⓒ Ⓓ	31. Ⓐ Ⓑ Ⓒ Ⓓ	51. Ⓐ Ⓑ Ⓒ Ⓓ	71. Ⓐ Ⓑ Ⓒ Ⓓ	91. Ⓐ Ⓑ Ⓒ Ⓓ
12. Ⓐ Ⓑ Ⓒ Ⓓ	32. Ⓐ Ⓑ Ⓒ Ⓓ	52. Ⓐ Ⓑ Ⓒ Ⓓ	72. Ⓐ Ⓑ Ⓒ Ⓓ	92. Ⓐ Ⓑ Ⓒ Ⓓ
13. Ⓐ Ⓑ Ⓒ Ⓓ	33. Ⓐ Ⓑ Ⓒ Ⓓ	53. Ⓐ Ⓑ Ⓒ Ⓓ	73. Ⓐ Ⓑ Ⓒ Ⓓ	93. Ⓐ Ⓑ Ⓒ Ⓓ
14. Ⓐ Ⓑ Ⓒ Ⓓ	34. Ⓐ Ⓑ Ⓒ Ⓓ	54. Ⓐ Ⓑ Ⓒ Ⓓ	74. Ⓐ Ⓑ Ⓒ Ⓓ	94. Ⓐ Ⓑ Ⓒ Ⓓ
15. Ⓐ Ⓑ Ⓒ Ⓓ	35. Ⓐ Ⓑ Ⓒ Ⓓ	55. Ⓐ Ⓑ Ⓒ Ⓓ	75. Ⓐ Ⓑ Ⓒ Ⓓ	95. Ⓐ Ⓑ Ⓒ Ⓓ
16. Ⓐ Ⓑ Ⓒ Ⓓ	36. Ⓐ Ⓑ Ⓒ Ⓓ	56. Ⓐ Ⓑ Ⓒ Ⓓ	76. Ⓐ Ⓑ Ⓒ Ⓓ	96. Ⓐ Ⓑ Ⓒ Ⓓ
17. Ⓐ Ⓑ Ⓒ Ⓓ	37. Ⓐ Ⓑ Ⓒ Ⓓ	57. Ⓐ Ⓑ Ⓒ Ⓓ	77. Ⓐ Ⓑ Ⓒ Ⓓ	97. Ⓐ Ⓑ Ⓒ Ⓓ
18. Ⓐ Ⓑ Ⓒ Ⓓ	38. Ⓐ Ⓑ Ⓒ Ⓓ	58. Ⓐ Ⓑ Ⓒ Ⓓ	78. Ⓐ Ⓑ Ⓒ Ⓓ	98. Ⓐ Ⓑ Ⓒ Ⓓ
19. Ⓐ Ⓑ Ⓒ Ⓓ	39. Ⓐ Ⓑ Ⓒ Ⓓ	59. Ⓐ Ⓑ Ⓒ Ⓓ	79. Ⓐ Ⓑ Ⓒ Ⓓ	99. Ⓐ Ⓑ Ⓒ Ⓓ
20. Ⓐ Ⓑ Ⓒ Ⓓ	40. Ⓐ Ⓑ Ⓒ Ⓓ	60. Ⓐ Ⓑ Ⓒ Ⓓ	80. Ⓐ Ⓑ Ⓒ Ⓓ	100. Ⓐ Ⓑ Ⓒ Ⓓ

Total Number of Questions   100
Total Incorrect —
Total Correct   × 1 = _____%
Score

EFFECTIVE EXPRESSION

DIRECTIONS: Since language is a living, active thing, your grasp of correct and effective expression is best measured by a type of question which tests a multitude of grammatical skills. That's why these questions are so very important and useful to you. They draw upon your practical ability to discern and correct errors in punctuation, incomplete sentences, run-on sentences, split infinitives, dangling participles, double negatives, confusion of adjectives and adverbs, disagreement in number between subject and verb, incorrect use of homonyms, lack of clarity, inappropriate choice of words, clumsy phrasing.

In each of the following passages, some portions are underlined and numbered. Corresponding to each numbered portion are three different ways of saying the same thing. Read through each passage quickly to determine the sense of the passage, then return to the underlined portions. If you feel that an underlined portion is correct and is stated as well as possible, choose alternative A, NO CHANGE. If you feel that there is an error in grammar, sentence structure, punctuation or word usage, choose the correct answer. If an underlined portion appears to be correct, but you believe that one of the alternatives would be more effective, mark that choice. Remember, you are to choose the best answer. Correct answers to this test will be found at the end of the chapter.

Sample Exercise

If a person were to try stripping the disguises from
<u> </u>
1
actors while they play a scene upon the stage, showing to

1. A. NO CHANGE
   B. Person were to try
   C. Person was to try
   D. person was to try

the audience there real looks and the faces they were born
2   3

2. A. NO CHANGE
   B. their real looks
   C. there Real Looks
   D. their "real looks"

with. Would not such a one spoil the whole play? Destroy
3

3. A. NO CHANGE
   B. born to—would
   C. born. Would
   D. born with, would

the illusion and any play was ruined.
4

4. A. NO CHANGE
   B. any Play was
      ruined
   C. any play is ruined?
   D. any play is ruined.

The Correct Answers in This Example Are:

1. (A) The passage is correct as shown and therefore NO CHANGE is the best selection.
2. (B) The possessive pronoun is spelled *their.*
3. (D) The comma corrects the sentence fragment.
4. (D) The present tense *is* is consistent with the present tense *destroy.*

PASSAGE I

The standardized educational or psychological tests,
<u>that are</u> widely used to aid in selecting, classifying, assign-
1

ing, or <u>promoting students</u>, employees, and military person-
2
nel have been the target of recent attacks in books, maga-

zines, and <u>newspapers that are printed every day</u>. The tar-
3

get is wrong, for in attacking the tests, critics <u>revert atten-</u>
4
<u>tion from</u> the fault that <u>lays with illinformed</u> or incompetent
4   5

users. The tests themselves are merely <u>tools; with</u> character-
6

istics that can be <u>assessed reasonably precise</u> under specified
7
conditions. Whether the results will be valuable, meaning-

less, or even misleading <u>are dependent partly upon</u> the tool
8
itself but largely upon the user.

PASSAGE II

The forces that generate conditions conducive to crime
and <u>riots, are stronger</u> in urban communities <u>then in rural</u>
9   10

1. A. NO CHANGE
   B. tests that are
   C. tests, which are
   D. tests; which are

2. A. NO CHANGE
   B. promoting of students
   C. promotion of students
   D. promotion for students

3. A. NO CHANGE
   B. the daily press
   C. newspapers that are pub-
      lished daily
   D. the daily newspaper press

4. A. NO CHANGE
   B. revert attention to
   C. divert attention from
   D. avert attention from

5. A. NO CHANGE
   B. lies with poorly-informed
   C. lays with poor-informed
   D. lies with ill-informed

6. A. NO CHANGE
   B. tools with
   C. tools, possessed of
   D. tools; whose

7. A. NO CHANGE
   B. assessed as to its reasonable
      precision
   C. assessed reasonably and with
      precision
   D. assessed with reasonable pre-
      cision

8. A. NO CHANGE
   B. is dependant partly upon
   C. depend partly upon
   D. depends partly upon

9. A. NO CHANGE
   B. rioting, are stronger
   C. riots are more strong
   D. riots are stronger

areas. Urban living is more anonymous <u>living, it</u> often re-
   10   11
leases the individual from community restraints more com-

mon in <u>tradition, oriented societies.</u> <u>But</u> more freedom
                      12   13
from constraints and controls also provides greater freedom

to deviate. In the more impersonalized, <u>formally, controlled</u>
                                                14
urban society regulatory orders of conduct are often directed by distant bureaucrats. The police are strangers

<u>which execute</u> these prescriptions on, at worst, an alien sub-
   15

community and, at best, an <u>anonymous and unknown</u> set of
                                    16
subjects. Minor offenses in a small town or village are often

handled <u>without resort to</u> official police action. As disput-
        17

able as such action may seem to be, <u>you will find it results</u>
                                            18
in fewer recorded violations of the law compared to the
city.

10. A. NO CHANGE
    B. then in rural communities
    C. than in rural areas
    D. then they are in the country

11. A. NO CHANGE
    B. living. It
    C. living; which
    D. living. Because it

12. A. NO CHANGE
    B. traditional oriented socieities
    C. traditionally, oriented societies
    D. tradition-oriented societies

13. A. NO CHANGE
    B. Moreover
    C. Therefore
    D. Besides

14. A. NO CHANGE
    B. formally controlled
    C. formalized controlled
    D. formally-controlled

15. A. NO CHANGE
    B. they execute
    C. executing
    D. who conduct executions of

16. A. NO CHANGE
    B. anonymously
       unknown
    C. anonymous
    D. anonymous,
       unknown

17. A. NO CHANGE
    B. without their having to resort
       to
    C. without needing
    D. outside the limits of

18. A. NO CHANGE
    B. they say it results
    C. you will say, "It results
    D. it nonetheless
       results

PASSAGE III

Human beings are born with a desire to <u>communicate</u>
19

<u>with</u> other human <u>beings, they</u> satisfy this desire in many
19   20

19. A. NO CHANGE
    B. communicate to
    C. communicate about
    D. communicate

20. A. NO CHANGE
    B. beings. They
    C. beings, who
    D. beings which

ways. A smile communicates <u>a friendly feeling,</u> a clenched
21

21. A. NO CHANGE
    B. a friendly, feeling;
    C. friendship,
    D. a friendly feeling;

<u>fist anger;</u> tears, sorrow. From the first days of life, <u>pain</u>
22   23

<u>and hunger are expressed by baby's</u> by cries and actions.
23

22. A. NO CHANGE
    B. fist an angry
       feeling,
    C. fist, anger;
    D. fist, angriness,

23. A. NO CHANGE
    B. babies express pain or
       hunger
    C. a baby's pain or hunger are
       expressed
    D. pain and hunger is expressed
       by babies

Gradually they add expressions of pleasure and <u>smiling for</u>
24

24. A. NO CHANGE
    B. smiled
    C. smiles
    D. he may smile

a familiar face. Soon they begin to reach out <u>for picking up.</u>
25

25. A. NO CHANGE
    B. to pick up
    C. and pick up
    D. to be picked up

<u>Those people who are human beings</u> also use words to com-
26

26. A. NO CHANGE
    B. (BEGIN new paragraph)
       Those people who are hu-
       man beings
    C. (BEGIN new paragraph)
       Human being babies
    D. (BEGIN new paragraph)
       Human beings

municate. Babies eventually learn the language of there
                                                      27
parents. If the parents speak English, the baby will learn

to speak English. If the parents speak Spanish, a Spanish-
                                                         28
speaking baby will result. An American baby who is taken
      28   29
from his natural parents and brought up by foster parents
who speak Chinese, Urdu, Swahili, or any other language

will talk the language of the people around them instead of
  30   31
English.

Words are important tools of learning. It enables chil-
                                                     32
dren to ask questions and understand the answers; they can
  32

tell about their discoveries and to express their likes and
                                 33
dislikes.

PASSAGE IV

A high school diploma by itself is not sufficient preparation for many occupations. But neither is a college de
                                       34
gree. Different fields of work require different types of
training. Just as there are occupations that require college

degrees, so to there are occupations for which technical
         35

27. A. NO CHANGE
    B. their
    C. they're
    D. OMIT

28. A. NO CHANGE
    B. their baby will speak Span-
       ish.
    C. the baby will learn spanish.
    D. there baby will speak Span-
       ish.

29. A. NO CHANGE
    B. American Baby
    C. american baby
    D. american-born baby

30. A. NO CHANGE
    B. will be speaking
    C. will learn
    D. will talk of

31. A. NO CHANGE
    B. him
    C. themselves
    D. himself

32. A. NO CHANGE
    B. It provides children with the
       means to
    C. That makes it possible for
       children to
    D. Once children learn to use
       language they can

33. A. A. NO CHANGE
    B. use it to express
    C. express
    D. to talk about

34. A. NO CHANGE
    B. Nor a college
       degree.
    C. No more a college degree.
    D. Nor a degree from a four-
       year college.

35. A. NO CHANGE
    B. so to are there
    C. so too there are
    D. there are to

training or work experience <u>are the most important</u> entry
                                                    36
requirement. Employers always wish to hire the best qualified applicants, but this does not mean that the jobs always

go to those applicants <u>which are most educated.</u> The type of
                                        37

education and training an individual <u>has had is as important</u>
                                                            38
as the amount. For this reason, a vital part of the career

planning process is deciding <u>what kind as well as how much</u>
                                                          39
education and training to pursue.
    Persons who have definite career goals may not find

this decision <u>difficult, many</u> occupations have specific edu-
                            40
cation requirements. Physicians, for example, must gener-

ally complete at least 3 years of college, <u>4 years of Medical</u>
                                                            41
<u>School,</u> and in most states 1 year of residency. Cosmetolo-
gists are required to complete a state-approved cosmetology

course that generally lasts 18 months. <u>For most people,</u>
                                                          42
<u>however,</u> the decision is more difficult. Either they have yet
to choose a field of work, or the field they have selected
many be entered in a variety of ways. Making career decisions requires not only specific information about the types
of education and training preferred for various occupations,
but also <u>to know one's own</u> abilities and aspirations.
              43

PASSAGE V
    Everyone has at one time or <u>another</u> felt the need to
                                              44

36. A. NO CHANGE
    B. is the most
       important
    C. are more
       important
    D. are of the utmost importance
       as an

37. A. NO CHANGE
    B. that are most educated of all
    C. that have the most years of
       school
    D. who have the most educa-
       tion.

38. A. NO CHANGE
    B. has had are as important
    C. have had is important
    D. had had was as important

39. A. NO CHANGE
    B. what kind of as well as how
       much of
    C. what kind of as well as how
       much
    D. what and how much

40. A. NO CHANGE
    B. difficult. Many
    C. difficult many
    D. difficult being that many

41. A. NO CHANGE
    B. four years of Medical School
    C. 4 years in Medical School
    D. 4 years of medical school

42. A. NO CHANGE
    B. However, for most people
    C. (Begin new paragraph)
    D. For most persons, however,

43. A. NO CHANGE
    B. a knowledge of one's own
    C. the knowing of ones' own
    D. you must know your own

44. A. NO CHANGE
    B. the other
    C. an other
    D. one other

express <u>himself</u>. What must <u>you</u> do in order to learn to say
      45   46

<u>exactly what <u>you want</u> to <u>say</u>. <u>You will have to</u> study <u>very</u></u>
           47   48   49   50

<u>careful</u> the English language and especially <u>it's</u> <u>grammer.</u>
 50   51   52

<u>Some</u> people think that <u>Good English</u> is fancy English, but
 52   53

45. A. NO CHANGE
    B. theirself
    C. themself
    D. theirselves

46. A. NO CHANGE
    B. they
    C. he
    D. one

47. A. NO CHANGE
    B. we want
    C. one wants
    D. everyone wants

48. A. NO CHANGE
    B. say?
    C. say!
    D. say:

49. A. NO CHANGE
    B. They ought to
    C. We should
    D. One must

50. A. NO CHANGE
    B. with care
    C. carefully (inserted after language)
    D. OMIT

51. A. NO CHANGE
    B. its
    C. its'
    D. their

52. A. NO CHANGE
    B. grammer; some
    C. grammar. (begin a new paragraph with Some)
    D. grammer. (begin a new paragraph with Some)

53. A. NO CHANGE
    B. good english
    C. good English
    D. English that is good

this contention <u>isnt true.</u> Just because a person uses long
54

54. A. NO CHANGE
    B. isn't true.
    C. aint so.
    D. aren't true.

<u>words it does not mean that</u> <u>he speaks good.</u> The person
55   56

55. A. NO CHANGE
    B. words, it does not mean that
    C. words, you don't know that
    D. words, he does not necessar-
       ily

56. A. NO CHANGE
    B. he speaks well.
    C. speak correct.
    D. speak well.

<u>whom</u> uses simple words and phrases <u>which say</u> exactly
57   58

57. A. NO CHANGE
    B. who
    C. what
    D. which

58. A. NO CHANGE
    B. what say
    C. which says
    D. who say

what he means is using better English <u>than the</u> individual
59

59. A. NO CHANGE
    B. from
    C. then
    D. instead of

who shows off with <u>hard to understand expressions.</u>
60

60. A. NO CHANGE
    B. hard to understand expres-
       sions.
    C. hard-to-understand expres-
       sions.
    D. hard-to-understand-expres-
       sions.

PASSAGE VI

The <u>most serious threatening</u> to modern <u>man it would</u>
61   62

61. A. NO CHANGE
    B. most seriously threatening
    C. most serious threat
    D. seriously threatening

seem is not physical annihilation but the alleged meaning-
62

lessness of life. This latent vacuum becomes manifest in a
63

state of boredom. Automation will lead to more and more
64
freer time and many will not know how to use their liesure
64   65
hours, this is evidenced today by what a prominent psychia-
65

trist refers to as Sunday Neurosis the depression that
66
inflicts people who become conscious of the lack of content
67
in their lives when the rush of the busy week stops. Nothing

in the world helps man to keep healthy so much as the
68

knowledge of a life task. Nietzsche wisely said "he who
69

knows a Why of living surmounts over every How."
70

62. A. NO CHANGE
     B. man; it would seem that
     C. man. It would seem that
     D. man, it would seem,

63. A. NO CHANGE
     B. latent vacuum
        become
     C. latent vacuum have become
     D. latent vacuole
        becomes

64. A. NO CHANGE
     B. more freer time
     C. more and more free time
     D. more or less free-time

65. A. NO CHANGE
     B. liesure hours, that
     C. leisure hours, that
     D. leisure hours. This

66. A. NO CHANGE
     B. Neurosis, the
     C. neurosis. The
     D. Neurosis. The

67. A. NO CHANGE
     B. inflicts people whom
     C. afflicts people who
     D. afflicts people whom

68. A. NO CHANGE
     B. so much so
     C. so much that
     D. so much as that

69. A. NO CHANGE
     B. said "He who
     C. said, "he whom
     D. said, "He who

70. A. NO CHANGE
     B. surmounted over
     C. surmounts
     D. surmount

PASSAGE VII

The cynical <u>some times</u> are critical. But <u>I do not know</u>
            71   72

71. A. NO CHANGE
    B. some of the times
    C. sometimes
    D. at sometimes

72. A. NO CHANGE
    B. I know of no more worthy
    C. I don't know of no more worthy
    D. I can't know of any more worthy

<u>of no more</u> worthy motive or purpose that a <u>human being</u>
   72   73
<u>can have had</u> than <u>to try to lie out</u> as your goal <u>a Program</u>
   73   74   75

73. A. NO CHANGE
    B. human being could have had
    C. human being could be going to have
    D. human being can have

74. A. NO CHANGE
    B. to try to layout
    C. trying to lie out
    D. trying to lay out

75. A. NO CHANGE
    B. a "Program" that will
    C. a program, that will
    D. a program that will

<u>that will</u> educate the mind, that will conquer disease <u>in the</u>
   75   76
<u>body. That</u> will permit your children <u>and you're people to</u>
   76   77

76. A. NO CHANGE
    B. in the body; that
    C. in the body, but
    D. in the body, and that

77. A. NO CHANGE
    B. and Your People to
    C. and you are people to
    D. and your people to

live in an atmosphere and <u>an environment of</u> beauty and
                                78
culture—and enjoy the better things of life.

78. A. NO CHANGE
    B. environs of
    C. the environs of
    D. environments of

We cannot conquer disease <u>nor we cannot</u> educate all
                              79

79. A. NO CHANGE
    B. or we cannot
    C. nor we can
    D. nor can we

humanity. We can't not have a symphony in every town and
80   81

we cannot have a mellon art gallery in every capitol. But we
            82   83   84

can hope for these amenities and be working for them, and
                                    85

we can give what we have to them. And we can urge them
                            86   87

and provide leadership and ideas and try to move along.
                                    88

80. A. NO CHANGE
B. We can not
C. We can't
D. When can we

81. A. NO CHANGE
B. Symphony in
C. Symphony, in
D. Symphony, in

82. A. NO CHANGE
B. a "mellon art gallery"
C. a Mellon "Art" gallery
D. a Mellon Art Gallery

83. A. NO CHANGE
B. every capitol?
C. every capital.
D. every capital?

84. A. NO CHANGE
B. Therefore we
C. Moreover we
D. Since we

85. A. NO CHANGE
B. work for them
C. have them work
D. keep them working

86. A. NO CHANGE
B. to them; and we can
C. to them. We can also
D. to them. Also we can

87. A. NO CHANGE
B. encourage them
C. urge it
D. encourage development of the arts

88. A. NO CHANGE
B. and try to move up.
C. and try to move them up.
D. OMIT

DIRECTIONS: Questions 89 to 100 consist of a single sentence with all or part of the sentence underlined. Following each sentence are four different ways of phrasing the underlined part. Select the one phrasing that makes the sentence both correct and effective. If you feel that there is no error in the original sentence, select NO CHANGE as your answer. Blacken the letter of your choice on the answer sheet.

89. They were very kind to my friend and I.
    A. NO CHANGE
    B. to my friend and me.
    C. to me and my friend.
    D. to both I and my friend.

90. We tried to quickly finish the work.
    A. NO CHANGE
    B. We quickly tried to finish the work.
    C. We tried to finish the work quickly.
    D. We tried to finish the work quick.

91. People get use to prosperity easily.
    A. NO CHANGE
    B. get easily use to prosperity.
    C. get use to prosperity easy.
    D. get used to prosperity easily.

92. I saw neither the books or the pencils on the desk.
    A. NO CHANGE
    B. I saw neither the books nor the pencils
    C. I did not see neither the books nor the pencils
    D. Neither did I see the books or the pencils

93. This is John Smith, the man who I was telling you about yesterday.
    A. NO CHANGE
    B. about who I was telling you
    C. I was telling you about
    D. about whom I was telling you

94. Is this the book you want me to copy from?
    A. NO CHANGE
    B. from what you want me to copy?
    C. from which you want me to copy?
    D. from whom you want me to copy?

95. If you disobey traffic regulations, you will loose your driver's license.
    A. NO CHANGE
    B. lose your drivers' license.
    C. lose your driver's license.
    D. your driver's license lose.

96. The exhausted animal lay there, sick.
    A. NO CHANGE
    B. animal lied there,
    C. animal laid there,
    D. animal layed there,

97. Was it him that you called yesterday?
    A. NO CHANGE
    B. he who you called
    C. he whom you called
    D. him who you called

98. I and him went to the football game.
    A. NO CHANGE
    B. Him and I went
    C. He and I went
    D. He and me went

99. Irregardless of the weather, classes will be held tonight.
    A. NO CHANGE
    B. Irregardless what the weather,
    C. Regardless of the whether,
    D. Regardless of the weather,

100. Some students believe the sum of the figures should be included in the final averages.
    A. NO CHANGE
    B. the some of the figures
    C. that some of the figures
    D. that sum of the figures

CORRECT USAGE TEST
ANSWER KEY

TEST 1

1. Ⓐ ● Ⓒ Ⓓ   3. ● Ⓑ Ⓒ Ⓓ   5. Ⓐ ● Ⓒ Ⓓ   7. Ⓐ Ⓑ Ⓒ ●
2. Ⓐ Ⓑ ● Ⓓ   4. Ⓐ Ⓑ ● Ⓓ   6. ● Ⓑ Ⓒ Ⓓ   8. Ⓐ Ⓑ Ⓒ ●

TEST 2

1. ● Ⓑ Ⓒ Ⓓ   3. Ⓐ Ⓑ Ⓒ ●   5. ● Ⓑ Ⓒ Ⓓ   7. Ⓐ Ⓑ Ⓒ ●   9. Ⓐ ● Ⓒ Ⓓ
2. ● Ⓑ Ⓒ Ⓓ   4. ● Ⓑ Ⓒ Ⓓ   6. Ⓐ ● Ⓒ Ⓓ   8. Ⓐ Ⓑ Ⓒ ●

TEST 3

1. Ⓐ ● Ⓒ Ⓓ   3. Ⓐ Ⓑ ● Ⓓ   5. Ⓐ Ⓑ ● Ⓓ   7. Ⓐ ● Ⓒ Ⓓ   9. Ⓐ ● Ⓒ Ⓓ
2. ● Ⓑ Ⓒ Ⓓ   4. Ⓐ Ⓑ ● Ⓓ   6. Ⓐ Ⓑ Ⓒ ●   8. Ⓐ Ⓑ ● Ⓓ

TEST 4

1. ● Ⓑ Ⓒ Ⓓ   3. Ⓐ Ⓑ ● Ⓓ   5. Ⓐ Ⓑ ● Ⓓ   7. Ⓐ Ⓑ ● Ⓓ   9. ● Ⓑ Ⓒ Ⓓ
2. Ⓐ ● Ⓒ Ⓓ   4. ● Ⓑ Ⓒ Ⓓ   6. Ⓐ Ⓑ Ⓒ ●   8. Ⓐ ● Ⓒ Ⓓ   10. ● Ⓑ Ⓒ Ⓓ

TEST 5

1. Ⓐ Ⓑ ● Ⓓ   3. Ⓐ Ⓑ ● Ⓓ   5. Ⓐ ● Ⓒ Ⓓ   7. Ⓐ Ⓑ Ⓒ ●
2. Ⓐ Ⓑ Ⓒ ●   4. ● Ⓑ Ⓒ Ⓓ   6. ● Ⓑ Ⓒ Ⓓ   8. Ⓐ Ⓑ ● Ⓓ

TEST 6

1. Ⓐ Ⓑ Ⓒ ●   3. Ⓐ Ⓑ ● Ⓓ   5. ● Ⓑ Ⓒ Ⓓ   7. Ⓐ Ⓑ Ⓒ ●   9. Ⓐ Ⓑ ● Ⓓ
2. Ⓐ ● Ⓒ Ⓓ   4. Ⓐ Ⓑ ● Ⓓ   6. ● Ⓑ Ⓒ Ⓓ   8. Ⓐ Ⓑ ● Ⓓ   10. Ⓐ Ⓑ Ⓒ ●

TEST 7

1. Ⓐ Ⓑ ● Ⓓ   3. Ⓐ Ⓑ ● Ⓓ   5. Ⓐ ● Ⓒ Ⓓ   7. Ⓐ Ⓑ ● Ⓓ
2. Ⓐ Ⓑ ● Ⓓ   4. Ⓐ Ⓑ Ⓒ ●   6. ● Ⓑ Ⓒ Ⓓ   8. Ⓐ ● Ⓒ Ⓓ

TEST 8

1. ● Ⓑ Ⓒ Ⓓ   3. Ⓐ ● Ⓒ Ⓓ   5. Ⓐ Ⓑ Ⓒ ●   7. Ⓐ ● Ⓒ Ⓓ   9. ● Ⓑ Ⓒ Ⓓ
2. ● Ⓑ Ⓒ Ⓓ   4. Ⓐ ● Ⓒ Ⓓ   6. Ⓐ Ⓑ ● Ⓓ   8. Ⓐ Ⓑ Ⓒ ●   10. Ⓐ Ⓑ ● Ⓓ

CORRECT USAGE TEST
ANSWER KEY

TEST 9

1. Ⓐ Ⓑ Ⓒ ●	3. ● Ⓑ Ⓒ Ⓓ	5. Ⓐ Ⓑ Ⓒ ●	7. Ⓐ ● Ⓒ Ⓓ	9. Ⓐ Ⓑ ● Ⓓ
2. Ⓐ ● Ⓒ Ⓓ	4. Ⓐ Ⓑ ● Ⓓ	6. ● Ⓑ Ⓒ Ⓓ	8. Ⓐ Ⓑ ● Ⓓ	10. Ⓐ Ⓑ Ⓒ ●

TEST 10

1. Ⓐ Ⓑ Ⓒ ●	5. ● Ⓑ Ⓒ Ⓓ	8. Ⓐ Ⓑ Ⓒ ●	11. Ⓐ ● Ⓒ Ⓓ	14. Ⓐ Ⓑ Ⓒ ●
2. Ⓐ Ⓑ Ⓒ ●	6. Ⓐ Ⓑ ● Ⓓ	9. Ⓐ Ⓑ Ⓒ ●	12. Ⓐ Ⓑ ● Ⓓ	15. ● Ⓑ Ⓒ Ⓓ
3. ● Ⓑ Ⓒ Ⓓ	7. Ⓐ ● Ⓒ Ⓓ	10. Ⓐ ● Ⓒ Ⓓ	13. Ⓐ ● Ⓒ Ⓓ	16. ● Ⓑ Ⓒ Ⓓ
4. Ⓐ ● Ⓒ Ⓓ				

TEST 11

1. Ⓐ ●	5. ● Ⓑ	8. Ⓐ ●	11. ● Ⓑ	14. ● Ⓑ
2. ● Ⓑ	6. Ⓐ ●	9. ● Ⓑ	12. ● Ⓑ	15. Ⓐ ●
3. Ⓐ ●	7. Ⓐ ●	10. Ⓐ ●	13. Ⓐ ●	16. ● Ⓑ
4. Ⓐ ●				

TEST 12

1. ● Ⓑ	5. Ⓐ ●	8. Ⓐ ●	11. Ⓐ ●	14. Ⓐ ●
2. Ⓐ ●	6. ● Ⓑ	9. ● Ⓑ	12. ● Ⓑ	15. Ⓐ ●
3. ● Ⓑ	7. Ⓐ ●	10. ● Ⓑ	13. ● Ⓑ	16. ● Ⓑ
4. ● Ⓑ				

PARAGRAPH ORDER ANSWER KEY

1. (A) ● (C) (D)
2. ● (B) (C) (D)
3. (A) (B) (C) ●
4. (A) (B) ● (D)
5. (A) (B) (C) ●
6. (A) ● (C) (D)

7. ● (B) (C) (D)
8. (A) (B) ● (D)
9. (A) ● (C) (D)
10. (A) (B) (C) ●
11. (A) ● (C) (D)

12. (A) (B) ● (D)
13. ● (B) (C) (D)
14. (A) (B) ● (D)
15. (A) (B) ● (D)
16. ● (B) (C) (D)

Total Number of Questions 16

$$\frac{\text{Total Incorrect}}{\text{Total Correct}} \times 6.2 = \underline{\quad}\% \atop \text{Score}$$

EFFECTIVE EXPRESSION TEST
ANSWER KEY

#	Ans	#	Ans	#	Ans	#	Ans	#	Ans
1.	B	21.	D	41.	D	61.	C	81.	A
2.	A	22.	C	42.	C	62.	D	82.	D
3.	B	23.	B	43.	B	63.	A	83.	C
4.	C	24.	C	44.	A	64.	C	84.	A
5.	D	25.	D	45.	D	65.	D	85.	B
6.	B	26.	C	46.	D	66.	B	86.	C
7.	D	27.	B	47.	C	67.	C	87.	D
8.	D	28.	B	48.	B	68.	A	88.	D
9.	D	29.	A	49.	D	69.	D	89.	B
10.	C	30.	C	50.	D	70.	C	90.	C
11.	B	31.	B	51.	B	71.	C	91.	C
12.	D	32.	C	52.	C	72.	B	92.	B
13.	A	33.	C	53.	C	73.	D	93.	C
14.	B	34.	A	54.	B	74.	D	94.	C
15.	C	35.	C	55.	D	75.	D	95.	C
16.	C	36.	B	56.	D	76.	D	96.	A
17.	A	37.	D	57.	B	77.	D	97.	C
18.	D	38.	A	58.	A	78.	A	98.	C
19.	A	39.	B	59.	A	79.	D	99.	D
20.	B	40.	B	60.	C	80.	C	100.	A

EFFECTIVE EXPRESSION TEST
EXPLANATORY ANSWERS

1. **B.** The phrase following *tests* is an essential part of this sentence and should not be set off by commas.

2. **A.** This is correct.

3. **B.** The three words *the daily press* say everything that is said by the other, more wordy choices.

4. **C.** *Divert*, meaning "to turn from one course to another," is the most appropriate choice. *Revert* means "to return" and *avert* means "to turn away or prevent."

5. **D.** The present tense of the verb *to lie,* meaning "belonging to," is required here.

6. **B.** It is not necessary to separate the prepositional phrase from the rest of the sentence.

7. **D.** This is the clearest and least awkward choice.

8. **D.** The subject of the verb here is implied—the subject is actually the significance of the results. Thus, a singular verb is needed, and D gives the only singular verb construction that is spelled correctly.

9. **D.** Do not use a comma to separate a subject and a verb (except when the subject contains a nonessential clause, an appositive or other phrase which is set off by two commas).

10. **C.** *Than,* a conjunction, is used after the comparative degree of an adjective or adverb. *Then,* an adverb, means "at that time" or "next."

11. **B.** To correct this run-on sentence, it is necessary to add a period after *living.* Beginning the next sentence with *Because*

creates a sentence fragment, rather than a complete sentence.

12. **D.** Use a hyphen in unit modifiers immediately preceding the word or words modified. *Tradition-oriented* is a unit modifier.

13. **A.** *But* is correct to indicate a contrasting idea. *Moreover* and *besides* mean "in addition to what has been said." *Therefore* means "for that reason."

14. **B.** Do not use punctuation between the terms of a unit modifier when the first term is an adverb modifying the second term.

15. **C.** The participle *executing,* meaning "carrying out," not "putting to death," is the correct word for this sentence. *Which* refers to things, not to people. Choice **B.** creates a run-on sentence.

16. **C.** *Anonymous* means "unknown."

17. **A.** This is the most concise and correct way to make this statement.

18. **D.** As written, this sentence illustrates a needless shift in subject (from *action* to *you*) which results in a dangling modifier.

19. **A.** This is correct.

20. **B.** As written, this is a run-on sentence. To correct it, add a period after *beings* and start a new sentence with *They.*

21. **D.** Use a semicolon to separate sentence parts of equal rank if one or more of these parts is subdivided by commas.

22. **C.** Use a comma to indicate the omission of a word or words. This phrase actually means "a clenched fist (communicates) anger."

23. **B.** Avoid the shift from the active to the passive voice. The possessive *baby's* is incorrectly substituted for the plural *babies*.

24. **C.** *And* is used to correct similar grammatical elements, in this case the noun *expressions* and the noun *smiles*.

25. **D.** The present infinitive is correct because the action of the infinitive is present or future in relation to the action of the finite verb *begin*.

26. **D.** The introduction of a new topic—the use of words to communicate—indicates the need for a new paragraph. *Human beings* are people and so the phrase *Those people who are* is unnecessary.

27. **B.** The possessive pronoun needed here is *their*. *There* refers to place and *they're* is a contraction for *they are*.

28. **B.** A comparison is being drawn between English and Spanish-speaking families. The two sentences that form the comparison should be parallel in structure. *Spanish* is a proper noun and must begin with a capital letter.

29. **A.** *American* is a proper noun and should be capitalized; *baby* is merely a noun and, therefore, needs no capital letter.

30. **C.** *Talk* means to use *language* for conversing or communicating.

31. **B.** The subject of this sentence, which is also the antecedent of the pronoun, is singular (*baby*); therefore, the pronoun must also be singular.

32. **D.** Avoid the indefinite use of *it*. In standard written English, *it* requires a stated antecedent for clarity.

33. **C.** Items presented in series should be parallel in structure.

34. **A.** This is correct.

35. **C.** Don't confuse the homonyms *to*, *two* and *too*. *To* means "in the direction of." *Two* is the numeral 2. *Too* means "more than" or "also."

36. **B.** Use a singular verb (*is*) after two singular subjects (*training, experience*) joined by *or* or *nor*.

37. **D.** The relative pronoun *who* refers to persons; *which*, to animals or things; *that*, to persons, animals or things.

38. **A.** This is correct. *Individual* is singular and therefore takes the singular verb form *has had*. *Type* is also singular and therefore takes the singular verb is.

39. **C.** The preposition *of* is needed after the word *kind*. It is incorrect to say "what kind education."

40. **B.** To eliminate the comma splice, add a period after *difficult* and start a new sentence with *Many*. Choice **D.** is incorrect because *being* is a participle, not a conjunction.

41. **D.** Capitalize only the name of a specific medical school, not medical schools in general.

42. **C.** There is a change in emphasis from persons who do not find career decisions difficult to those who do. Such a subject change indicates the need for a new paragraph.

43. **B.** The *not only . . . but also* construction should connect words or phrases of equal rank, in this case two nouns (*information* and *knowledge*).

44. **A.** The idiom is correctly written. *Another* is always one word.

45. **A.** *Everyone* is singular; therefore the pronoun must be singular. Furthermore, none of the incorrect choices is a legitimate word.

46. **D.** Avoid use of the word *you* when not addressing a specific person or group of people.

47. **C.** As in question 46, avoid the use of *you*.

48. **B.** A question must end with a question mark.

49. **D.** Again, see question 46.

50. **D.** The sentence is incorrect as written because *careful* is an adjective and what is needed is an adverb to modify the verb *study*. Choices **B.** and **C.** are correct but awkward. Since studying implies care, no modifying adverb is required.

51. **B.** The possessive form of *it* is *its*. *It's* is the contraction for *it is*. *The English language* is singular.

52. **C.** The author is introducing a new idea, so a new paragraph is required.

53. **C.** *English* is the name of the language, so it must be capitalized. There is no reason to capitalize the adjective *good*. Choice **D.** is verbose.

54. **B.** *This contention* is singular, so the singular verb *is* must be used. The correct contraction for *is not* is *isn't*.

55. **D.** *It* is an expletive (a pronoun subject with no antecedent). An expletive is always weak, but especially when it occurs in the middle of a sentence. Unless a sentence is compound, try to maintain the same subject throughout the sentence, as in **D.**

56. **D.** Because the passage continues from choice **D.** of question 55, the subject *he* has already been stated. *Correct* is an adjective and thus cannot modify the verb *speak*.

57. **B.** *Who* is the subject of the verb *to use*. *Which* cannot apply to people.

58. **A.** The subject, *words and phrases,* is plural, requiring use of the plural verb *say*.

Who cannot refer to things. *What* is not a relative pronoun.

59. **A.** *Than* is a pronoun expressing comparison. *Then* is an adverb expressing progression in time.

60. **C.** *Hard-to-understand* is a made-up adjective, and its parts must be connected by hyphens.

61. **C.** The noun form needed to serve as subject of this sentence is *threat*, not *threatening*.

62. **D.** *It would seem* is used here as a parenthetical expression and should, therefore, be set off from the main part of the sentence by commas.

63. **A.** This is correct.

64. **C.** The comparative degree is formed either by adding *-er* to the adjective or by using an expression such as "more and more" before the adjective. Use one or the other of these comparative methods, but not both.

65. **D.** It is necessary to begin a new sentence after *leisure hours* because a new thought is being introduced.

66. **B.** A comma is needed to separate the term *Sunday Neurosis* from the appositional phrase that follows. The appositional phrase does not express a complete thought and therefore is not a sentence.

67. **C.** This sentence requires the verb *afflict* meaning "to trouble," not *inflict* which means "to impose." Because *people* is the subject of the verb *become, who*, not *whom*, is correct.

68. **A.** This is correct.

69. **D.** When using a direct quotation, use a comma to separate the beginning of the quotation from the preceding phrase. Except in rare cases, the first word of a quotation is capitalized.

70. **C.** The phrase *surmount over* is repetitive, because surmount means "to overcome." To avoid a switch in verb tense, use the present, *surmounts*.

71. **C.** *Sometimes* is written as one word.

72. **B.** All other choices are double negatives.

73. **D.** All that is needed is a simple present tense.

74. **D.** The general rule for the verbs *to lie* and *to lay* is: Use *lay* when you can substitute *put*. One would *put down* a goal.

75. **D.** No capitalization or punctuation is necessary.

76. **D.** *That will permit* is the beginning of the final item in a list. *And* precedes the last item in an inclusive list.

77. **D.** The possessive form of *you* is *your*. *You're* is the contraction for *you are*. The capital form, as in **B.**, is used only when referring to a deity.

78. **A.** One lives in only one environment.

79. **D.** D. is the correct idiom.

80. **C.** A. constitutes the double negative. *Cannot* would be correct, but it must be written as one word.

81. **A.** No punctuation or capitalization is necessary.

82. **D.** Mellon Art Gallery is the name of an art gallery. Each word of a name must begin with a capital letter.

83. **C.** *The Capitol* is the domed building in Washington, D.C. All other uses of *capital* are spelled *al*.

84. **A.** Because this sentence contrasts in tone with the previous sentence, *but* is the correct transition word.

85. **B.** C. and D. change the meaning of the sentence. A. is verbose.

86. **C.** A. is correct but confusing in its repeated use of *and*. D. would be correct, but a comma would be needed after *also*.

87. **D.** *Them* refers to *these amenities*. One does not "urge" or "encourage" amenities, nor can one introduce a new pronoun, *it*, without an antecedent. Therefore **D.** is the only correct answer.

88. **D.** This last clause provides only confusion and verbosity.

89. **B.** *I* is the nominative case, and the objective case—*me*—is needed.

90. **C.** The adverb *quickly* should modify the verb *finish*, not the verb *tried*.

91. **D.** The past participle *used* is required.

92. **B.** The *neither . . . nor* construction is needed.

93. **C.** Use of relative pronoun creates wordiness; eliminate whenever possible.

94. **C.** Avoid ending sentences with prepositions.

95. **C.** *Lose* is the correct verb; *loose* means "not tight."

96. **A.** NO CHANGE.

97. **C.** A predicate nominative *he* is needed after linking verb *was*.

98. **C.** The nominative case is needed for a compound subject.

99. **D.** *Regardless* is correct; *irregardless* is not an accepted word.

100. **A.** NO CHANGE.

ARCO Books to Improve your Office Skills

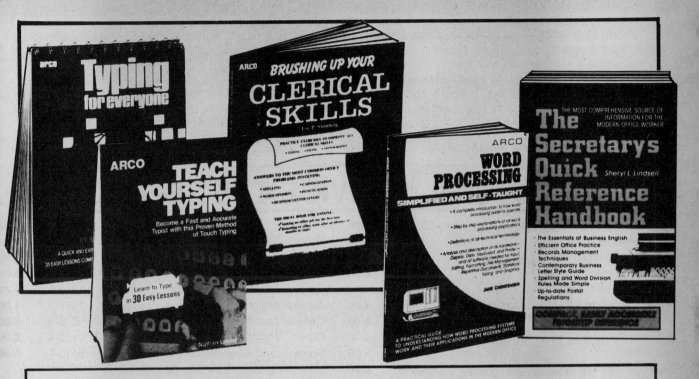

BRUSHING UP YOUR CLERICAL SKILLS
Eve P. Steinberg. Practice exercises to bring back typing speed and accuracy. Drills to improve filing efficiency. Dictation practice to shore up stenographic skills. Ideal for anyone seeking a first office job or a return to office work after a long absence.
ISBN 0-668-05538-3 Paper **$5.95**

WORD PROCESSING SIMPLIFIED AND SELF-TAUGHT
Jane Christensen. Introduction to how word processing systems operate. Explanations of all word processing applications. Analysis of all hardware.
ISBN 0-668-05601-0 Paper **$4.95**

THE SECRETARY'S QUICK REFERENCE HANDBOOK
Sheryl L. Lindsell. Concise guide to the basics of business English, the fundamentals of business letter writing and the essentials of office practice and procedure.
ISBN 0-668-05595-2 Paper **$3.95**

TYPING FOR EVERYONE
Nathan Levine. A quick and expert way to learn touch typing. Thirty-five easy lessons with timed-typing score sheets.
ISBN 0-668-04975-8 Easel-back **$6.95**

TEACH YOURSELF TYPING
Nathan Levine. A brief self-teaching guide to touch typing. Thirty short lessons lead to maximum proficiency in a minimum amount of time.
ISBN 0-668-05455-7 Paper **$3.95**

QUICKSCRIPT: THE FAST AND SIMPLE SHORTHAND METHOD
Adele Booth Blanchard. Complete instruction and numerous practice exercises for mastering the quickscript shorthand method.
ISBN 0-668-05572-3 Paper **$5.95**

For book ordering information refer to the last page of this book.

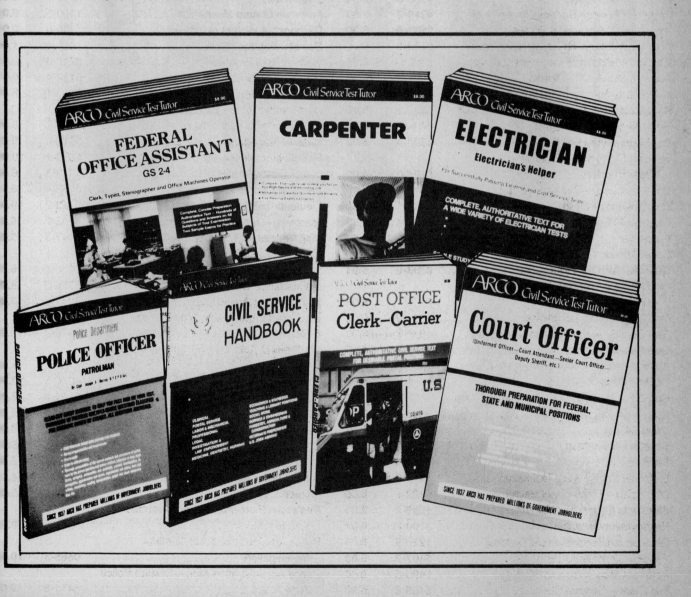

For book ordering information refer to the last page of this book.

ARCO Books For
College Entrance Preparation

PREPARATION FOR THE COLLEGE ENTRANCE EXAMINATION SAT (SCHOLASTIC APTITUDE TEST)

Brigitte Saunders, Gabriel P. Freedman, Leonard J. Capodice, Margaret A. Haller. Six full-length practice exams with detailed explanatory answers to all questions. Expert review material for both verbal and mathematics sections of the exam. Comprehensive word list.
ISBN 0-668-04920-2 Paper **$6.95**

VERBAL WORKBOOK FOR THE SAT

Gabriel P. Freedman and Margaret A. Haller. Comprehensive review for the verbal and TSWE sections of the SAT. Hundreds of graded practice questions for review in each area. Five full-length practice tests with explanatory answers. Progress charts for self-evaluation.
ISBN 0-668-04853-0 Paper **$6.00**

MATHEMATICS WORKBOOK FOR THE SAT

Brigitte Saunders. Authoritative instructional text and extensive drill in all math areas covered on the SAT. Diagnostic tests in each area to spotlight weaknesses; post-tests to measure progress. Three sample tests with complete solutions.
ISBN 0-668-04820-4 Paper **$6.95**

PSAT/NMSQT PRELIMINARY SCHOLASTIC APTITUDE TEST/NATIONAL MERIT SCHOLARSHIP QUALIFYING TEST

Eve P. Steinberg. Four full-length sample exams and extensiv practice with every type of examination question. Every answe fully explained to make practicing for the test a valuable learnin experience.
ISBN 0-668-04980-4 Paper **$6.00**

PAGE-A-DAY™ SAT STUDY GUIDE

Frances C. Bennett and Sunny Chang. Perforated pages pull out and take along for study anytime, anywhere. Each pag contains both verbal and math practice complete with answe to all questions.
ISBN 0-668-05196-5 Paper **$4.95**

PRACTICE FOR THE SCHOLASTIC APTITUDE TES

Martin McDonough and Alvin J. Hansen. The essentials SAT preparation condensed into one compact, easy-to-us study guide that fits into pocket or purse. Complete coverage every question type, 1000 word SAT vocabulary list, one fu length practice exam with explanatory answers for all question:
ISBN 0-668-05425-5 Paper **$2.95**

For book ordering information refer to the last page of th book.

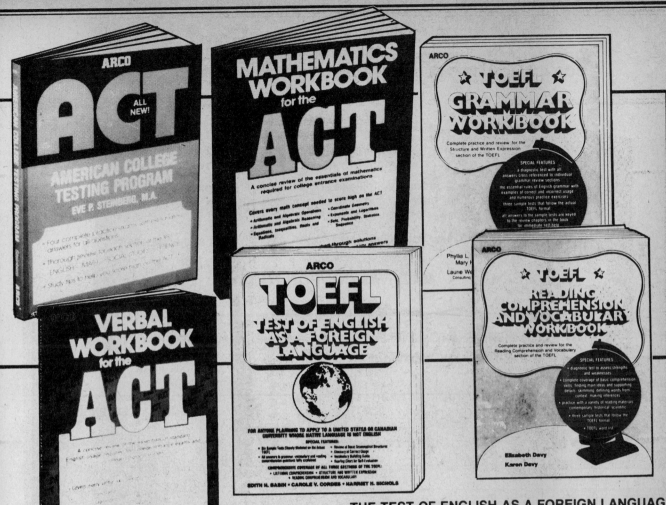

THE TEST OF ENGLISH AS A FOREIGN LANGUAGE (TOEFL)

Edith H. Babin, Carole V. Cordes, and Harriet H. Nichols.
Complete preparation for the college entrance examination required of students whose native language is not English. Six simulated sample tests covering all sections of this important exam. Separate cassette tape available for practice with the listening comprehension section.
ISBN 0-668-05446-8 (book) **$8.95**
ISBN 0-668-05743-2 (cassette) **$7.95**

TOEFL GRAMMAR WORKBOOK

Phyllis L. Lim and Mary Kurtin; Laurie Wellman, Consulting Editor. Intensive review for the Structure and Written Expression section of the TOEFL. Concise explanations of the points of English grammar covered by the test. Diagnostic test to direct study. Three practice tests for review.
ISBN 0-668-05080-2 Paper **$6.95**

TOEFL READING COMPREHENSION AND VOCABULARY WORKBOOK

Elizabeth Davy and Karen Davy. Graded practice in reading comprehension and vocabulary to build these essential English skills. Numerous exercises for practice with a variety of reading materials. Three sample Reading Comprehension and Vocabulary Tests with explanatory answers for all questions.
ISBN 0-668-05594-4 Paper **$6.95**

For book ordering information refer to the last page of this book.

AMERICAN COLLEGE TESTING PROGRAM (ACT)

Eve P. Steinberg. Four full-length practice test batteries with explanatory answers for all questions. Skills reviews and practice questions in each subject area of the exam. Detailed directions for scoring and evaluating exam results. Valuable test-taking tips.
ISBN 0-668-05151-5 Paper **$6.95**

VERBAL WORKBOOK FOR THE ACT

Joyce Lakritz. Intensive review for the English Usage and Reading Comprehension sections of the ACT. Three full-length sample ACT English Usage Tests with explanatory answers to help candidates assess their readiness for the ACT.
ISBN 0-668-05348-8 Paper **$6.95**

MATHEMATICS WORKBOOK FOR THE ACT

Barbara Erdsneker and Brigitte Saunders. In-depth review of the mathematical concepts essential to scoring high on the ACT. Diagnostic tests in each area, followed by instructional text and practice problems, with re-tests to measure progress. Three sample ACT Mathematics Tests with detailed solutions.
ISBN 0-668-05443-3 Paper **$6.95**

ORDER THE BOOKS DESCRIBED ON THE PREVIOUS PAGES FROM YOUR BOOKSELLER OR DIRECTLY FROM:

ARCO PUBLISHING, INC.
215 Park Avenue South
New York, N.Y. 10003

S.F.H.S.

To order directly from Arco, please add $1.00 for first book and 35¢ for each additional book for packing and mailing cost. No C.O.D.'s accepted.

Residents of New York, New Jersey and California must add appropriate sales tax.

MAIL THIS COUPON TODAY!

ARCO PUBLISHING, INC., 215 Park Avenue South, New York, N.Y. 10003
Please rush the following Arco books:

NO. OF COPIES	TITLE #	TITLE	PRICE	EXTENSION
			SUB-TOTAL	
			LOCAL TAX	
			PACKING & MAILING	
			TOTAL	

I enclose check ☐, M.O. ☐ for $ _____
☐ Is there an Arco Book on any of the following subjects: _____
☐ Please send me your free Complete Catalog.

NAME _____

ADDRESS _____

CITY _____ STATE _____ ZIP _____

Every Arco book is guaranteed. Return for full refund within ten days if not completely satisfied.

NOT RESPONSIBLE FOR CASH SENT THROUGH THE MAILS